THE FALL OF THE US EMPIRE

Vassilis K. Fouskas is Professor of International Relations at Richmond University, London, and the founding editor of the *Journal of Balkan and Near Eastern Studies* (quarterly). He is the author of *Cyprus: The Post-Imperial Constitution* (with Alex O. Tackie, 2009), *The New American Imperialism* (with Bülent Gökay, 2005), *The Politics of Conflict* (editor, 2007, 2010), *Zones of Conflict* (2003) and *Italy, Europe and the Left* (1998). He is an editor of globalfaultlines.com and a member of the editorial board of *Debatte*.

Bülent Gökay is Professor of International Relations and Head of the School of Politics, International Relations and Philosophy at Keele University. He is the author of *The Politics of Caspian Oil* (2001), *Eastern Europe Since 1970* (2005, 2006), *Soviet Eastern Policy and Turkey, 1920–1991* (2006), *Politics of Oil – A Survey* (2007), and *Muslims and Communists in Post-Transition States* (with Ben Fowkes, 2011). He is the founder and managing editor of globalfaultlines.com.

The Fall of the US Empire

Global Fault-Lines and the Shifting Imperial Order

Vassilis K. Fouskas
and
Bülent Gökay

PlutoPress
www.plutobooks.com

First published 2012 by Pluto Press
345 Archway Road, London N6 5AA

www.plutobooks.com

Copyright © Vassilis K. Fouskas and Bülent Gökay 2012

The right of Vassilis K. Fouskas and Bülent Gökay to be identified as the author of this work has been asserted by them in accordance with the Copyright, Designs and Patents Act 1988.

British Library Cataloguing in Publication Data
A catalogue record for this book is available from the British Library

ISBN	978 0 7453 2644 3	Hardback
ISBN	978 0 7453 2643 6	Paperback
ISBN	978 1 84964 658 1	PDF
ISBN	978 1 84964 660 4	Kindle
ISBN	978 1 84964 659 8	ePub

Library of Congress Cataloging in Publication Data applied for

This book is printed on paper suitable for recycling and made from fully managed and sustained forest sources. Logging, pulping and manufacturing processes are expected to conform to the environmental standards of the country of origin.

10 9 8 7 6 5 4 3 2 1

Designed and produced for Pluto Press by Curran Publishing Services, Norwich.
Simultaneously printed digitally by CPI Antony Rowe, Chippenham, UK and Edwards Bros in the United States of America

To the memory of Peter Gowan
Teacher, mentor and comrade

CONTENTS

Acknowledgements		*ix*
List of abbreviations		*xii*
Introduction		*xv*
Box: a definition of global fault-lines		*xviii*

1	**Global fault-lines**	**1**
	Preliminary observations	1
	Beyond conventional wisdom	9
	Marxisant discourses on the financial crisis	14
	The tragedy of globalization: the end of the 'long twentieth century'?	25

2	**From Bretton Woods to the abyss of globalization, 1944–71**	**33**
	Background to Bretton Woods	33
	The US empire-state responds to the great slump	38
	Determinants of the rise and fall of the 'Golden Age'	43

3	**The failure of financial statecraft (1), 1971–91**	**57**
	A note on Ernest Mandel	57
	Business strategies dealing with stagflation	61
	An unstable 'petrodollar'/'weapon-dollar' regime	65

4	**The failure of financial statecraft (2), 1991–2011**	**77**
	Towards a periodization of imperial orders	77
	The explosion of financialization and how it undermined growth	83
	The internationalization of the US treasury	87
	The implosion of financialization and the case of the United Kingdom	96

5	**The power shift to the global East**	**111**
	Issues between the United States and China	113
	The growth of emerging economies	114
	Control over resources	117
	The growing consumer classes	119

Brazil's experience 121
Projected results of the shift in economic power 125
Analysis and interpretation 129

6 Resource depletion and environmental degradation 133
Oil 134
Oil scarcity and its impact 137
The environment in crisis 138
Responses to environmental challenges 140

Conclusion 142
Summing up the argument 142
Prospects for the future 145

Notes 153
References 176
Websites 188
Index 189

ACKNOWLEDGEMENTS

Vassilis K. Fouskas would like to thank:

All the participants in the Richmond University colloquium on 'Understanding the Global Financial Crisis' (March 2011), especially Robert Wade (LSE), Costas Lapavitsas (SOAS, University of London), Stephen Haseler (London Metropolitan University) and Engelbert Stockhammer (Kingston University).

The librarians at Richmond University; my students at Richmond, especially Stefan Kurtev Atanasov, and my colleagues, especially the teaching team of our MA in IR. In particular, I would like to thank my colleagues Alex Seago and Wolfgang Deckers. Thanks are also due to Martin Winter in Richmond's reprographics, for tirelessly producing draft copies of the manuscript during a hot London summer, and Tryfon Chiotis and Kalliopi Moumgi of the Citizens' Advice Bureau, Petra, Lesvos, for the same reason (but this time the heat was in Greece).

Kees van der Pijl (Sussex University) for many discussions on the financial crisis and for his contribution to the December 2009 Athens workshop on the financial crisis held in honour of Peter Gowan.

Alex Tackie (Kingston University) for endless discussions on critical and heterodox political economy matters since 1999, and for reading the entire first draft of this work, helping me to deal with problems I was blind to.

Donald Sassoon for being a constant source of advice for 20 years now, and for asking me frequently to review key books in IR for the *Political Quarterly*.

The editorial teams of the *Journal of Balkan and Near Eastern Studies* (Routledge, quarterly) and *Global Fault-lines* (an online publication initiated by my visionary co-author and long-time academic collaborator).

Participants in workshops and discussion groups at venues, such as the Graduate Center (CUNY), Woodrow Wilson Center and the Program in Hellenic Studies (Princeton University), SOAS (especially the annual 'Historical Materialism' Conference), Goldsmiths University of London, Queen Mary University of London, LSE (especially the 2011 Millennium Conference), and Sussex University (especially the workshop organized by Justin Rosenberg under the auspices of BISA's historical sociology group).

Last but not least, my wonderful, appreciative and tolerant wife, Maritsa V. Poros (City College, CUNY), for having to persevere with motherhood without the father, yet actively encouraging me and inspiring me with countless discussions and advice, both social and scholarly, in order to 'write a good book with Bülent'.

Bülent Gökay says:

This book has long been in the making. Vassilis and I began to discuss in the 1990s aspects of the US global hegemonic system in our various joint articles and seminars. Since this time I have personally benefited from the assistance, ideas and enthusiasm of so many people, who have shared my interests in the global political economy and the rise and fall of hegemonic systems. I cannot attempt to thank all of them, but here, briefly and incompletely, is an attempt to thank some of those sources of inspiration and friendship.

Ben Fowkes – my tutor, mentor and close friend since the 1980s – has consistently been most generous with his time, knowledge, materials and support. I owe a great debt to his works on modern history, in particular his work on the late communist and post-communist period.

I acknowledge a very special debt of gratitude to Darrell Whitman, my colleague and friend, for many hours of invaluable intellectual companionship, which has played a huge role in shaping my ideas and writing about global fault-lines over the last ten years. Special thanks are also due to Vildan Serin, whose fantastic advice on many aspects of the history of finance and economics added much to the development of my understanding of these issues. My colleagues in SPIRE and my students in my 'IR of Eurasia' class at Keele University over the last four years have been a great source of inspiration with their sharp observations, for which I thank them individually and collectively.

Above all I would like to thank my family who make everything possible: my daughters – Ada, Leyla and Saira – whose love and support made this project even more enjoyable; and Farzana for her continued encouragement, and keen editorial eye, which made all the difference.

Joint comments:

We both are solely responsible for the arguments advanced in this book. We have decided to dedicate this, our second joint book, to Peter Gowan. Peter prefaced our first work *The New American Imperialism* (2005). Since the early 1990s, he has been a constant source of inspiration for us, a scholar of high calibre and moral standards, whose immense intellectual powers have been, among others, in the right services of educating youth against the obscurantism of nationalisms and imperialisms of all sorts.

We also thank Susan Curran and her team at Curran Publishing Services Ltd for their work on the book.

ABBREVIATIONS

ACC	The seven most industrialized countries during the 'Golden Age' (1950–70): the United States, Canada, the United Kingdom, France, West Germany, Italy and Japan
ASEAN	Association of South-East Asian Nations
BP	British Petroleum
CBI	Confederation of British Industry
CDS	credit default swaps
CIPD	Chartered Institute for Personnel and Development (UK)
COMAC	Commercial Aircraft Corporation (China)
COMECON	Council for Mutual Economic Assistance
DWSR	Dollar–Wall Street regime
E-7	Emerging seven economies (Brazil, China, India, Indonesia, Mexico, Russia, Turkey)
ECB	European Central Bank
EEC	European Economic Community
EIA	Energy Information Administration (US)
EU	European Union
FIRE	finance, insurance and real estate
FDI	foreign direct investment
FTA	free trade agreement
GATT	General Agreement on Tariffs and Trade
GCSE	General Certificate of Secondary Education
GDP	gross domestic product
GNP	gross national product
IEA	International Energy Agency
IMF	International Monetary Fund
IPE	international political economy
IR	international relations
ISIC	International Standard Industrial Classification
KPMG	global network of professional firms providing tax and advisory services

MER	market exchange rate
NAFTA	North American Free Trade Association
NATO	North Atlantic Treaty Organization
NSC	National Security Council (US)
OECD	Organisation of Economic Co-operation and Development
OPEC	Organization of Petroleum Exporting Countries
PCI	Italian Communist Party
PDVSA	Petróleos de Venezuela S.A.
PPP	purchasing power parity
RMF	Research on Money and Finance (Research group on political economy at the School of Oriental and African Studies, University of London)
REE	rare earth elements
SIVs	structured investment vehicles
TARP	Toxic Asset Relief Programme
UK	United Kingdom
UN	United Nations
US	United States (of America)
USSR	Union of Soviet Socialist Republics
WEO	World Energy Outlook
WTO	World Trade Organization

INTRODUCTION

Imperialism is civilization unadulterated.
Oswald Spengler, *The Decline of the West* (1917)

In our first joint work, *The New American Imperialism* (2005), we predicted that globalization/financialization could not survive under a dollar-based regime of accumulation, and that it threatened the fundamentals of US global supremacy established in the 1940s under the influence of Dean Acheson and Paul Nitze. *The Fall of the US Empire* provides, in a historically and theoretically informed way, a review of the gradual and painful decline of the Anglo-American political economies since the late 1960s, a period in which they have been beset by the rise of a number of other capitalist caucuses around the world, especially in Southeast Asia. It identifies the visible shifts and less visible fault-lines that lie beneath the disintegrative tendencies of the Atlantic economies.

We reinterpret the past in light of the 'event': our point of departure is the global financial crisis that hit the Anglo-American heartland in summer 2007, and still continues by way of becoming a crisis of the real economy and of the political classes that are trying – unsuccessfully – to manage it. We argue that the roots of the crisis are to be found in the late 1960s and early 1970s, and that they are consubstantial with the relative economic decline of the United States as the key imperial power in the capitalist world order. Both the United States and the United Kingdom, the first and second powers of the imperial order, attempted to respond to their crisis and decline. But the two main policy responses to their own structural crisis, globalization and neoliberalism, did not succeed in reversing the course of their downturn. In fact, quite the opposite: instead of undoing decline, globalization – we use the term here as synonymous with US-led financialization – and neoliberalism weakened their political economies further. At the same time, it propped up the rise of other political economies, which have recently embraced capitalism (for instance China and Russia), or have previously been under a US-led 'debt fetter' (for example, Latin America). Economies burdened by artificially imposed debt could not sufficiently stimulate domestic demand. These political economies have now risen to such prominence as to directly challenge US supremacy. In short, this is the tragedy of globalization: a US-led policy undermining the very dominance of the United States in the world socio-economic system.

There is, in other words, a remaking of the imperial order as power shifts from its Western caucuses to the global East (China, India, Russia, Brazil and so on). The rise of other (than the United States) centres and regional caucuses of capital accumulation is a structural feature of the global system that Marxian discourses, following Leon Trotsky's insights, theorized as 'uneven and combined development' – which, in a way, assumes that the developmental impetus for the universe derives always from the West. The US-led accumulation regime was first undermined by (West) German and Japanese competition in the 1950s and 1960s, whereas it has been outperformed by China, India and other emerging economies from the 1980s onwards.

Our work aims at going beyond the notion of 'uneven and combined development'. If the power shift to the global East is other than linear and symmetrical, then what is it that is pulling the global imperial system in all sorts of geographical and regional directions, refashioning its class and power relations? This, we argue, is a structural, all-encompassing force for which we use the term 'global fault-lines'. It refers to the uneven and combined economic, geopolitical, environmental, political and even ideational developments that have taken place under social and class struggles since the 1970s. These developments, among others, include such events as the collapse of the USSR, the policy processes of financialization and neo-imperialism, the continuous destruction of the environment, the constructivist moment of US grand strategy after 9/11 – that is, the fabricated and ideational 'war on terror' myth – and so forth. Never before in modern history has the world been in such a shape. This study distinguishes three of all these developments and considers them as being the key vulnerabilities not only of the US empire-state, but of all new rising and aspiring global powers:

- A historically unusual and complicated type of globalization (for example, pension funds in Texas and Montana hold Greek debt, and what if Greece defaults on its debt?).
- The world is on the verge of environmental catastrophe (for example, the climate change problem).

- The finite nature of raw materials is in full swing (is the hybrid car the future?).

These three observable developments are systemic. The explosive growth of the financial system relative to manufacturing and the economy as a whole, and the proliferation of speculative and destabilizing financial instruments of parasitic wealth accumulation, have shattered the Anglo-American heartland. Eventually, however, this vulnerability is becoming manifest in the West, but it should not be surprising if it appears in the global East too, in the event that it adopts similar instruments and methods for dealing with a possible crisis of profitability in its industrial sector in the future.

In terms of their long-term effects, the greatest vulnerabilities of the world system as a whole are probably resource depletion and environmental degradation. The availability and distribution of critical resources such as oil, food and water, and the continuing degradation of the ecosystem at least from the 1970s onwards, speak volumes about the inability of the ruling classes around the world to control the discursive structural powers of global fault-lines. Patently, these all are constraints/vulnerabilities not just upon the United States, but upon all global powers and the world system as a whole. The world system may not have the capacity to sustain another full-fledged major developmental impetus led by China and India, so the prospect of a democratically and regionally/locally planned world economy, oriented towards satisfying social need rather than maximizing profit, at least in the major centres of global capital accumulation (Europe, the Western hemisphere, South and East Asia) arises as the only feasible alternative.

Having said this, global fault-lines go beyond any concept developed so far by international relations (IR) literature, especially its progressive Marxist and Marxisant branches, to describe hegemonic transition and global crises. Inspired by Andre Gunder Frank's work, this concept may well lead IR research to new theoretical and empirical avenues, overcoming even the restrictions of such useful concepts, such as that of 'combined and uneven development'. Such concepts, we argue, despite their relative heuristic value, are subject to pro-Western, and not truly global, approaches (the Box that follows this Introduction makes explicit the definition of the concept as we used it throughout the book as well as its advantages compared to the notion of 'uneven and combined development').

Our narrative unfolds as follows.

Chapter 1 looks at methodological issues, defines the key

concepts of our work and reviews critically the relevant literature on the subject. Our theses and views are tested against major works in the field of international political economy, such as those by Robert Brenner, Leo Panitch and Giovanni Arrighi. Chapter 2 is a critical presentation of the so-called 'Golden Age of capitalism', and lays the foundation for a thorough examination of globalization and neoliberalism that, as clusters of policy led by the Anglo-American core, came into being straight after the collapse of the Bretton Woods regime in 1971, if not before. Chapters 3 and 4, entitled 'The failure of financial statecraft (1) and (2)', reflect a division of the developmental trajectory of the West which we have opted to follow. From 1971 to 1991 growth was very weak and profitability very low. But during the Clinton era, seemingly, growth picked up as well as the rates of profit in both manufacturing and financial sectors. These two chapters show, among others, that globalization and neoliberalism, as policy responses to the crisis of the previous accumulation regime driven by Keynesianism and fixed exchange rates, failed to reverse the declining profit rates in the West, as most of the aggregate growth achieved, especially in the 1990s, was debt-driven.

As we pointed out earlier, if financialization is a key vulnerability of the global capitalist system affecting all great powers, whether declining or rising, then resource depletion and environmental degradation are the other two. In Chapters 5 and 6 we examine these two key vulnerabilities of the United States and potentially of new rising powers, first and foremost of China, whereas the Conclusion of the book outlines the main findings and explains the necessity for a new economic system geared to sustainable human development, ecological plenitude and the cultivation of genuine human relationships.

A DEFINITION OF GLOBAL FAULT-LINES

Global fault-lines is inspired by the late Andre Gunder Frank's work, in particular his *ReOrient* (1998). We conceive of the term as referring to a post-Hegelian and post-Marxian totality across historical time and space, and whose elements and instances (political, economic, cultural, ideational, societal, geopolitical, geographical and ecological) are discursively interconnected, articulated and mingled, invariably generating political and economic change, global hegemonic transitions and power shifts. Just like the movements in the tectonic plates originating in Earth's radioactive, solid iron inner core, the vast shifts in the structures of the international system are the outcome of changes that have been taking place beneath the surface of social life for decades, if not centuries and millennia. These ongoing movements, mostly happening beneath the surface of social life, but becoming more visible in times of acute crisis, constitute and codetermine 'global fault-lines'.

The term applies to premodern and precapitalist epochs, despite the fact that there is a different articulation of the elements composing the post-Hegelian totality then. We do not accept that there was a 'premodernity' first and a 'modernity' that followed. Rather, we believe that elements and structures of premodern eras exist in modern times and vice versa. Human history has never been singular, linear and uniform.

The 'prime mover' – to use an Aristotelian notion – of global fault-lines is social and class struggle, as they develop both within the ensemble of dominant power structures *and* between ruling and dominated classes. Struggles (agencies in action) and political economies and states (structures mobilized by agencies) may determine in the *first* but not in the *last* instance the elements and articulations of the post-Hegelian/post-Marxian totality. Capitalists (agents) do not control capitalism (structure). There are other forces in play that we disclose empirically with the theoretical employment of this new concept. Global fault-lines rest on a plural, not singular determination of social and historical continuity, change and hegemonic transitions. In this sense, Marx is still useful: 'the concrete is concrete', he wrote in the 'Introduction' to *Grundrisse* (1857), 'because is the concentration of many determinations, hence unity in diversity'.

Global fault-lines do not have a Eurocentric point of departure, as seems to be the case with the notion of *uneven and combined development* (UCD). First launched by Leo Trotsky and further elaborated by George Novack, Ernest Mandel, Michel Löwy and Justin Rosenberg, UCD has partial heuristic and explanatory powers. Although it is extremely useful in capturing global capitalist developments, it abstracts from global political, societal, cultural and ideational structures upon which such developments rest. It attributes primacy to (uneven and combined) economic development as if unable to get rid of the 'determination in the last analysis' by the economic instance.

Historically, and with the exception of Rosenberg, all aforemen-
tioned thinkers seem to have conceived of the term as having its
point of departure in British capitalism, which then spreads in
an uneven and combined developmental way around the globe.
In other words, it reads as a Eurocentric concept. Accordingly,
the world is divided into 'the West' and 'the rest', and a system
of knowledge is constructed around a series of binary hierarchies
with Europe unfailingly occupying the higher position, whether
culturally or otherwise. Even Trotsky, the most brilliant mind
of the Bolshevik revolution, could not escape this Eurocentric
bias.

We introduce a new concept in the progressive and scholarly
literature and we are employing it specifically in order to
understand not just the current financial crisis but what lies
beneath it, both historically and structurally. The concept helps
us to analyse the transformations that have been occurring
discursively and in various geographical caucuses of capital
accumulation – what we call 'the global East' – and to examine
the impact of such significant changes on the hegemonic
structure(s) of post-1945 international political economy. In
his *Global Shift* (2007), Peter Dicken describes this ongoing
process as 'the changing global economic map', arguing that
'old geographies of production, distribution and consumption
are continuously being disrupted and that new geographies are
continuously being created'. We argue that 'global fault-lines'
has the intellectual might to explain this process, in the sense
that the strength of a hegemonic power can only be properly
measured relative to other powers and political economies, and
that hegemonic ascendancies and declines correlate strongly
to available resources and politico-economic durability. Paul
Kennedy was not far off the mark when he argued that military
overstretch and a concomitant relative decline is the consistent
threat facing hegemonic and imperial powers, whose ambition
and security requirements come to be greater than the resource
base they can amass.

1

GLOBAL FAULT-LINES

The most specific feature of this social group, which separates it
from the proletariat and the bourgeoisie alike, is its alienation
from economic life. This group does not participate in productive
activities or in commercial transactions; its representatives, at
times, do not even bother to show up to cash out the bonds with
their own hands. This is why we can consider this group as being
one that becomes active only *in the sphere of consumption*. The
foundation of the entire life of the rentier is consumption – and
the psychology of 'pure consumption' becomes their 'lifestyle'.
Nikolai Bukharin, *Die Politische Ökonomie des Rentners*,
1914 (Verlag für Literatur und Politik, 1926)

PRELIMINARY OBSERVATIONS

There is some analytical confusion concerning the literature on
globalization (a term invented in the West to serve specific
purposes), financialization and the state. Here, we confine ourselves
to setting out some conceptual and methodological propositions/
clarifications in order to pave the ground for a critique of some of
the most influential works on the current financial crisis.

A good starting point could be to clarify the linkages between the
domestic and *external* domains of state activity, what old-fashioned
realist theory in international relations (IR) calls 'second' and 'third'
(or systemic) 'images'.[1] These two analytical instances of social and
political action are intrinsically interlinked, and at the same time
relatively distinct, not least because of the differing policy practices,
institutional structures and jurisdictions that pertain to each one
of them. But mainstream IR does not take into account a 'fourth
image', that of the empire-state. This 'image'/category or ideal-
type is as significant as the other two categories, not least because

it determines the key structures, practices and actions of them. For instance, as we have shown elsewhere, the US empire-state determines the policy and ideational contours of its key Eurasian allies (Europe, Japan, Middle Eastern and Latin American states) through hub-and-spoke arrangements, although the subordinate states in the imperial chain maintain a relative autonomy in order to organize class hegemony and other security interests in their respective domestic/national domains.[2] In other words, subaltern states can question and challenge each other on certain issues, and they can also implement certain policies independently, but all these initiatives cannot challenge the fundamentals of supremacy of the empire-state – its class and security interests – by, for example, allying with a major rival. Having said this, we would put forward at this point three important propositions reflecting contemporary reality and settings:

- What came to be called as neoliberalism/neoconservatism in the wake of the Margaret Thatcher and Ronald Reagan 'revolutions' since 1979 applies, predominately but not exclusively, to the domestic environment of the capitalist state.
- What has commonly been called globalization, a term popularized under the Bill Clinton administration in the 1990s, should be seen as a policy of rampant financialization that, predominately but not exclusively, applies to the external environment of the capitalist state.
- The US empire-state is the lead agency of this Atlantic/ Eurocentric globalization/financialization and neoliberalism, dictating policy to other core, but not all, capitalist states and peripheries via hub-and-spoke arrangements, even if those states and regional blocs maintain a relative autonomy for class, and sometimes security/military, purposes. For example, these states or regions need a relative autonomy from the US hub in order to organize political hegemony over their respective populations. They do not always succumb to US pressure. In fact, at times, they oppose US policies (for instance, the conflict between the European Union and the United States on trade issues).

But globalization did not begin in the 1990s. Strictly speaking, globalization is directly linked to the process of the liberalization of banking and finance that began in the wake of the collapse of the Bretton Woods system in the late 1960s and early 1970s. This breakdown was not the result of a spontaneous collapse of the dollar–gold parity. In fact, it was a politically conscientious decision taken by the Richard Nixon administration as a response to the pressure exercised on the dollar's gold link by the other two caucuses of capitalist accumulation, notably Japan, on the one hand, and France and Western Germany on the other.[3] The move away from the fixed exchange rates regime and the ability of the US state to set the price of the dollar without any obligation to any constraint, initiated new forms of money circulation and profiteering on the basis of what we can call *'financialization via dollarization'*. This means that since the end of Bretton Woods, financial operators (individuals, investment banks, hedge funds and so on) could take advantage of the freed money markets and set benchmarks of moving cash and paper around – in the form of securities, derivatives, bonds, gambling in the stock market and so on – on the basis of the floating dollar, now the key global and unfettered reserve currency. This is a key feature of the post-1971 phase of globalization/financialization. It is interesting to note that Nixon's decision to place the entire global capitalist economy on a dollar standard was immediately accompanied by an agreement with the Saudi oligarchy that oil trade be denominated in dollars.[4] Among others, the aim of this agreement was that the surplus of dollars resulting from petroleum trade be invested in US Treasury bills, which in turn would help the United States to refinance its current account deficit and other debt obligations, including defence spending. This is exactly what has been happening since, the sole difference being that other US Treasury bill buyers became increasingly important, most notably Japan in the 1980s and 1990s and China more recently. Having said this, we would argue that both policies, that of globalization/financialization (predominately systemic) and that of neoliberalism (predominately domestic), were initiated by the Anglo-American alliance, trying to relaunch and revamp the policy envisaged in Bretton Woods and which Richard Gardner had accurately called 'sterling–dollar diplomacy'.[5]

As we know from the work of Adam Smith, Karl Marx and other social theorists, forms of globalization and financialization are innate to capitalist modernity, and so they existed before the 1970s – we will also review Giovanni Arrighi's work later.[6] Yet the period that started in the 1970s assumed different structural characteristics, the most important of which is the high degree of interpenetration of international finance and speculative arbitrage across frontiers and states.[7] The Bretton Woods period was the only time in US imperial history since the 1890s that the US 'open door' policy was somewhat constrained by the gold standard and the fixed exchange rate regime.[8] But since at least 1968, the United States, manipulating the dollar, began unleashing the 'open door' in a most ferocious and aggressive manner, encouraging and fostering high levels of speculation, financialization and both domestic and international institutional engineering towards neoliberal reforms (liberalization of the banking and financial sectors, abolition of capital controls, privatizations, reform of the General Agreement on Tariffs and Trade, GATT, wage and welfare state retrenchment, and so on). The aim was the transformation of the domestic environment of subaltern states after the image of US and UK neo-capitalisms.

Any further attempt at generalization might be problematic, the reason being that financialization in the Anglo-American world of free markets and shadow banking does not have the same functions and institutional connotations as in the Eurozone dominated by Germany, and the Japanese model. When Rudolf Hilferding in his classic *Finance Capital* (1910) defined finance as the merger of banking and industrial capital, he had in mind the institutional framework of Germanic states and empires (Germany, Austria), not that of Wall Street. According to Hilferding, *finance capital* should be distinguished from *financial capital*, the latter being the capital that characterized the epoch of competitive capitalism which Marx wrote about (Marx distinguished between *industrial, merchant* and *financial capital*). But finance capital dominates the era of monopoly capitalism as industrial capital merges with banking capital under the dominance of the banks. Thus, it is vital not to confuse finance capital with financial capital, the former being the fusion of industrial and banking/financial capital, the latter being banks and all sorts of capitalist enterprises/individuals dealing with money.[9]

The problem is that German/Japanese capitalisms (with a substantive institutional and even state presence in commodity markets) operate on a different institutional base than the Anglo-American model (unregulated market and 'open door' primacy).[10] The Anglo-American model still runs the first reserve currency in the world, the US dollar, with UK sterling losing its second position to the euro after its introduction in 1999. We find it, therefore, extremely problematic to try to produce a general definition of the concept of financialization, and wherever we use the term here we intend it to mean the way finance operates in the internationalized markets of – strictly speaking – the United Kingdom and the United States. To put it differently, we use the term financialization as a movement that, stemming from its US–UK core, aims at penetrating other markets across the world. Thus, Anglo-American paper assets, liquid, deals and all sorts of banking practices and regulations of the so-called 'new political economy' penetrate Asian and European markets, contaminating their institutional frameworks, yet this has to do with the effects of globalization, rather than being the source of it.

This is now the time to make clear that profits resulting from financialization should not be confused with profits emanating from material production (for instance, manufacturing). Profits generated from rentier and commercial activities (such as speculative arbitrage in currency markets, interest-based profits and so on) do not stem from production of use values, although they may be invested for such a purpose. Along with classical economists, Marxists and other Marxisants, such as Andrew Glyn and Robert Brenner, we use the concepts of *profit, profit rate* and *average rate of profit* only if applicable to material production of use values. In particular, we define as *rate of profit* the percentage return on capital employed in material production. In this respect, profit and *surplus value* are forms, expressions of the social relations of production and exchange, but surplus value is only extracted during the process of material production, where direct producers (labour power) are legally dissociated/dispossessed from the means and objects of their labour.

Unlike mainstream world system theory (for example, Immanuel Wallerstein and others following him), or realist/neorealist international policy economy (IPE) (for example Robert Gilpin and Stephen Krasner), which privilege the process of commodity circulation over material production in the definition of capitalist social orders, and unlike orthodox Marxists that see production determining circulation in the 'last instance', we counter by arguing that material production determines circulation only in the *first instance*. In this way – as we shall see in more detail later and with a plethora of empirical evidence – we avoid a twin fundamentalism: the fundamentalism of the market relation, whether commodity or money market relation, and the fundamentalism of the relations of production.[11] Having said this, we are very sceptical of the official statistical information we have obtained in the course of research for this book. Thus, the tables and the statistics we have opted to use here are either carefully selected, or are elaborated by authors with whom we share our views about the manner in which real gross domestic product (GDP) and other aggregate data are measured. In any case, we use all quantitative data, statistics, tables and graphs as a way to indicate *historical trends*, not absolute extractions of solid conclusions and dogmas.

We can now formulate a theoretical proposition upon which we base our main contention in this work: there is a fundamental power shift to the global East (Russia, Brazil, South Africa, Indonesia, China, India), and the reasons for this are to be found not in the current crisis of financialization alone, but in the configuration of the totality of social and production relations that have been emanating from the Anglo-American core since the late 1960s. It is virtually impossible for the United States to regain the power it enjoyed in the 1940s and 1950s by, say, falling back on a path of sustainable growth and prosperity under whatever policy initiative, post-Keynesian or otherwise, inasmuch as the erosion of its productive, industrial, material basis seems to be historically irreversible. The United States may well turn out to be a great power among others, but not the super-power of the 1950s.[12] This erosion of the industrial base of the Anglo-American economy has been accompanied by the outsourcing of labour power to the global East, especially China and India, which increasingly operate through economies of scale that 'could dwarf those currently enjoyed with the US market'.[13] This reflects the potential for sustained growth and determines the money-capital in circulation and the political power embedded in these. Our insistence on the significance of manufacturing is not just an axiomatic 'article of faith', as Giovanni Arrighi put it in his debate with Robert Brenner (see our analysis below). Manufacturing is the ontological social base for the reproduction of life, and it is as significant in modernity, however defined, as it has been in all social systems that preceded modernity, East and West. In short, our claim that the remaking of the imperial order after the tragedy of globalization is under way has its foundations here.

This erosion of manufacturing, in turn, especially the deepening of the Chinese market through economies of scale, creates immense problems for the United States with the management of aggregate demand in periods of crisis, making even partial economic recovery very hard and nearly impossible.[14] In addition, it has enormous repercussions on the ability of the US–UK axis to shape the security contours of the world. Almost three months after we wrote that the United States could not take the lead in the Libyan war because of financial constraints, thus making way basically for France, US Defence Secretary Robert Gates admitted exactly the same in his outgoing speech. He warned that NATO is facing the real possibility of military and security irrelevance, if European powers do not increase and rationalize their defence spending, adding that: 'any successor who advocated a land war in Asia or the Middle East should have his head examined'.[15] Meanwhile, in June 2011, China announced the construction of its first aircraft carrier. In addition, during the 49th Paris Air Show in June 2011, the largest event in aviation and space in the world with over 2,100 exhibitors and nearly half a million visitors, the Chinese manufacturer COMAC (Commercial Aircraft Corporation of China) presented models of its future planes, which compete directly especially with the Airbus A320 and Boeing B737.[16]

We contend that the current crisis should be seen as a systemic crisis of a particular form of capitalism, neoliberal capitalism.[17] It is the outcome of the exhaustion of the (false) responses employed by the Anglo-American elites to deal with the over-accumulation crisis of the 1970s. It is, therefore, the outcome of deep-seated contradictions within the uneven/asymmetrical structure of the global economic system. But it should not be seen as a failure of the global system as a whole. Crises such as the one we are experiencing today are central to the mode of functioning of the global system itself, with the global East assuming pride of place in the international and technical division of labour. New caucuses of capitalist accumulation have been developed, especially in South and Southeast Asia. Furthermore, other combinations of capitalist cooperation – not necessarily between states with close geographical proximity – have emerged, balancing out the declining capitalist core centred on the US–UK axis.[18] We argue that the most defining security characteristics of the present era are not the fall of the Soviet Union or 9/11, but Russia's and China's transition to capitalism, giving a new impetus to global economic competition between regional hubs around large states – the Western core, on the one hand, and the new rising caucuses such as Russia, China, India, Indonesia, Brazil, South Africa and Turkey on the other.

It is in this respect that, arguably, the 'law' of uneven and combined development, coupled with environmental degradation and the depletion of natural resources, is acquiring new forms and impetuses, disintegrating the Anglo-American economic primacy even further.[19] The transition of Russia and China to capitalism has not been such great news for the United States after all. In the main, this is what we exemplify here as 'global fault-lines'. Mainstream economists and policymakers, such as Alan Blinder, Joseph Stiglitz and Larry Summers, have a different way of putting all this: they express 'concerns' about whether globalization – see open door in the form it acquired since the 1970s – works to the benefit of the United States.

As far as the European Union is concerned, and given the plight of the Eurozone especially from 2009 onwards, the only country that seems to have substantial global industrial significance and economic clout is Germany. This crisis, therefore, is the result of an uneven, combined and 'long' historical/developmental process, pertaining to transitions from one imperial power to another, from one dominant state or group of states to another.[20] We adopt a structuralist reading of capitalist history according to which all previous epochs are present in the 'long' (Arrighi) or 'short' (Hobsbawm) twentieth century, and are subject to the fault-lines created by uneven and combined development, social struggles, the relative and continuous decline of the United States since the late 1960s, the fall of authoritarian socialism in 1989–91, the ecological crisis and the depletion of natural resources, especially of raw materials, such as oil. To use an analogy to the complex motions of large plates of the Earth's outer shell, the lithosphere, this is a discussion of shifting tectonic plates in the world economy, longer-term movements together with some more sudden and unexpected eruptions. At this moment of acute systemic crisis, great shifts are taking place in the balance of economic strength among the global powers, and all this is hemmed in by the problems of resource depletion and environmental degradation. However, global fault-lines act as a constraint on all great powers, old and new: nobody can escape class struggle, resources depletion and the looming ecological crisis.

New fault-lines can be discerned in the global economic and political system. Just like the movements of the tectonic plates originating in Earth's radioactive, solid iron inner core, the vast shifts in the structures of the international system are the outcome of changes that have been taking place beneath the surface of social and economic life for decades. Yet social and class struggle, widely perceived, has been and is central to these movements, as opposed to a certain 'dialectics of nature' implied in the analogy here. Social struggles cut across the national and international levels, ramified in the spatial contours of the social and technical division of labour and capital as the West and the East penetrate each other's domains and social power structures. There are class struggles that are taking place among capitalists, as well as class struggles that manifest themselves between capital and labour, all of which are inscribed and effected onto/into state apparatuses and international institutions. But we are able to observe that current struggles within the business and political executives of the victorious powers of the Second World War are not in a position to be absorbed by those executives, as they lack the means to economically support any meaningful expansion at both national and international levels, which would have diffused the crisis. It is, in other words, a question of development: the United States cannot act as a lever for the development of other societies as it did after the Second World War. As we shall illustrate below, Anglo-American power is a debtor power and has been so since the 1960s. In other words we should be counting the years and days of this *neoimperialism without credit*.[21]

In order to grow further, the world economy needs qualitative changes and leadership that the US–UK axis can no longer provide. There are limits to reform in the global economic system, but at no other time in the last half-century have those limits seemed more flexible. The crisis has already brought irreversible geopolitical consequences. The US economy and the rest of the US-centred economies of the West are fast losing ground. China, India and other large emerging economies, have been strengthening considerably. The underlying feature of the current situation is this historical shift: the 'unipolar' phase of US dominance is being replaced by a 'multipolar' phase, in which the United States will continue to remain one of the most prominent powers – we do not know for how long – but has to share this position with China and India as the biggest and fastest growing rising economic powers. One of the most interesting results of the global crisis, so far, is the acceleration of the global economic power shift toward emerging economies.[22] The economies to watch now are the E-7 (Emerging Seven): China, India, Brazil, Russia, Mexico, Indonesia and Turkey, or what we call here 'the global East'. The rest of the twenty-first century will be increasingly dominated by this relationship between the United States and China, India, Russia and other rising powers, and it is this that determines the process of the remaking of the global imperial order.[23]

We have laid down our main theses and we are now in possession of the conceptual and methodological apparatuses needed in order to examine some views about the current financial crisis.

BEYOND CONVENTIONAL WISDOM

On September 15, 2008, the supposedly safe and perpetually prosperous world of globalized finance and banking structures blew itself up when Lehman Brothers filed for Chapter 11 bankruptcy. True, the credit crunch kicked in earlier (in summer 2007) with the collapse of Fannie Mae and Freddie Mac in the United States and Northern Rock in the United Kingdom, but this 158-year old iconic investment bank was forced into this act of extremes, when the initial breakdown of the US mortgage market turned securitized mortgage-backed debt obligations into toxic assets. Initially, $7.8 billion of mortgage-related bonds were considered worthless. The bank also admitted that it still had $54 billion of exposure to hard-to-value mortgage-backed securities. Triumphant post-industrial Anglo-American capitalism, free of labour-power contestations that kept recording defeats since the late 1970s, seemed to have been brought to its knees by none other than itself. Unlike the crisis in the mid-1970s which liberal orthodoxy attributed – certainly mischievously – to the 'powerful labour movement and its high wages', the 2007–08 global credit crunch could not be attributed, purposefully or not, to such a cause: this crisis was entirely centred upon a rentier capitalist class, Anglo-American in origin and inspiration. Since the breakdown of the Bretton Woods system this class had proved incapable of managing the contradictions of globalization and neoliberalism it created, and envisaged both as a response to the over-accumulation crisis of the 1970s. In other words, this crisis is linked to the structural contradictions produced and reproduced historically within the dominant economic structures.

The crisis has already generated a vast amount of commentary – some polemical and some more measured. Mainstream analysts in the United States and the United Kindom have converged around subprime mortgage lending as being the immediate cause of the crisis, which was exported to other countries, especially in the Eurozone, through an interconnected web of global financial instruments propped up by new laws facilitating globalization. Others focused on the lessening of regulations on the financial system and the very low interest rates introduced by the US Fed to counter the effects of the 2000 'New Economy' stock market bubble – which was eventually replaced by the housing bubble.

We disagree with these interpretations, and find them superfluous and even dangerous, as the policy recommendations accompanying them are often along the lines 'we need less state, not more', or 'the financial services authorities regulating bond markets failed to do their job properly'.[24] Instead, we argue that the subprime lending itself was one of the many manifestations of a crisis registered in the broader processes of financialization and liberalization, which were put forth as policy responses to the crisis of profitability in the late 1960s and early 1970s. The tragedy of globalization, among others, regards the inability of Anglo-American agencies, whether state or otherwise, to solve the over-accumulation crisis of the 1970s by resorting to the liberalization of finance and banking, and to the manipulation of monetary instruments, such as interest rates, while curtailing welfare spending.[25]

Concentration/accumulation and circulation of industrial/productive capital are not the same as concentration/accumulation and circulation of money capital, especially in the Anglo-American world. Whereas the former tends to create crises of profitability, the latter is responsible for bubbles and illusions of profitability, and therefore illusions of prosperity and growth. Hence it leads to the 'boom and bust cycles', as Robert Brenner put it. It is clear, therefore, that we cannot treat financialization and production as an integrated and cumulative form of capital, as do most mainstream economists, and also those whose work is inspired by Antonio Negri's post-structuralist theories of empire. 'The thesis that is being put forth here', Christian Marazzi – one of Negri's followers – writes, 'is that financialisation is not an unproductive/parasitic deviation of growing quotas of surplus-value and collective saving, but rather the form of capital accumulation symmetrical with new processes of value production.'[26] In other words, production/circulation of commodities and speculation/circulation of money are dealt with in an integrated way, as if both are carriers of value.

Subprime lending and various types of the so-called 'self-certified mortgages' are spinoffs of financialization for the sake of easy and greedy profiteering or, one might say, the new 'hype' that jumped into markets in the wake of the bust of the 'dot.com' bubble in 2000. (Previous crashes include the US stock market crash of 1987 and the late 1990s, the Japanese financial crisis of the early 1990s and the Southeast Asian panic of 1997–98.) As such, 'easy lending' did not cause the current tragedy of Atlantic capitalism. Rather, it was the entire complex macro-historical and contradictory process of ecologically unfriendly deindustrialization, and the move away from Keynesian regimes of accumulation, that were responsible for the plight of Anglo-American political economy today.

A number of authors, including Marazzi, have argued that Keynesianism has always been in operation, inasmuch as the switch from the 'public' to the 'private' has had the same operational effect, namely the boosting of aggregate demand and consumer power via the creation of bubbles and access to easy credit. This may be quite misleading. Bubbles are, in fact, quite political. As a political matter, subprime lending was encouraged by governments and private agencies alike, both because it served the interests of the system in maximising fictitious profits and because it generated an illusion of value in private property that reinforced capitalist values of growth for growth's sake among the middle and the working classes, and even among the totally pauperized. But this does not mean that Keynesian policymaking is the flipside of the neoconservative/neoliberal policy: that is, the type of state policy that has been taking place since the late 1970s, and that was initiated by Margaret Thatcher and Ronald Reagan. Keynes himself was very aware of the catastrophic economic potential of financialization, when in one of his most perceptive comments in the *General Theory* he wrote: 'Speculators may do no harm as bubbles on a steady stream of enterprise. But the position is serious when enterprise becomes the bubble on a whirlpool of speculation.'[27] (We analyse the wider policy context of this statement below.)

As we shall explain in more detail below, we are not subscribing to certain analyses that stem directly from a Kalleckian–Minskyan–Keynesian 'instability hypothesis', according to which the current crisis is the result of the mismatch between state regulation and the new economy of financial capitalism that tends to damage the so-called 'real economy'.[28] Although we recognize the scholarly and positive contribution of this trend to the study of international political economy, and we have certainly benefited from these contributions, we argue that the whole issue is far more complicated. Finance is not simply a 'superstructure' of production, but a class relation penetrating social life and production itself.

The fusion/interaction between banking and industrial capital – what Hilferding called 'finance capital' – finds such a historical expression mainly in a German/continental institutional context, but this is not predominantly the case with Anglo-American capitalism. In the Anglo-Saxon world of freedom and liberty, especially in 'switching periods' in which finance comes to dominate the social economy after an over-accumulation crisis in industry, the key to understanding finance and its contradictions is to treat them separately from the realm of capitalist production. As we stated earlier, the interpenetrative function of industrial, banking, commercial and financial capital does not have the same effects upon the formation of money markets in the Anglo-American world as in Germany and/or Japan. In the dollar–sterling world of finance and free enterprise, shadow banking, hedging, bond markets and other financial instruments acquire a life of their own that pertains to the Marxian equation 'M-M', with minimal institutional or other real commodity-type mediation.[29] In the event, those who fail to make this distinction, tend either to propose as policy solutions more financial regulations by way of using financial instruments (bailouts, 'quantitative easing', interest rate manipulation across currency zones and so on), or a robust state intervention along Keynesian lines, forgetting that none of the alternatives provides a long-term solution. As Saskia Sassen has pointed out, using financial instruments to solve a financial crisis is not at all adequate, not least because the real causes of the crisis lie elsewhere.[30]

Most of the debates in the media are related to 'how much' and 'what kind' of new financial regulation is needed. Even more critical and nuanced commentators ended up explaining the crisis by the 'stupidity, poor economic analysis and sheer ignorance' of central bankers, politicians and auditing agencies, and even the greediness of bank managers and directors with their sky-high bonuses.[31] Such explanations, focusing on the blatant deceit and corruption of financial players, run the risk of downplaying the structural features and tendencies of international political economy in the twenty-first century, which indeed breeds such financial meltdowns. For example, Madoff's Ponzi scheme did not cause anything. It simply took advantage of a reality structured around a flow of liquidity and paper money sustained, through acts of omission and commission, by national and international agencies and policies.[32]

There are certain requisites for a capitalist economy to function smoothly. Capital is a social relation and a process of circulation in which capitalists throw in money in order to collect it back with a robust profit on top. This profit, or part of it, then goes back to circulation and investment, seeking more profit and so on. It has been estimated that, through this process of capital circulation, investment and profit generation, the economy needs a compound rate of growth of around 3 per cent.[33] This rate of growth is necessary, if not vital, for capital and the capitalist economy as a whole to avoid being in a recession.

Another important and related requisite is the following: in a depression-free capitalist economy the wealth being produced throughout the system must be sold. If investment falls below savings, a gap opens up between what has been produced and what is being sold. Some producers cannot sell what they produced, and they have to scale down or even close, as a result of which their workers lose their jobs. This reduces still further what can be sold in the system. This did not happen until the recent crisis in the United States, because easy lending to US and UK consumers had provided an easy domestic market and absorbed the surplus production. The credit crunch put a stop to this, because banks and mortgage lenders, fearing that they will be unable to meet their own financial obligations, avoid lending money to one another and to customers in general. Mortgages are no longer as easily obtainable and now require a large deposit from the buyer as a guarantee against possible default. Even if credit institutions recover confidence (and capacity) in lending to each other, it is not likely that they would start lending to people again soon with the same relaxed attitude. Credit will not start flowing just because banks can access more liquidity. Instead, and most likely, banks will use the funds to shore up their own finances, fix up bad debts and build up their capital base in an attempt to achieve solvency.

Let us recap the main point we have made so far. What has been missing in mainstream explanations of the crisis (especially in the media) is any deep grasp of the underlying, complex historical and structural causes of the crisis and its Anglo-American 'dollar–sterling' context, which initiated everything. There is an overemphasis on proximate causes – the US housing bubble and the huge size of the US economy, persistent unresolved global imbalances, a lack of government regulation of the financial sector, lax regulation and insufficient regulation that led to widespread underestimation of risk.[34] We argue that all these are still symptoms or short-term precipitate causes. Explanations and solutions are put forward on the basis that the causes of the crisis are to be found in the contemporary managerial remit of credit and finance alone, whether national or international. As a result any solution framework that is proposed pertains to the sphere of circulation alone. But it is arguably not the case that these were the basic causes. What is missing in the current debate is any real grasp of the underlying causes of the crisis.

MARXISANT DISCOURSES ON THE FINANCIAL CRISIS

In times of crisis like this, where the organization of societies was and is being built on liberal economic dogmas, most schools of thought in IR and international political economy (IPE), from constructivists to all sorts of realists and liberals, opt for either aligning themselves with conventional wisdom and mainstream media views, or remaining silent. Some seem to want to defect, but do not quite do so.[35] Only critical theorists and those operating within the Marxist/ Keynesian tradition offer sound reflections and cogent argumentation about the causes and consequences of the crisis. This section of our study is committed to them, presenting a summary of their views and even critiquing them, as it is critique alone that can improve scholarship and provide a better understanding of social issues. Their views will be revisited in accordance with the specific topics dealt with in each chapter here, and as we move along with our concrete analyses and empirical material.

Every major capitalist crisis has both long-term structural/ systemic roots and shorter-term precipitate causes. A global crisis can be better understood when analysed in a long-term historical perspective together with a specific reference to short-term causes. From this perspective, one must be able to distinguish, as Antonio Gramsci did, between 'organic movements' and movements which may be termed 'conjunctural (and which appear as occasional, immediate, almost accidental').[36] To put this differently, we must distinguish *structural* sources of crisis/conflict from *contingent* sources of crisis/conflict.[37] We argue that the historical/structural roots of the current crisis are to be found in the expiration of the model of capitalist accumulation for the core countries in the West in the 1970s, whereas the short-term precipitate causes are to be found in the contradictions of financialization/globalization. Both sets of causes, seen as social and political processes, cross each other.

Having said this, and in order to achieve a clear sense of the present crisis and its origins, we should first look at a broad picture regarding the configuration of the world economy in a long-term historical perspective: that is to say, how the global economy has been organized, its contradictions and trends, as well as the kind of shifts that have been taking place since the inception of the global supremacy of the United States during the Second World War. Such a long-term perspective is essential because, as we shall show, the recent crisis is a clear expression of the structural transformations and deep-rooted contradictions which have occurred within the global system, particularly affecting the old capitalist core – that is, the economic regions of North America, Western Europe and Japan – since the late 1960s.

Ernest Mandel was perhaps the first intellectual who saw the breakdown of the Bretton Woods system and the dollar devaluation as the beginning of a perpetual crisis of US neo-imperialism.[38] Mandel's views were opposed, among others, by Nicos Poulantzas's influential work in France, Germany and the United Kingdom at the time, arguing that the thesis of the economic decline of the United States is wholly misleading. According to Poulantzas – whose views are in some important respects echoed today in the scholarly work by Leo Panitch, Sam Gindin and others – the supremacy and centrality of US capital over European social formations and Japan, as well as the forms in which such domination finds expression, leave no doubt as to the dominant position of the United States in the global imperial chain, hence the misleading character of any discourse about US decline.[39] In Germany, however, some theses put forth by Klaus Busch in the late 1970s espoused the Mandel position, arguing that the United States lost its post-war hegemonic position in the wake of the breakdown of Bretton Woods.[40]

Today, Panitch and other scholars working around the journal *Socialist Register,* and finding it rather difficult to establish concrete empirical evidence that undermines the thesis of the long-term, historical economic decline of the United States, would lay out a rather political thesis: 'to posit a terminal decline in US imperial power is to attempt to accomplish in theory what remains to be done in political struggle'.[41]

Interestingly, the position of this current of thought shares certain post-modern analyses on financialization, such as the one put forth by Marazzi. For Panitch, Sam Gindin and others, financialization and neoliberalism are seen as one and the same process emanating from the US core and articulated across the rest of the world, the main recipient regions of this imperial policy being Japan and the European Union. As such, and precisely because neoliberalism – after the 'Volcker shock' and the interest rate spike of 1979–83 – was a successful response to the over-accumulation crisis of the 1970s, the current crisis is a type of 'creative destruction' that empowers, rather than weakens, the US empire-state – although Panitch does not use this Schumpeterian term. Here is the argument in full:

> Quite the contrary to being a predatory breed of capitalists picking over the successes and ruins of a productive economy, financial capital represents and defends the interests of all capitalists in capitalism. The fault-line internal to financial capital of breeding financial crises and speculative bubbles – in the pursuit, as Marx phrased it, of 'money begetting money' – must be interpreted with these integral features in mind. This is the key to unlocking a central paradox of neo-liberalism within American capitalism: *financialisation gives rise to such financial volatility that crises actually become one of the developmental features of*

*neo-liberalism, and this therefore reinforces rather than under-
mines the central position of financial interests in capitalist power
structures* [emphasis by Albo, Gindin and Panitch.].[42]

The position of Panitch and others, therefore, has three defining
features:

• Financial capital is an all-embracing social money-capital relation
to the services of the productive capital. Yet if this is the case,
no distinction between finance and financial capital could be
discerned in reality. In other words, there would be no distinction between money capital employed for the production of use
values and money capital employed for the production of money
alone.
• Neoliberal financialization unblocked the crisis of over-
accumulation of the 1970s and unleashed a new phase of
capitalist prosperity and growth.
• The hegemonic position of the US empire-state has been reinforced
across the imperial chain of the core capitalist countries.[43]

Interestingly, this position is similar to a neo-Schumpeterian
approach, which sees the current financial crisis not as a systemic
default of the capitalist system but rather as a consequence of its
enormous success.[44]

In some respects, this position is challenged by that put forth by
authors working in the Marxian tradition of Paul Sweezy, Harry
Magdoff and Paul Baran, whose contributions appear in the influential journal *Monthly Review*. Despite the fact that this current,
due to its influences from the Marxism of the Second International –
especially from Karl Kautski's views of 'ultra-imperialism' – still tend
to see the US empire-state as an expansive and dominant politico-
economic force, their writings on financialization stand at the other
extreme of the Panitch position.[45] Adopting basically a Keynesian/
Kaleckian approach, this tendency decouples – especially in periods
of money supremacy – the market for financial assets from production. In addition, it embraces Hyman Minsky's 'financial instability
hypothesis'. Financialization, in this respect, is defined as 'the shift
in gravity of the economy from production to finance'.[46]

Whereas this grouping of scholars has the tendency to isolate
finance from production, political economists inspired by Panitch's
and Negri's work tend to see no distinction between productive
and financial capital, often confusing finance and financial capital.

We argue that money/paper capital, whether in fusion with industrial capital or not, should be seen as a superstructure of productive
capital whereby the latter determines the former in the first but not
in the last instance at all times. This is true especially in periods
whereby crises of over-accumulation in industry necessitate a capi-
talist-strategic switch to finance, that is a transition from M–C–M'
to M–M'. This 'determination in the first but not in the last instance'
means that the movement of productive/industrial capital does not
represent a permanent, structural and unaltered feature determining
ad infinitum the fate of capitalism and modernity in history, but it
has a contingent/conjunctural, albeit vital, function in the configuration of capital's circulation and its political-disciplinary attributes
across the world. This approach, as we shall see later, is crucial in
defining the characteristics of the present era of capital accumulation and monetary relations – what some call 'Bretton Woods II'
– especially in regions such as North America, Europe and China/
Southeast Asia.

The Foster–Magdoff thesis, precisely because it makes such a
sharp distinction between money markets and production, is in a
position to distinguish between profits in the financial sector and
profits in the manufacturing sector during the period 1970–2005.
As the stagnation of production and manufacturing necessitated the
switch to finance, so profits in the financial sector soared in contrast
with profits in industry:

> While in the 1960s financial profits accounted for about 15
> percent of all domestic profits in the United States, by 2005 it
> accounted for close to 40 percent of all profits. At the same time,
> manufacturing, which once accounted for 50 percent of domestic
> profits, now accounts for less than 15 percent of profits.[47]

The Paris-based 'Regulation school' has since the mid-1970s also
emphasized the fall in the rate of profit as an important consequence of the slowdown in productivity after the mid-1960s, which
in turn led to public policy responses and capitalist strategies such
as financialization and neoliberalism.[48] Poulantzas himself, in a
volume he edited in Paris in 1976, saw the shift in public policies
taking place at the time in France and Britain – what he called 'the
crisis of the capitalist state' – as a way for the capitalist class to
restore the tendency of the falling rate of profit at the time.[49] He
saw state intervention in the economy as a way for the bourgeois
state to counterbalance the tendency for a falling rate of profit – an

analysis Marx left incomplete in the third volume of *Capital*. Others place the rate of profit at the centre of their explanation schemata in understanding the shift of the US empire-state from the industrial corporation to extreme financialization of this corporation. This includes the important, and rather forgotten, work of such authors as Fred Moseley.[50]

Arguably, this line of thinking is very close to Robert Brenner's historical analysis of post-Second World War capitalism. Building, in many respects, on the important work and findings carried out in the 1980s by Andrew Glynn, Philip Armstrong, John Harrison and others, Brenner argued that at the roots of the current crisis is the inability of the US non-financial corporate sector to return to pre-1970 levels of profitability.[51] According to Brenner, 'from the start of the long downturn in 1973, economic authorities staved off the kind of crises that had historically plagued the capitalist system by resorting to ever greater borrowing, public and private, subsidizing demand'.[52] There had been a 'persistent stagnation' from 1973 to 1993 that the Clinton administration had only partially managed to stop, as indeed under Clinton briefly a return to profitability and growth seemed to be in hand. But Clinton's experiment did not take root, and to all intents and purposes it never matched, or even came closer to, the so-called 'Golden Age of Capitalism' of the 1950s and 1960s.

How did this Golden Age happen in the first place? Brenner tells us that this was the result of *uneven development*:

From the very beginning, then, uneven economic development did entail the *relative* decline of the US domestic economy. But it was also a precondition for the continued vitality of the dominant forces within the US political economy. US multinational corporations and international banks, aiming to expand overseas, needed profitable outlets for their foreign direct investment. Domestically based manufacturers, needing to increase exports, required fast-growing overseas demand for their goods. An imperial US state, bent on 'containing communism' and keeping the world safe for free enterprise, sought economic success for its allies and competitors as the foundation for the political consolidation of the post-war capitalist order, in the face of the anaemia of domestic ruling classes sapped by war, occupation, collaboration and defeat. All these forces thus depended upon the economic dynamism of Europe and Japan for the realization of their own goals.[53]

In other words, the profit squeeze of the 1970s was not due to high wages as neoliberal orthodoxy argued, but the result of global intercapitalist competition. Whereas Poulantzas, Aglietta and others discerned the state in the 1970s as acting as a counter-tendency to the tendency of the rate of profit to fall, Brenner confirms that state intervention, and US state intervention in particular, failed not only to stave off the crisis of – what he calls – 'over-capacity/over-production', but it also set capitalist states and economically integrating zones one against the other (United States–Western Europe–Japan). The result of this global capitalist competition was stagnation and a 'long downturn', the sole exception being the brief Clinton years.

Clinton, Brenner's argument goes, built on Reagan's Plaza Accord (September 22, 1985), when the G5 powers agreed to the US policy of reducing the exchange rate of the dollar in order to bring relief to US manufacturing.[54] Although the recovery under Clinton was rather spectacular and even, in politico-ideological terms, triumphalist (with the collapse of the Soviet Union, the 'unipolar moment' of the United States, the First Gulf War, human rights campaigns and 'humanitarian intervention'), it did not reverse the inherited problem of manufacturing 'overcapacity/overproduction'. This was partly due to a parallel financialization process, which continued unabated despite the partial recovery of profitability in manufacturing. The key feature of this financialization – the so-called 'New Economy' – was, in the words of Brenner, a 'reverse Plaza Accord' pushing up the value of the dollar while increasing the participation of East Asian states, especially Japan, into the purchase of shares on the stock market. Japanese authorities began massively buying US paper (government securities, treasury bills and so on).

From then on the story is well known, as one bubble followed the bursting of the preceding one: the stock market bubble burst, only to be followed by the 'dot.com' one. Then equity and security speculators, encouraged by the Fed chairman, Alan Greenspan, moved into housing markets. Brenner brings into context the 1997–98 East Asian panic too, but this is not the right place to dwell on that. Instead, we would like to point out that in his most recent writings Brenner expands his inquiry to include China, describing coherently the symbiosis and interdependence of US and Chinese capitalisms – what others have called 'Bretton Woods II', inasmuch as the gold standard was being replaced by the Treasury bill standard that the Chinese, after the Arabs and the Japanese, began buying in earnest.[55] He also recognises a relative economic power shift to Southeast Asia, with China as its main hub.

By opening up to foreign direct investment (FDI) and taking advantage of its cheap labour power – Arrighi would add that this labour power is highly skilled and educated, as opposed to the Italian, Greek and Turkish *gustarbeiter* of the 1950s – while at the same time appropriating all the trade and technological innovations of the region, China became a major world manufacturer. 'By 2004–05', Brenner argues in his 'Afterword' to *The Economics of Global Turbulence* (2006), 'foreign firms had come to account for no less than one third of Chinese manufacturing output and 50-60 per cent of its exports.'[56] With China as the main production hub and key exporter, the United States could act as the world's main consumer only via a fictitious boosting of domestic demand reliant on bubbles: the stock market, dot.com and then the housing market bubble. At the same time it was refinancing its current account deficit via the Treasury bills the Chinese and other surplus Asian and Arab producers were buying.[57] From this perspective, as we shall see below, Brenner's analyses stand very close to some of the key arguments we develop here.

Brenner is reluctant to step out of this short-term perspective with regard to his description of the US–China economic duopoly. He sees a relative economic powershift to Southeast Asia, but he is not willing to generalize a scheme along Braudelian or Kondratieff lines:

> The post-war golden age in the US was, in historical terms, unquestionably impressive, but it was not in a league of its own, as is evident when compared to the previous long upturn, between 1890 and 1913 .... By contrast, the long downturn after 1973 can be clearly and properly identified as such, because its economic performance was so weak, compared not only to that of the World War II boom but also to the pre-World War I long boom. It fell palpably short of both of these long expansions with respect to virtually all of the main macroeconomic indicators. The long downturn is precisely that, and, lasting through the end of the millennium, far too extended to be passed off as just another down phase of the latest Kondratieff cycle (leaving aside the vexed question of their existence).[58]

This is in sharp contrast to the (diverging) approaches adopted by Wallerstein and Arrighi. Wallerstein's essays on the current financial crisis adopt an outright Kondratieff perspective, but Arrighi's Marxisant contribution, especially his monumental trilogy, makes

the best possible use of Braudelian historiography, combined with
Gramsci's analysis of hegemony and Polanyi's 'double movement'
concept.[59] For the purposes of this chapter, we shall dwell on
Arrighi's contribution, beginning with his critique of Brenner.

In the first place, Arrighi's embrace of Braudelian historiography
makes him harsh on Brenner, especially when Brenner compares
long downturns and upswings over the last 100 years or so. For
instance, the long downturn of 1873–96 was caused not only
by inter-capitalist competition, but also by the strength of class-
based organizations. The same pattern, more or less, applies to
the beginning of the new downturn in the 1970s. In other words,
according to Arrighi, Brenner does not seem to have a comprehensive and holistic understanding of crises and historic downturns.
His account overplays 'horizontal pressures and conflicts' (inter-
capitalist competition) at the expense of 'vertical pressures and
conflicts' (labour versus capital).[60] Despite the fact that Brenner
states that he will offer a global and systemic analysis of capitalist
political economy since the Second World War, in fact his focus
remains on three key countries (the United States, Germany and
Japan), and tends to 'evict world politics from the analysis of
capitalist dynamics'.[61] Thus, a comprehensive analysis of China's
dynamics is missing – although Arrighi admits that Brenner includes
China to some extent in his 'Afterword' to *The Economics of
Global Turbulence* – and so is an analysis of the negative effects of
the escalation of the Vietnam war on the political economy of the
United States. Although Arrighi recognizes that Brenner does not
leave Vietnam completely out of his analysis, he nevertheless wants
to see it elevated as the most important political factor contributing
to the relative economic decline of the United States since the late
1960s. But why is the Vietnam war so important for Arrighi?

Arrighi, like many others who see the economic decline of the
United States through the prism of Braudelian historiography and
world system theory, considers the US debacle in Vietnam to be the
main cause for the deterioration of the US balance of payments. This
and the costs of war, coupled with the huge domestic opposition to it
in the United States and Western Europe, contributed not only to the
profit squeeze and the beginning of 'stagflation' (stagnation accompanied with high inflation), but also to the collapse of the Bretton
Woods system and the devaluation of the dollar that followed suit.[62]
In fact, Arrighi sees the costs of the Vietnam war as being 'the most
fundamental cause of the collapse of the Bretton Woods system of
fixed exchange rates'.[63] Leaving out of his 'research design' – as

he put it – this world political variable, Brenner commits a serious analytical mistake of omission.

Last but not least, Arrighi is in disagreement with Brenner inasmuch as Brenner seems to be analysing the dynamics of capitalist development 'by exclusively focusing on manufacturing':

> The theoretical and historical identification of capitalism with *industrial* capitalism appears to be for him [Brenner] – as most social scientists, Marxist and non-Marxist alike – an article of faith which requires no justification. Yet, the share of value added generated in manufacturing worldwide has been comparatively small, shrinking steadily from 28% in 1960 to 24.5% in 1998. Moreover, the contraction has been greater than average in Brenner's 'advanced' capitalist countries, the share for North America, Western Europe, Australasia and Japan combined having declined from 28.9% in 1960 to 24.5% in 1980, to 19.7% in 1998.[64]

Arguably, this contention is misleading. We discussed earlier the ontological significance of manufacturing for the production and reproduction of social life in all social systems. But beyond that, we would like to argue that the evidence given by Arrighi to support his claim against Brenner does not seem to be very sound.

Arrighi tells us that his percentage data on manufacturing are calculated from the World Bank, although he does not tell us how. Whereas he is correct in pointing out the decline in manufacturing in the Western core in a historical perspective, he is rather evasive in explaining how the World Bank measures GDP growth and its added value variable in manufacturing. In fact, the World Bank adopts a rather restricted definition of manufacturing, as follows:

> Manufacturing refers to industries belonging to ISIC divisions 15–37. Value added is the net output of a sector after adding up all outputs and subtracting intermediate inputs. It is calculated without making deductions for depreciation of fabricated assets or depletion and degradation of natural resources. The origin of value added is determined by the International Standard Industrial Classification (ISIC).[65]

ISIC (divisions 15–37) is a very restricted UN system for classifying economic data in manufacturing. The UN Statistics Division leaves much industry, including the iron, steel, chemical and petrochemical industries (divisions 20 and 21) outside its calculations. Whereas divisions 15–37 refer to manufacturing, industry corresponds to ISIC divisions 10–45, which *include* manufacturing. They comprise value added in mining, manufacturing (which Arrighi classifies as a separate subgroup), construction, electricity, water, and gas.[66] The way in which Brenner defines the rate of profit in relation to material production differs substantially from the definition of manufacturing by the World Bank, which Arrighi adopts in order to undo Brenner's argument concerning the relevance of manufacturing. In fact, Brenner says, 'the rate of profit is generally given for the "private economy", or "private business economy" or a specific major industry'. And, he continues, 'the private economy is, unless otherwise stated, always non-farm and non-residential, meaning that the value-added of farms and that attributed to the residential sector is excluded'. Brenner also excludes from his calculations the value added of government enterprises. Thus, whereas Brenner's definition is broader and closer to ISIC divisions 10–45, at the same time he does not inflate the percentage share of material production as such in order to prove its social and economic relevance. Brenner indicates that during the 1990s the 'US corporate manufacturing sector still accounted for 46.8% of total profits accruing to the non-financial sector',[67] and this is a time when industry was being outsourced to China, India and Southeast Asia. Further, Arrighi criticizes Brenner for not including profits in the corporate financial sector, and for failing to see – Arrighi is using Greta Krippner's work here – that manufacturing leads the trend towards financialization of the non-financial economy.[68]

Time and again, this is, at best, an oversight on the part of Arrighi. First, Brenner himself states clearly that late in the 1980s the 'manufacturing sector remained overwhelmingly dominated by the propensity to use financial resources for financial manipulation – above all borrowing for the purpose of leveraged mergers and acquisitions and stock buybacks, rather than for investment in new plant and equipment'.[69] Second, it would be a methodological mistake to confuse financial and non-financial corporate profits, as they correspond to two different forms of socially produced values and use values, whereas some financial profits do not have an impact on these two classical economy variables at all. Thus, it seems that it has taken a long way for Arrighi to meet all these writers who do not distinguish between *finance* and *financial* capital. This, in turn, is related to the distinction between *productive* and *unproductive* capital, as finance capital may well remain in a portfolio or hoarding and idle form, and it may also be the 'product' of pure speculative arbitrage of an M–M' relation, so having no contact with production of use values. Furthermore, the transformation of an industrialist into a financial agent for profit reasons should not be confused with the structural dimension of the rate of profit and its tendency to fall: the former is an agential function performed as a consequence of a structural tendency dissociated from the capitalist-agent.

THE TRAGEDY OF GLOBALIZATION: THE END OF THE *'LONG TWENTIETH CENTURY'*?

The discussion we summarized above has stimulated wider scholarly debates and led many writers to build on some of Brenner's conclusions, advancing innovative theoretical schemata, such as the 'stationary state' put forth by Gobal Balakrishnan.[70] This suggests that US-led Western capitalism has lost its propulsive force as its material-productive base has since the 1970s been eroded, so the present state of affairs can be characterized as a 'post-industrial stationary condition'.[71] Andrew Kliman too converges on Brenner's argument of the fundamental importance of the falling rate of profit for Anglo-American capitalism since the 1970s, while offering a new approach through Marx's concept of 'the destruction of capital though crises'.[72] Yet Brenner himself, as Michel Aglietta did not fail to mention, is not sure at all that there is a power shift to what we called here the 'global East'.[73] In other words, Brenner does not answer the question of whether or not the United States can recover from its 'long downturn' which began in the 1970s, and remake the global capitalist order after its image. On this issue, Arrighi is more than clear, namely that the US decline is definitive and irreversible. In fact, his main contribution is not his discussion of Brenner's argument on profitability. Arrighi's monumental trilogy captures the long historic and 'hegemonic' decline of the United States, which it is incapable of arresting. Drawing to a large degree on world systems theory and Braudel's historiography, Arrighi and Beverly Silver describe how great powers rise and fall through successive historical cycles linked to periods of economic crises. Both capitalist and commercial empires in history moved through phases of productive or commercial expansion and through phases of slowdown and deceleration marked by financial expansion. The key contention here is that each time, especially in capitalist history, empires expand their power, they do so on the basis of their lead in the industrial-productive sector, whereas when a phase of contraction and crisis opens they are forced to resort to financialization in order to stave off crises in commerce or industry. Resort to financialization, Arrighi and Silver argue, never manages to restore the global primacy of the empire; it simply delays the empire's decline, and this is the case with the US empire at present.[74]

This argument of cyclical and recurrent patterns is better refined in Arrighi's *Adam Smith in Beijing* (2007), and in two other contributions written shortly before his death (2009).[75] Arrighi adopts Braudel's periodization of capitalism, identifying three periods of financial expansion. The first was under the hegemony of Italian city-states in the mid-sixteenth century; the second was centred on Holland (in the mid-eighteenth century); and the third, in the late nineteenth century, was driven by the United Kingdom. We are interested here in discussing the third period, because it is a period that came into being as a result of the over-accumulation crisis in the United Kingdom (and other core Western capitalist centres), and ended with the 1929–32 financial crash. This is also a period in which *capitalism as a mode of production* was operating in full, whereas all previous 'Braudelian' periods described by Arrighi and other 'world systems' theorists are social and historical epochs structured alongside the dominance of *commodity exchange* relations.[76]

The beginning of each financial expansion, Arrighi says, indicates the 'signal crisis' of the global hegemon in the system. For example, the 'switch' to finance at the end of the nineteenth century signalled the beginning of the 'terminal crisis' of the British Empire. The financial meltdown of 1929–32 signalled the beginning of the end of the dominant regime of accumulation, or in other words the end of the hegemony of the UK system of global governance, and its subsequent succession by the new global industrial and credit power, the United States. Similarly, the US-led process of post-Second World War capitalist accumulation, centred on industrial development and growth in all core capitalisms, gave way to financialization and therefore a protracted period of US hegemonic decline, which began in the 1970s (with the 'signal crisis'). This crisis of financialization at present is but the 'terminal crisis' of the US-led system of accumulation. In short, this is Arrighi's *Long Twentieth Century* (1994) concept. His *Adam Smith in Beijing* (2007) is a courageous and powerful intellectual attempt to show that the new rising global leader to take over from the United States is China. China is the new global centre of material accumulation of wealth, and potentially of political/military power, a view to which Aglietta subscribes wholeheartedly, but without adopting a Braudelian perspective.

Our approach here is similar but not identical. There is indeed a relative powershift to the global East, but this shift is asymmetrical and uneven. It combines the articulation of national and international regimes of trade and accumulation, conflicting imperial projects, environmental degradation, resource depletion, and above all, the US military power that still backs the 'open door' and the centrality of the dollar. In other words, the relative economic power shift to the global East rests, as did the previous global shifts, on the fault-lines developed historically by the deep-seated contradictions of the global eco-socioeconomic system. This is itself a terrain of social and class struggles, a process in which it shows centripetal and centrifugal tendencies. The present tragedy of globalization is therefore directly related to the global fault-lines of the system and the social struggles it incorporates. But the United States is resistant to letting the system move forward by recognizing the fact that a new international/imperial order is already in the making. In the end, the tragedy of globalization is the tragedy of the open door: the latter no longer brings the desired results for the US economy.

The power of the declining hegemon to shape developments according to its class and security interests still remains paramount to some extent, at least for the time being. Nearly 100 years after its 'terminal crisis' in the inter-war period, the United Kingdom is still in a position, though in a much more limited way, to get away with outdated forms of colonialism – see, for instance, the case of its sovereign bases in Cyprus – and has a kind of major, albeit declining, role in US-led/NATO-led military ventures (Afghanistan, Iraq and Libya).

In this context, we need to consider the powerful drive of US open door imperialism since the 1970s, the role of US multinationals, massive retailers and offshore business, which bring new dynamism to US domestic capitalism as they repatriate their profits and become inserted into the IRS (Inland Revenue System).[77] The open door policy attacks aggressively the jurisdictions of other states, as it did with the political economies of the so-called 'Tiger States' of Southeast Asia, whose opening of capital accounts not only triggered the panic of 1997, but also led to the appropriation of economic assets by the United States and other OECD states.[78]

Open door imperialism is a structural and historical feature of the US system of global governance, and has been part and parcel of the strategic culture of US policy-making elites since at least the 1890s.

When the predominant features of the global economic system rest on industrialism, then open door is predominately targeting politico-economic environments and regimes based on the state–industry nexus. But ever since the predominant features of the global system have moved to financialization, open door has been attacking the state–finance nexus. Open door spreads around the globe the class interests of the US bourgeoisie – consider, for instance, retailers such as Walmart – dislocating the class interests of other states and imposing a market discipline after the image of the US market. Thus, one of our key objections to Arrighi's and other similar arguments is that they downplay the power of open door arrangements and the complex global spread of Anglo-American political economy via what Peter Gowan (and Robert Wade) called Dollar–Wall Street Regime (DWSR).[79]

In other words, although we share the macro-historical approach of a long-term decline of the United States (proposed by Arrighi and others), we would be cautious in underestimating the combined benefits stemming from a critical analysis of shorter historical periods and even conjunctures that make profitable use of established explanatory concepts in understanding the global political economy of the United States. In a way, what we are trying to do is to map the global structural shift from US/West-centred core economies to new emerging powerhouses. But since we are still at an early stage of this macro-historic shift it is important to identify the extent of influence and the specific policy aspects of the old hegemonic power(s) that are trying to arrest their decline.

A second objection is related to the recurrent character of his model of crisis and capitalist periodization and to the correspondence of this recurrent model to hegemonic transitions. From this perspective, we see no difference in principle between Braudelian–Arrighian cycles and Kondratieff waves. Although periodic crises, waves and cycles, long, medium and short, 'had been accepted by businessmen and economists rather as farmers accept the weather, which also has its ups and downs',[80] what is it that entitles us to make this descriptive historical observation an axiom with eternal validity and without any theoretical foundation?[81] The gist of Arrighi's thesis is that each period of crisis in the realm of money and finance is terminal and accompanied by a system-wide transition from one imperial power to another – although the term Arrighi uses is not 'imperial' but 'hegemonic'.[82]

This is very controversial, especially as far as US neo-imperialism is concerned, for three main reasons. The first, as we saw above, regards the open door imperial policy of the United States and the system of global governance it built on the basis of dollar primacy and hub-and-spoke arrangements, issues we have analysed elsewhere.[83] This is significant because the US imperial system of global governance differs substantially from that of its UK predecessor. Therefore we would argue that the likelihood of the United States 'bouncing back', albeit in a multipolar world, and at least for a short term (say, for example, via the initiation of a large-scale war in Asia), should not be completely excluded. Arrighi does not include this possibility in any of his future scenarios concerning the directions the world system might take.[84]

The second reason concerns the locus of periodic financial crises in the system. The terminal crisis of the British Empire marked by the 1929–32 crash did not happen in London but in New York. But today's tragedy of financialization did have its headquarters in Wall Street, only to trickle down to London (almost instantly) and the Eurozone (a few months later). The late Arrighi is at pains to address this problem, as well as to use open door class analysis in understanding the economic grand strategy of US neo-imperialism:

In a co-authored book published in 1999 entitled *Chaos and Governance in the Modern World System*, Beverly Silver and I argued that the inability of the Japanese economy to recover from the crash of 1990–92 and the East financial crisis of 1997–98 in themselves did not support the conclusion that the rise of East Asia had been a mirage. We noted that in previous hegemonic transitions it was the newly emerging centres of capital accumulation on a world scale that experienced the deepest financial crises, as their financial prowess outstripped their institutional capacity to regulate massive flows of mobile capital entering and exiting their jurisdictions. This was true of London and England in the late eighteenth century and even more of New York and the United States in the 1930s. No one would use the Wall Street crash of 1929–31 and the subsequent US Great Depression to argue that the epicentre of global processes of capital accumulation had not been shifting from the United Kingdom to the United States in the first half of the twentieth century. No analogous conclusion should be drawn from the East Asian financial crises of the 1990s. It does not follow, of course, that incumbent financial centres cannot themselves experience financial crises. From this standpoint, no generalization is possible. In the transition from British to US hegemony, the United Kingdom did not experience a financial crisis comparable to that of the United States. In the present transition, in contrast, in 2000–01 and again in 2008–09 the United States has experienced crises at least as serious as the East Asian crises of the 1990s.[85]

First, this long quote speaks volumes of the failure of Arrighi to capture the fact that the East Asian crises of 1997–98 were the product of US open door policy engineering and not of the weak institutions of local economies which could not manage 'massive flows of mobile capital entering and exiting their jurisdictions'. This is essentially a liberal argument. We therefore witness a lack of class analysis on the part of Arrighi: that is, a failure to understand open door as a dollar-led neo-imperial strategy appropriating international value.[86] Second, Arrighi himself recognizes the difficulty in putting forward a theoretical scheme about hegemonic transitions, inasmuch as the locus of financial crises may not occur inside the jurisdiction territory of the incumbent global hegemon. In other words, Arrighi's theoretical scheme, already a historical description and not a theory, fails even to qualify as such.

The argument of *The Fall of the US Empire* rests on a different approach, although we share with Arrighi and others the thesis of the gradual power erosion of the United States and the power shift to accumulation regimes dominated by other global and regional powers. First, we accept this with the important qualification that this decline is *relative*. Second, and as we saw earlier, the argument of global fault-lines suggests that twentieth-century history and beyond can be seen as an all-encompassing moment of convergence and divergence of all global history and social orders so far experienced in history. Under the supremacy of a US-led IPE, this structuralist approach entails a mode of operation alongside the notions of 'uneven and combined development' and social and political struggles at national, regional and international levels that erode the power of the US centre, buttressing the rising of new centres. In the event, it is the discursive development of global fault-lines that drives the process. The current global financial crisis (and serious economic downturn) is only one aspect of a multi-dimensional set of simultaneous, interacting and 'converging crises'. What is underlying the current situation, more than anything else, is a significant historical, structural shift that US policies (at the level of agency) cannot arrest. The 'unipolar' phase of US dominance is being replaced by a 'multipolar' phase, in which the United States will continue to remain one of the most prominent powers, but has to share this position with other new rising global superpowers and regional powers.

The new rising centres are not necessarily particular territorial states, but an ensemble of powers across the globe, which – for lack of a better term and because of an overuse of the term 'global South' – we call the 'global East'. This includes primarily China, India, Brazil and Russia. Our structuralist understanding of global history, in turn, does not underestimate the utility of the study of specific periods in capitalist history. Nor does it insinuate that the historical trajectory of the global system resembles a mere return to a 'new centre', whatever that centre might be, so that therefore no real distance can ever be covered, and no real prospects and progress can ever be registered, especially for the deprived and the subaltern world social classes. Quite the opposite: the tragedy of globalization and its underpinning system of global fault-lines that drive it are seen here as the outcome of modern social and economic struggles reverberating within the executives of core capitalist states. From this perspective, the struggles in the United States (see, among others, the Occupy Wall Street movement), Europe (especially in the periphery zone of Greece, Spain, Portugal and Ireland), China, the Middle East and Northern Africa today are as important for the progress of humanity as the scholarly prediction of a possible replacement of the Anglo-American imperium with a new form of global order, possibly centred, as Arrighi saw it building on Braudel's perspective, on China.

We argue in Chapter 5 that there is a power shift to the global East, and that China, for the time being, is indeed at the centre of that shift. We incorporate into our analyses the massive ecological crisis and the finite nature of raw materials, two aspects of the crisis today that have been lingering since the early 1970s. The chapters that follow attempt to substantiate our criticisms addressed to the works of the scholars reviewed here, while acknowledging their profound influence in shaping the undertaking and the argument of *The Fall of the US Empire*. Among others, it will become apparent that our contribution to these debates relates to the critical role of the connection between Anglo-American grand strategy and the international political economy of oil, gas and other hydrocarbons. We will show that control over extraction, production, refining, jurisdiction and transportation of oil and gas from petro-states to Western and Eastern markets at stable prices denominated in dollars is vital for Anglo-American global supremacy. Again, this is a matter of successful US open door neo-imperialism. In the end, agential strategies (financialization, neoliberalism and so on) cannot arrest long-term structural decline. If anything, they can only delay it.

2

FROM BRETTON WOODS TO THE ABYSS OF GLOBALIZATION, 1944–71

Lenin is said to have declared that the best way to destroy the capitalist system was to debauch the currency. By a continuing process of inflation, governments can confiscate, secretly and unobserved, an important part of the wealth of their citizens. By this method they not only confiscate, but they confiscate arbitrarily; and, while the process impoverishes many, it actually enriches some. Lenin was certainly right. There is no subtler, no surer means of overturning the existing basis of society than to debauch the currency. The process engages all the hidden forces of economic law on the side of destruction, and does it in a manner which not one man in a million is able to diagnose.

John Maynard Keynes, *The Economic Consequences of the Peace* (1919)

BACKGROUND TO BRETTON WOODS

The over-accumulation crisis that hit the industrial core in the last decade of the nineteenth century gave birth to one of the most enduring features of emerging US neo-imperialism, namely its open door policy. US secretary of state John Hay issued his open door notes in September and November 1899, a political move that should not be seen, primarily, as a result of a systemic competition between the United States and European imperialist powers over China and Southeast Asia. Rather, open door originated from within the US socioeconomic system as a consequence of the first serious crisis of the US accumulation regime after the Civil War and the victory of the industrial North over the agrarian and populist

33

South. 'Never before', the *Commercial and Financial Chronicle*
wrote in August 1893, 'has there been such a sudden and striking
cessation of industrial activity …. Mills, factories, furnaces, mines,
nearly everywhere shut down in large numbers … and hundreds of
thousands of men [were] thrown out of employment'.[1] The way out
of the crisis, as US industrial and financial elites saw it, was imperial
expansion abroad, penetrating more markets for the consumption
of the commodities that could not be sold at home. And if this
could not happen by means of economic diplomacy, then bold
military intervention forcing other states to open their markets to
US industry and finance was the second best preferred solution. In
this respect, we could surmise that the US polity, despite its admin-
istrative federal complexity and convoluted physiognomy, refracted
the interests of the capitalist class from its very beginning and in the
clearest possible way – in contrast, for example, to Britain's Crown
system and feudal remnants. In the words of Williams:

> In a less well-known episode, businessmen such as William
> Rockefeller of Standard Oil had urged the Cleveland
> Administration to intervene boldly in the Brazilian Revolution
> of 1893. Determined to protect and expand the trade with Brazil
> that was beginning to develop, Cleveland deployed ships of the
> United States Navy in a way that helped defeat the rebels who
> were opposed to the pattern of unequal economic relations with
> America.[2]

At the dawn of the twentieth century, US supremacy in the Western
hemisphere was complete and the US economy was the largest in
the world. By 1902 Europeans were already speaking of 'American
invasions', and by 1914 US direct investment abroad amounted
to 7 per cent of US GNP – the same percentage as in 1966, when
Europeans once again felt threatened by an 'American challenge'.[3]
The First World War (1914–18) turned the United States into a huge
financial and credit power, and in fact the United States entered
the war in 1917 when it became apparent 'that to stay out would
entail at least an interim economic collapse as American bankers
and exporters found themselves stuck with uncollectible loans
to Britain and its allies'.[4] Yet after the end of the war, a vicious
circle concerning war debt payments became evident, as the United
Kingdom and France could not pay back their war debts to the
United States, because Germany did not abide by what she signed
up in Versailles – as John Maynard Keynes predicted – namely to

pay war reparations to the United Kingdom and France.[5] By the Lausanne Conference of summer 1933, it was clear to France and the United Kingdom that they could not extract any more war reparation money from Germany.

As far as Russia's debt was concerned, which represented 'more than 75 per cent of Britain's $3.3 billion of net war credits',[6] this had to be written off as Lenin's revolutionary government could not pay it back, and had no intention of trying. This, coupled with the overall effects of Russia's withdrawal from the international capitalist system, created a major instability in the system of European and international political economy between the wars, as the Russian (weak) link of the global imperialist chain turned socialist.

During the war, the dollar became a world currency, equal in strength to the British pound.[7] The US Federal Reserve system was established in 1913. European merchandise exports to Latin America were severely curtailed by the war, with the United States occupying an even more prominent economic and political position there. US policy continued to put pressure on France, the United Kingdom and Italy on the basis of the open door policy, especially as the Europeans were secretly dividing up the Middle Eastern oil market and at the same time drawing up the petro-borders of the Ottoman Empire.[8]

Europe was short of capital, and capital scarcity in Europe meant high rates of return for the United States, which strengthened the dollar, buttressed financialization and forced the French and the British to peg their currencies against the dollar at depreciated rates, especially during the war. But both countries suspended convertibility, as their gold reserves began eroding. From then on, a long period of instability set in: a period of floating exchange rates, which ended with Britain's return to gold in April 1925; a short period of fixed rates ending in September 1931, when Britain abandoned the gold standard under the pressure of the Great Depression; and, finally, the floating system of rates until the outbreak of the Second World War.[9] Gold convertibility was essential for the Europeans to fight inflation – caused mainly by the issuing of paper money – and to stop the United States acquiring more and more gold. It is no accident that 'among the first countries to re-establish gold convertibility where those that had endured hyperinflation', such as Germany (1924), Austria (1923), Poland (1924) and Hungary (1925).[10] This meant the issuing of new currencies reflecting gold-standard equivalences because, as Karl Polanyi put it, 'banknotes have value because they represent gold'.[11] The French mania to buy and hoard gold began in those years, a trend that continued, as we shall see below, in the post-war years under de Gaulle's leadership.

In the main, all this meant that liberal imperialism could no longer support a viable regime of capital accumulation, especially the demand side of it. The system collapsed and switched to autarky and self-sufficiency not because there was no central hegemon to buttress its new imperial foundations (as argued by Charles P. Kindleberger), but primarily because 'mass demand could not keep pace with the rapidly increasing productivity of the industrial system in the heyday of Henry Ford, the result being over-production and speculation'.[12] But this discussion should not be seen in isolation from the issue of war debt and reparations, or from the US concept of the open door, for one key feature of the open door is the opening of other states' markets to US business, while protecting US business at home from foreign competition. In fact, as Michael Hudson points out, 'the United States refused to permit Europe to pay off its World War I debt by exporting more goods to the United States'. He continues:

> The country's tariffs were raised in 1921 specifically to defend US producers against the prospect of Germany and other countries depreciating their currencies under pressure of their foreign debts. In May of that year prices began their collapse in the United States, following the drying up of European markets that had been supported by US War and Victor loans. An emergency tariff on agricultural imports was levied, followed in 1922 by the Fordney Tariff which restored the high level of import duties set by the Payne-Aldrich Act of 1909. Tariffs on dutiable imports were raised to an average 38 per cent, compared to 16 per cent in 1920.[13]

Further, the Smoot–Hawley tariff law of 1930 closed off US markets and pushed other countries to retaliatory measures. It was not Nazi Germany that first closed itself off from the outside world, but the liberal and open door United States.[14] Thus, the structural contradictions of capitalist modernity were unleashed beyond control: a war-torn European continent with a weak demand side and unstable monetary system was forced into a corner by the US open door, which required payment of war debts at the same time as it closed its market to European producers in order to protect domestic class interests.

We can discern two dramatic and opposing consequences, both of which should be seen as *political* strategies attempting to address the problem of a weak aggregate demand. First, weak demand was 'beefed up by means of an enormous expansion of consumer credit',[15] including a stock market and speculative real estate boom, so familiar to us after the 2007–08 experience. Roosevelt's attack on the so-called *haute finance* was ferocious. One of his most significant financial reforms was the Glass–Steagall Act of 1933, which separated investment from commercial banking, regulated the housing market and dealt a severe blow to the house of Morgan, which dominated the US financial market. This move away from the power of financial markets was bringing back in the political power of the US state, with most other states following suit.

The second consequence of the contradictions of the system was that it pushed states to autarchy and self-sufficiency in as much as after 1930 in particular, with the collapse of world trade, each country took protectionist measures. These led in some cases to authoritarianism (Italy and other regimes in Southern and Central Europe) and even extreme violent racism (Nazi Germany). Britain suspended gold convertibility on September 21, 1931, whereas France kept *commodity money* in place until 1936 – that is, gold convertibility – mainly because of its obsession with buying gold. Other countries employed exchange controls to defend the exchange rate. Greece defaulted on its debt obligations in 1932 for a second time in its modern history – the first being in 1893 – embarking on a dictatorship in 1936 under Ioannis Metaxas. Similar developments followed in Spain after its dramatic civil war (1936–39) and Portugal, both of which were taken over by dictators, Franco (in 1936) and Salazar (in 1932) respectively. In January 1934 the United States increased the gold–dollar parity from $20.67 to $35 an ounce, and this eventually forced France and, among others the Netherlands, to abandon convertibility.

It is interesting to note that, precisely because of the extreme financial speculation, monetary instability and high inflation, industrial production began a free fall in all core countries and unemployment rose massively. In 1929–30 US industrial production fell by 48 per cent and unemployment peaked at 25 per cent. Just before Hitler came to power, Germany's industrial production fell by 39 per cent and unemployment in industry soared at 44 per cent. In 1931, the British set up the Macmillan Committee to propose solutions for reconnecting industry and finance, a link that was apparently broken.

From this perspective, Keynes' efforts were arduous and unique: he had set himself to producing an economic theory and political programme going beyond the curses of liberal financialization and authoritarianism – whether, as he saw it, of the Bolshevik or the fascist authoritarian type – while rescuing the fundamentals of capitalism. In the end, the Keynesian platform outlined in his *General Theory* (1936) and widely adopted by parties of the left and right in Europe after the Second World War, succeeded in boosting aggregate demand management while undermining the ability of the working classes to lead the process of transition towards a new, socialist regime of accumulation. As far as the medium of international exchange was concerned, this was settled at Bretton Woods and rather against Keynes' (and Britain's) wishes.

THE US EMPIRE-STATE RESPONDS TO THE GREAT SLUMP

Once the dominance of the industrial North over the agrarian South was established after the Civil War, the United States patiently built its world system of control, first in Latin America and the Philippines, and then in Europe, Japan, Korea and the Middle East. Its superior army, weapons systems and intelligence networks have been essential to this project. But equally important, if not more so, has been its economic control of the world economy, mainly through the role of the dollar as the world's reserve currency.

Dollar supremacy has always been critical to the future of US global dominance, even more so than its overwhelming military power. Spread all over the globe today in key geostrategic locations and chokepoints, US military power and projection is ultimately financed by dollars produced outside the United States. Thus, the US economy is intimately tied to the dollar's international status as a reserve currency. And the continuing dominance of the US dollar is not a matter of simple economics, but is also deeply rooted in the global geopolitical role of the country today. But how did this all come about, and even more importantly, is it sustainable in the long run? In this section, we shall deal only with the process that laid the foundation stones of the dollar supremacy, namely the fundamentals of the Bretton Woods system.

The central place that the United States still occupies today in the global system rests on a particular convergence of structure and history. The crucial phase in this process occurred during and after the Second World War. Only after the twin disasters of the Great Depression and the Second World War did international capitalism gain a new life under the supremacy of the new US system of imperial governance. This reorganization of capitalism could not

have been accomplished without the uneven and combined development of certain structural characteristics that also shaped the
post-war leadership of the US neo-imperial state. The post-war state
of physical and economic ruin in much of Europe, Asia and parts
of Africa represented a challenge, but more an opportunity, for the
United States to lead post-war reconstruction in the world system in
a manner different from that pursued after the First World War. The
economic and financial system in France was shattered, the whole
of the German state had collapsed, the United Kingdom was on the
brink of bankruptcy, and Japan was prostrate, hit by the atomic
bomb and entirely disorganized after the collapse of its imperial
state which had claimed a Greater East Asia Co-Prosperity Sphere.[16]
Under these circumstances, only the United States remained as a
stable and powerful capitalist state capable of determining the terms
of a new world economic order. And this is exactly what had been
crystallized in the Bretton Woods arrangements.

   The key task to rescuing the global capitalist order was to
recompose the nations of Western Europe and Asia as member states,
and then place the US empire-state at the centre of the system via
hub-and-spoke arrangements. From an economic perspective, this
required that the United States create a new international monetary
system buttressing new trade regimes and spearheading new developmental perspectives with the purpose of regenerating new open
door conditions. Both the post-war international political economy
(IPE) and the domestic political economies of US allies had to abide
by open door requirements. How did this new international order
come about, and what were these new open door requirements? We
will reconstruct some important events and policy-making decisions
here that show precisely the strength of the US empire-state as the
globe's new centre of power after the Second World War.

   Mainstream IPE approaches portray the Bretton Woods arrangements as an event concerned with technicalities and currency
realignments in order to facilitate free trade flows on the basis of
the new global commodity money pegged to gold, the US dollar.
The scope of the international institutions launched, such as the
International Monetary Fund (IMF), the World Bank and the
General Agreements on Tariffs and Trade (GATT) system was large,
and their aim was noble: to assist the reconstruction of war-torn
Europe, Japan/Asia and Latin America, while protecting the world
from sliding back to the protectionism of the inter-war period and
the political authoritarianism that had ensued.[17] Classic accounts
such as that by Richard Gardner focus on the US–UK 'special

relationship' which arose out of these arrangements in an effort to dominate global multilateral trade.[18] Despite the useful and scholarly information contained in these mainstream works, we argue that they miss the central point, namely that Bretton Woods and the new institutions formed as a result were driven by the US state and the new orthodoxy of the primacy of Washington over Wall Street and global finance in an effort to revive open door via a global developmental policy. In this respect, it is rather misleading to present them as 'multilateral' achievements which mutually benefited all the participants.[19]

The key to understanding the post-war 'multilateral' trade order is the 'Lend-Lease' agreements devised in December 1940 and then more formally established under Edward R. Stettinius Jr., whom Roosevelt made head of the Lend-Lease Administration seven months later. Lend-Lease should be seen as hand in glove with the Atlantic Charter, signed in August 1941 between Churchill and Roosevelt. The participation of Keynes and the economist and US Treasury Department official Harry Dexter White in these schemes and agreements began during that period. In the main, Lend-Lease was not about providing war material to an ailing Britain after the sudden fall of France to Nazi forces in order to expand the defence frontiers of the US state. Lend-Lease was about article VII, which stipulated an open door arrangement: the opening up of the British Empire to US industry. The Lend-Lease Master Agreements provided for:

(1) [the] expansion, by appropriate international and domestic measures, of production, employment, and the exchange and consumption of goods, which are the material foundations of the liberty and welfare of all peoples; (2) the elimination of all forms of discriminatory treatment in international commerce; and (3) the reduction of tariff and other trade barriers.[20]

To all intents and purposes, these provisions undermined the imperial preference system of low tariffs within the British Empire, which had been developed in 1932 to offset disruptions caused by the inter-ally war debt and the Great Slump. Keynes called article VII 'the lunatic proposals of Mr. Hull', Cordell Hull being the super-liberal and longest-serving US secretary of state (1933–44). Churchill himself eventually accepted the article only reluctantly. The United States had already laid out the post-Second World War global order on its own terms.

In July 1944, delegates from 44 countries gathered at Bretton Woods, New Hampshire, to discuss the economic and monetary arrangements for a new world order. The Soviet Union took part in the negotiations but eventually left the proposed scheme to form COMECON (the Council for Mutual Economic Assistance).[21] Since 1940 the US aim had been the founding of an international stabilization fund – what later was called the IMF – able to maintain a predictable regime of foreign exchange rates and act, in periods of crisis, as a 'lender of last resort'. Dexter White argued that the voting power of each country-member of the fund must reflect the size of its quota (that is, its contribution to the fund), and insisted that the United States must have a quota greater than 25 per cent of the total. The US delegation won the argument, and the result was that the United States was able to veto and block any proposed changes in currency value, thus becoming the decisive political power in the fund.

With this issue settled, the discussion at Bretton Woods moved onto the degree of freedom the fund would have to move exchange rates up and down. Keynes wanted to have as much flexibility as possible on that in order to apply trade and other restrictions 'as required to reconcile full employment with payments balance'.[22] On these grounds, Keynes proposed a Clearing Union from which debtor countries could draw credit to finance their balance of payments deficits, subject to conditions and penalty interest rates. But with the United States being a net creditor running huge surpluses for decades, all debtor countries would have special drawing rights obliging the United States to finance the debt of all other countries. In this context, Keynes went as far as to propose a new international currency, the 'bancor', based on the model of domestic banking. This, he argued, would be a unit of account defined on the basis of gold, but gold would have no other utility or function. Keynes wanted to 'sever all ties to the gold standard', while the United States wanted to place the gold at the centre of the global system, pegged against the dollar at its pre-war parity ($35 an ounce) in order to control international transactions, markets and investments. Dexter White aimed at having an international price structure that was as predictable and stable as possible.

The result of this debate was a compromise, which arguably worked in favour of the US empire-state. Bretton Woods Conference delegates agreed to the pre-war parity value of the dollar with gold, fixed at $35 an ounce, and member states would only be able to change the value of their currency by 10 per cent should they want to adjust it in order to try to improve their balance of payments.[23] But in the main, the exchange rate system would be fixed and all countries would need to use dollars – or gold – to pursue their international trade (gold was tradable too). Effectively, among other things, this system supplanted:

> German reparations as the vehicle through which to provide the allies with institutionalized means to sustain their demands for US products, while maintaining the discipline of gold in international relations .... After WWII, Europe's payments to the US were principally for actual goods and services, not for reparations or inter-ally debts.[24]

The door was open for the institutionalization of the international domination of the United States over all other capitalist states. This was reinforced by the creation of other institutions, such as the World Bank – at the time called International Bank for Reconstruction and Development and with a primary responsibility to finance economic development and post-war reconstruction – the GATT system, and later the European Payments Union and Marshall Aid. All these institutions and policies aimed at financing European and Asian capitalist economies, solving the dollar shortage of those countries and open up their markets to US manufacturing. They had 'much the same effect in the context of the capitalist world economy', Ernest Mandel wrote in 1972, 'as Keynesian policy in the national context: a large quantity of additional purchasing power was injected into the international area which – given a great deal of unutilized capacity – inevitably led to a major expansion of world trade'.[25] Those who had no dollars could not buy US produce, and the United States had to provide dollars to avoid another depression once the war was over, while together with the United Kingdom it led the new war against unemployment. But above all else, the United States, by providing dollars to the buyers of its products, was essentially financing itself through its money-printing press. A small favour was paid to the United Kingdom alone. The IMF articles of agreement, Michael Hudson observed, 'required signatories not to enter into bilateral monetary agreements or other forms of protectionism, save for the Sterling area, which was to be left intact'.[26] Herein lies the key explaining a great part of the so-called 'special relationship' between the United Kingdom and the United States.

In short, the concessions made by the United States were minimal, and Dexter White got what he wanted at Bretton Woods: to place the US state, its Treasury and the dollar at the power centre of the global financial and economic structures, opening up the war-torn economies of Europe and Asia to US trade and investment, and making the political economies of those regions conducive to US industrial production and export capacity. US corporations had evolved into hubs of increasingly dense host-country and cross-border networks among suppliers, financiers and final markets. This worked to secure an even tighter international network of production, and arguably promoted the *internationalization* of the US state, with the open door becoming more and more embedded across the globe. Increasingly, US 'national'/class interests were defined in terms of acting not only on behalf of the United States, but also on behalf of the extension and reproduction of the global capitalist order. By the mid-1940s, the United States was in possession of 75 per cent of the world's gold reserves and 60 per cent of the world's total manufacturing output. There is a lot a creditor imperial power can do with all these advantages, but this is precisely what has stopped being the case since the 1970s. Let us now turn to examine the 'economic miracles' of the 1950s and 1960s in order to explore the way in which this US economic power system had been eroded.

DETERMINANTS OF THE RISE AND FALL OF THE 'GOLDEN AGE'

Interestingly, Bretton Woods institutions as such had very little operational value in the 1950s and 1960s. In fact, they became relevant only after the United States suspended formally the dollar–gold convertibility in August 1971. This was no accident. Monetary institutions perform their aggressive capitalist assignments better when they are free of constraints and fetters, and this was the kind of environment opening up to them after 1971. The IMF and the World Bank began to participate increasingly in the creation of Yugoslav and Latin American debts in the 1970s and 1980s, with these reaching their climax in the 1990s as pure instruments of the US Treasury for the implementation of 'shock therapy' neoliberal doctrines in Eastern Europe. In other words, the Bretton Woods arrangements should be seen as monetary vehicles for the expansion of US power via dollarizing the European and Asian markets. Insofar as the key operational instruments were dollar–gold parity, with the dollar as the global reserve currency, and the fixed exchange rates regime, money was fettered. When gold convertibility ended, this unleashed the ability of all sort of business actors to exploit the advantage of the dollar's floating exchange rate. The key contradictions and disintegrative tendencies of the capitalist system began to be manifest at two levels simultaneously: at the international monetary/financial level and at the level of industrial production. The result was a manifestly serious fiscal crisis of core capitalist states in the West. Let us first look at what characterized the 'golden age of capitalism', a period that ran roughly and full-steam from 1950 to 1970.

Beyond uneven and combined development

The slowdown in US growth during the 1930s following the Great Depression was offset by the accelerated production rates during the Second World War. As we saw earlier, the United States came out of the war as a huge credit and industrial machine, the only power capable of assisting the reconstruction of the destroyed economies of Europe and Asia. The Marshall Plan did not only carry out a large-scale economic aid programme to help the recovery of Western Europe; it also promoted a preferential regime for European products to be exported to the United States. This assisted Europe and Japan with their problems of dollar shortage. The United States could supply dollars and other forms of dollarized aid in exchange for imports. In Germany's case, for example, 57 per cent of that country's imports between 1947 and 1949 were financed by US aid and other dollarized assets.[27] The tendency towards uneven and combined development had already been set in motion. Yet appreciating this is not enough in order to comprehend holistically how the world operated during that period. From the anti-colonial struggles of the 1950s and 1960s to Arab nationalism and the policies of détente and Östpolitik, and from Latin American developments to Mandela's anti-racist struggles, global fault-lines were in full operation during that period.

From 1938 to 1950 the index for the US gross national product (GNP), at constant prices, rose from 100 to 179, as opposed to 128 for the USSR, 114 for the United Kingdom, 127 for Holland, 121 for France, and 72 for Japan.[28] At any rate, the United States 'ended the war with almost two thirds of the world's industrial production'.[29] In 1945 the share of profits in the value of output was 22 per cent.[30] Between 1950 and 1958 the foreign exchange component of world reserves increased by nearly $7 billion, all of which took the form of US dollars, turning the dollar into the 'world's reserve currency and the US the world's central bank' – at least for that period.[31] Based on its technological and military lead, innovative research and development programmes, the mass of its gold reserves and the powerful position of the dollar in global currency and trade markets, the United States was the undisputed leader of the capitalist world: it overpowered the United Kingdom in the Bretton Woods arrangements, took the lead in the GATT negotiations on trade liberalization and set out the rules for European and Japanese reconstruction processes, including rules and institutional arrangements regarding security and military matters, such as the formation of the North Atlantic Treaty Organization (NATO) in 1949 and the bilateral treaty with Japan in 1951, which allowed for the establishment of US military bases there, especially in Okinawa.

In the 1950s and 1960s US capital in Western Europe and Japan assumed particular relevance, and 'was largely centred on manufacturing, especially petrochemicals'.[32] Initially led by the United States, foreign direct investment (FDI) flows more than doubled between 1950 and 1957 – from $11.8 billion to $25.4 billion – and then doubled again between 1957 and 1966 to $51.8 billion.[33] Multinational corporations expanded even more than during the pre-war years by way of dollarizing returns and profits, then partially repatriating them to the United States, and also creating a number of subsidiaries in the host countries. (Offshore companies and tax havens for companies became prominent in the 1960s following the relaxation of the fixed exchange rate system.)

These developments, coupled with strong state investment policies, increased the potential for endogenous industrial development of the European and Japanese political economies proper. For example, by 1970, 'the share of Europe in total US FDI outflow balance increased to 33.5 per cent from 14.7% in 1950, and the share of manufacturing industry increased to 41.1%'.[34] Similar developments occurred in Japan, although the Japanese state employed an interesting strategy: it focused on building a network of multinational corporations in Southeast Asia and other peripheral regions, creating solid foundations for further expansion into the European and US markets. The environment, obviously, was the first to suffer. Between 1950 and 1973 carbon dioxide emissions almost tripled, paving the way for what was later to become known as global warming.[35] Chemicals affecting the ozone layer, such as chlorofluorocarbons, were released massively into the atmosphere each year. Ecological movements and the number of environmentalists began to grow, and by the late 1960s environmentalism had a place next to other new social movements, such as feminism and youth movements.

Intra-European immigration grew at a fast pace, creating ideal conditions for an economic take-off. Southern Italian, Turkish, Spanish and Greek emigrants poured into the European industrial North, quickly becoming available to industrial capital as a source of cheap labour. In order to gain access to cheaper labour, and also to escape external tariffs after the founding of the European Economic Community (EEC) in 1957, US manufacturing investment in Europe grew from $1 billion in 1950 to $14 billion in 1970. The United States was becoming the engine of growth for the rest of the world economy in the 1940s and 1950s, not least because it needed developed consumer markets to export and sell its products. These markets needed to be conducive to its new, dollar-centred, open door policy.

But building a European and Japanese consumer market for US manufacturing proved to be difficult, because growth in this period was asymmetrical, and was higher outside the United States than inside it. This period saw the rapid expansion of primarily West German and Japanese manufacturing. State investment played a paramount role in the pro-growth strategies of post-war political elites during the years in question. During the 1950s, Germany's manufacturing output grew by an average of 10 per cent per year, and its GDP by 8 per cent (the highest rates in Europe). In Japan the numbers were more miraculous: manufacturing output during the same period grew at an average annual rate of 16.7 per cent, and GDP at about 10 per cent (the highest rates in all capitalist economies).[36] Average annual growth rates in the United States, Western Europe and Japan in the 1950s and 1960s were nearly 6 per cent, whereas the growth in the volume of trade was 'eight times faster than in the period 1913–50 and twice as great as in the century from 1820. Trade among the Western industrial economies was the most dynamic element in this, with trade and output growth especially marked in manufactures.'[37]

Finance capital – that is, the merging of banking with industrial capital – played a leading role in investment, especially in infrastructure, a process that took place under the aegis of the state.[38] The capitalist state, in other words, controlled banking and financial capital, led domestic economic development, organized hegemony and absorbed and refracted social struggles and discontent. In addition, this means that most 'economic miracles' were based on the developmental and export-led capacities of core capitalist states: that is, on the dollarization of global markets via the fixed exchange rate mechanism established at Bretton Woods.

It is very important to understand the full implications of this, because one of the problems of the 1944 regime was that dollars began accumulating not just in the United States but also, above all, *outside* it. This is the 'dollar-glut problem', which became a problem as US competitiveness was undermined, mainly but not exclusively by the core capitalist economies of Western Europe and Asia. We shall deal with this issue below. For the time being, we would add that one of the reasons why the 'Golden Age' was golden 'was that the price of a barrel of Saudi oil averaged less than $2 throughout the entire period from 1950 to 1973'.[39] Cheap oil fuelled the fast growth of the core capitalist economies of the United States, Europe and Japan. When the oil market collapsed in 1973, the United States created a new link with the dollar, leading to further dollarization. Let us now look at some qualitative policy instruments that buttressed the uneven and combined economic take-off in core global capitalist states.

In terms of domestic policy requirements, the Western (and Japanese) capitalist states, although each one of them operated within the sociopolitical constraints of its own traditions, adhered to Keynesian policy making. This, first and foremost, entailed a rationalized management of aggregate demand in order to stave off market disequilibria. It entailed the development of welfarism and the control of interest rates and inflation through fiscal/budgetary instruments. Under Keynesian policy making, the state assumed major entrepreneurial and financial roles by acting directly as an organizer of production and the reproduction of social capital. Increases in real and nominal wages under the aegis of the state were to be offset by an increase in the level of consumption and by continuous investment strategies. As Andrew Glyn, Philip Armstrong and John Harrison pointed out, the rise of wages during the 'Golden Age' is a complex phenomenon.[40] Rising wages did not damage the conditions of production, but they helped to encourage the introduction of new means of production in capitalist enterprises, so they could limit their employment numbers and maintain high levels of profitability. Glyn, Armstrong and Harrison went on to argue:

Regardless of their importance in sustaining accumulation by providing a growing market for consumer goods, wages must be regarded as a basically passive element in the process of realisation [reification – *our addition*]. The development of wages is largely a product of the process of accumulation itself. A capitalist boom requires surplus to be realised [reified]. Workers' spending as a whole provides the demand which realises [reifies] the profits of capitalists producing consumer goods. But the pay of their employees is an expense which reduces profits, not a source of demand which realises [reifies] them. Only the spending of workers employed elsewhere realises [reifies] profits in the consumer goods industries. These workers will only be employed if there is demand for the products they make – for export, from the government or from the employers themselves. So the realisation [reification] of all the surplus ultimately depends on sufficient spending by the employers (on investment or consumption), the government or by those purchasing exports.[41]

Fordism was the sister-structure of Keynesianism, a 'perfect' match of it. 'Mass production for mass consumption' was Fordism's cornerstone, itself based on a set of industrial relations on the shop floor regulated by new management techniques first proposed by Frederick Taylor, a worker in the Ford car factory in the United States before the First World War. The essence of those new techniques was to subsume labour to a quantifiable metric system of the assembly line, mainly but not exclusively by way of counting the working time in relation to output per worker. This involved a new industrial discipline under a new regime of exploitation of labour, corresponding to the extended form of the reproduction of capital assumed under Keynesianism. The aim was clear: to make available as many products as possible on the market by exploiting as much as possible the physical and mental abilities of workers, with their only reward being high wages. 'The striking feature of [the] Ford contract', John Holloway wrote, 'is the trade off between the acceptance of disciplined, soul-destroying monotony during the day and a relatively comfortable consumption after hours, the rigid separation between the death of alienated labour and the "life" of consumption'.[42] That was how the desired result of *mass production for mass consumption* could be achieved.

Once in power, V. I. Lenin admired Taylorism/Fordism and saw it as the best means by which the newly formed Soviet state could develop its social productive forces.[43] Antonio Gramsci, the leader of the Italian Communist Party and one of the most important Marxist theoreticians of the twentieth century (who was imprisoned under Mussolini from 1926 to 1934) basically abhorred it.[44] European and Japanese industries, whether public or private, applied it *en masse* during the Golden Age, not least because such a system of labour discipline on the shop floor contributed greatly to an increase in the

margins of profit, while fitting perfectly Keynesian policy requirements – including the integration of labour-power into the capitalist
system of decision making, what neoliberals in the 1980s began,
rather derogatively, to call 'corporatism'. It is precisely the complex
articulation of Taylorism/Fordism and Keynesianism that produced
what John Kenneth Galbraith called '*technostructure*' in the context
– as he saw it – of the 'new industrial state'.[45] Technostructure was
the intellectual superstructure/extension of qualified knowledge and
skills acquired from the new organization of labour and production,
which was embodied in a new, 'technocratic', managerial decision-
making class. Arguably, the fundamental aim of this comprehensive
system was twofold: to consolidate 'an aggregate volume of output
corresponding to full employment as nearly as is practicable',[46]
and to avoid a 'flight'/transformation of industrial capital to *haute
finance*, whose tendency is to become an independent structure of
money generation and to indulge in speculative arbitrage without
any connection with material production. Keynes himself had an
interesting way of putting it:

> Speculators may do no harm as bubbles on a steady stream of
> enterprise. But the position is serious when enterprise becomes
> the bubble on a whirlpool of speculation. When the capital devel-
> opment of a country becomes a by-product of the activities of a
> casino, the job is likely to be ill-done. The measure of success
> attained by Wall Street, regarded as an institution of which the
> proper social purpose is to direct new investment into the most
> profitable channels in terms of future yield, cannot be claimed
> as one of the outstanding triumphs of *laissez-faire* capitalism –
> which is not surprising, if I am right in thinking that the best
> brains of Wall Street have been in fact directed towards a different
> object.[47]

The above discussion is directly linked to the political and ideational structures of global capitalism in the 1960s and 1970s. As
we have shown elsewhere, the United States's defeat in Vietnam
and the beginnings of its economic decline induced the country to
launch the foreign policy of *détente*, thus transforming the ideational binary of the Cold War – 'the free West against the evil force
of Communism'.[48] The United States' economic competitor, West
Germany, took advantage of *détente* to launch its own *Östpolitik*,
improving its relations with the USSR on a number of issues,
especially on energy matters, in view of unifying Germany. This

development disturbed the United States, which saw a *rapprochement* between Germany and the USSR as detrimental to its own European interests and the Cold War balance of power in Eurasia. The United States eventually stopped it by placing intercontinental ballistic missiles on West German soil, reviving the Cold War. Developments and revolutions in Latin America and elsewhere, the rise of Arab nationalism, Vietnam and a series of other events can be inserted in the same constellation of a truly global, progressive dynamic undermining US supremacy. All in all, the entire global system in the 1960s and 1970s can be captured better by the concept of global fault-lines, rather than that of uneven and combined development. The latter seems to apply only to deciphering global economic trends – although Trotsky himself had conceived of it in a rather Eurocentric way.[49]

Over-accumulation, balance of payments and debt

The euphoria was not meant to last. The contradictions of the global economic system erupted at two interconnected levels. The first was an over-accumulation crisis typically manifested in a falling rate of profit across the core economies, especially in the United States; the second was an uncontrollable development in the US balance of payments and trade balance, which began registering persistent deficits as early as 1950, and a concomitant rise in US debt.

The uneven (and combined) character of the capitalist development meant that rivals of the United States in Europe and Japan 'were accumulating capital at a faster rate and were doing so on the basis of far lower wage costs'.[50] In 1960, 'hourly manufacturing labour costs, including social security contributions, were around three times as high in the USA as in Europe, and ten times as high as in Japan'.[51] The international competitiveness of US business began to erode in the face of the rapid development of other economic centres, namely Western Europe, Japan and Southeast Asia. This resulted in a relative fall in profitability, which became even sharper towards the second half of the 1960s because of the inability of excess capital to find profitable outlets. The open door policy was undermined by the rise of Arab nationalism and the completion of decolonization in the Third World, creating a new chain of states wanting to assert national sovereignty and impede the US desire to wield continuing influence via open door arrangements. Following the Cuban revolution Castro's government managed to maintain its grip on power, whereas by 1975 the United States had completely withdrawn from Vietnam: 'Goliath had been felled by the slingshot of David', as Hobsbawm put it.[52] The rate of profit in US manufacturing and business in general began a sustained fall after 1966 (see Table 2.1), and 'between 1965 and 1973, the rates of profit in the manufacturing and private business sectors fell by 40.9% and 29.3% respectively'.[53] As Armstrong, Glyn and Harrison underscore:

> Taking into account the rise in unemployment, the rise in capital stock per head (an index of increased mechanisation) was 38% in the US, 87% in Europe, and 203% in Japan. New investment per employed worker in the US manufacturing in 1955 was running at about 1.6 times the European level, and nearly five times that of Japan; by 1970 US manufacturing was investing about the same per worker as European industry and one-third less than Japanese. In the US average productivity rose by less than one-half between 1954 and 1970, in Japan it rose three and a half times and in Europe it doubled.[54]

It should be noted that the fall of profitability in Europe began earlier (1960), and that this was not caused primarily by the widespread industrial conflict and social unrest that culminated in the events of May 1968 in France and in Italy's Hot Autumn (1969).[55] Rather, profitability began falling earlier in Europe as a result of

Table 2.1 Percentages of profit rates, 1960–73

	ACC[1]	USA	Europe	Japan
Business				
Peak year[2]	17.2[3]	22.3[4]	16.3[5]	32.0[6]
1973	13.6	14.8	11.3	19.6
1973/peak year	0.79	0.66	0.69	0.61
Manufacturing				
Peak year[2]	23.6[3]	34.9[4]	19.9[5]	46.5[6]
1973	19.3	22.5	12.1	33.5
1973/peak year	0.82	0.64	0.61	0.72

Source: Armstrong, Glyn and Harrison (1984, p. 257).

Notes
1   The seven most industrialised countries at the time (United States, Canada, United Kingdom, France, Germany, Italy and Japan).
2   Year before sustained decline in profitability.
3   1968   4   1966
5   1960   6   1970.

the competition between the global 'triad' (Western Europe, the United States, Japan/Southeast Asia), which created a 'dollar glut' in European markets. That is, this period saw an accumulation of US dollars in the hands of European producers that could not find profitable investment outlets for them. Let us consider this case carefully.

From the late 1950s and early 1960s, the US balance of payments moved into persistent deficit. Even worse, there was a flurry of speculation in gold led by Gaullist France (see Table 2.2). But the balance of payments deficit alone does not represent the real weakness of the dollar as a means of international payment for the United States. What makes this variable (balance of payments) important is the connection it has with the issue of US government and private debt.

Table 2.2 US balance of payments ($ billion)

	1950–59	1960–67
Merchandise trade	29.3	39.6
Services and remittances	-5.3	-8.5
Net military transactions	-23.1	-20.5
US government grants (ex. military)	-20.5	-14.8
Net interest and dividends received	25.5	36.5
Current account balance	6.0	32.3
Direct investment (net)	-17.2	-27.9
Investment in shares and bonds (net)	-3.7	-6.4
Government loans	-4.1	-10.6
Long-term capital	-25.0	-44.9
Balance on current and long-term capital	-19.0	-12.6
Dollars held abroad by private sector[1]	1.5[2]	-2.8
Financed by		
Dollars held abroad in official reserves	13.0[3]	8.1
Reduction in US reserves	4.5	6.7
(of which gold)	(5.1)	(7.4)

Source: *US Survey of Current Business,* June 1975–October 1972, quoted in Armstrong, Glyn and Harrison (1984, p. 229).

Notes
1   Includes net short-term capital.
2   US liquid liabilities to private foreigners are not included.
3   Includes US liquid liabilities to private foreigners.

It was this that made the dollar weak. Ernest Mandel was entirely aware of this:

> The real weakness of the dollar rests in the enormous govern-mental and private indebtedness in the United States, without which the formidable American productive machine could no longer sell its flood of commodities. The American private debt went from $140 billion in 1945 to $753 billion in 1963. It came to 78% of US gross private production in 1945; it went to 143% of this in 1963. In 1951 the average American paid out 14% of his disposable income on debts and interest. This now reached almost 25%! It is clear that this debt spiral, which is a genuine inflationary spiral, cannot continue indefinitely without threatening the underpinnings of the system.[56]

Well into the 1960s, and in order to finance its military venture in Vietnam, as well as President Johnson's Great Society programme, the United States inflated the global economy by printing more dollars, contributing further to the 'dollar glut'.[57] This policy encountered the strong opposition of de Gaulle among others, since he realized that the uneven value of the dollar in Europe and the United States was placing a heavy burden on the European taxpayer, who in essence was financing the disastrous US war in Vietnam. Moreover, Europe's dollar glut cultivated inflation and reduced profitability. 'The dollar', as Treasury Secretary John Connally put it during the Smithsonian Conference in Washington in December 1971, 'may be our currency, but it's your problem.'[58]

But gold was an alternative tradable commodity, as it was fixed to the dollar. Since the Genoa Conference in 1922, 'France had opposed any scheme conferring special status on a particular currency.'[59] Its opposition at Bretton Woods counted for very little, though, as Roosevelt did not even want France to be a member of the UN Security Council. But in the 1960s France could not be ignored. In 1965 de Gaulle, breaking away from the tradition of 'dollar buying', demanded gold from the United States in return for $300 million, setting the tone for others to follow.[60] The US gold stock fell from $22.7 billion in 1950 to $17.8 billion in 1960 and $10.7 billion in 1970. Yet 'foreign official holdings of dollars grew by much more than foreign gold holdings, reaching $26.1 billion in 1970',[61] a fact that US policy makers took seriously into consideration when they pushed US President Richard Nixon to break away from the Bretton Woods system, closing the gold window once and for all.[62] Beginning with Japan, the United States attempted to put an embargo on its 'gold buyers', but it was already too late. As early as 1947, Belgian monetary economist Robert Triffin anticipated this run on US gold by the country's capitalist competitors, when he argued that US balance of payments deficits could be sustained without eventually undermining the commitment of the United States to sell gold for dollars. In fact, Triffin did nothing more spectacular than remind us that history and societies are dynamic, and not static, processes.

With the erosion of US competitiveness, the dollars accumulated in Europe and Asia outnumbered those circulating in the United States proper. As capitalists in Europe and the United States moved to raise the price of commodities in order to offset profitability losses, inflation inevitably moved in. In the United States inflation jumped from 1.5 per cent in the early 1950s to 5.9 per cent in 1970. By the mid-1970s, and because of the events of 1973–74 when the Organization of Petroleum Exporting Countries (OPEC), in coordination with the United States, quadrupled oil prices, inflation skyrocketed to double-digit numbers across the capitalist core. This proved very damaging especially for European and Japanese competitiveness. Further state intervention in the aggregate demand in the United States and the United Kingdom had the sole effect of widening fiscal disequilibria, thus initiating a permanent cycle of fiscal crises for the US federal state. Budget deficits in the United States began rising steadily as a result of debt financing (by 1980, the federal deficit was approximately 5 per cent of US GDP).[63]

To bring in a more macro-historical view, whereas 'in the early 1950s, the United States, with 6% of total world population, accounted for approximately 40% of the gross world product, by 1980 the American share had dropped by half to approximately 22%'.[64] This shift reflected substantially a process of deindustrialization, as Anglo-American manufacturing started to move offshore where tax exceptions were substantial and labour-power much cheaper. In 1957, 74 of the top 100 global firms were from the United States, but this number dropped to 53 in 1972.[65] The sales of the largest 100 US firms were nearly double the sales of the largest 100 non-US firms in 1962, but in 1972 they were only 40 per cent more. In the case of the car industry the numbers are equally telling. In 1962 the largest three US producers accounted for 67.5 per cent of the sales of the top 20 global producers, but 'in 1972 the share was 58.1%'. In 1957 the biggest three car firms sold 11.6 times as much as their three biggest rivals, yet 'in 1972 the difference was 4.2

times'.[66] In the iron and steel industries the ratio fell from 4.7 to 0.9 respectively.

Stagnation in investment, particularly in renewing the means of production, became endemic, and the result was a sharp rise in unemployment. The process of deindustrialization assumed colossal proportions in the United States in the 1980s as the result of an overvalued dollar, the interest rates spike (the 'Volcker revolution') and the subsequent high cost of capital. The United States began increasingly to consume more imported goods and services from Europe, Asia and the rest of the world, and to produce less. Meanwhile, new US multinational corporations based in Europe and Southeast Asia began pioneering cross-cutting equity ownership, cross-licensing of technology and joint venture schemes, increasingly targeting the so-called 'developing world". Thus, an interpenetration of each other's home market began, with the beneficiaries being the 'laggards' of the 'developing' world who were fast catching up. All in all, by the late 1960s the United States began to move steadily from being a credit superpower to a debtor one, from an economic giant to merely being the first among equals in economic terms.

The main policy determinants of the rise and fall of the 'Golden Age of capitalism' can be summarized as follows:

- Full employment policies, mass production for mass consumption and the avoidance of a casino/Ponzi capitalism via control of the exchange rate mechanism and banking capitals. Unemployment was almost non-existent during the years in question, the partial exception being the United States and Canada with an average rate of unemployment at about 4.7 per cent.[67] It is no accident that European social democracy flourished precisely by accommodating itself within the policy perimeters of Keynesianism/Fordism, thus obtaining the best possible results for the mass of working people – high wages, universal welfare, free education, healthcare and progressive pension schemes.
- The internationalization of the US state, the institutionalization of the primacy of the dollar via Bretton Woods institutions, large capital flows in intra-core political economies and the creation of colossal transnational corporations also contributed, together with the demand-led policies of the state, to creating an explosive developmental mix in each end of Eurasia, relatively eroding the primacy of the United States in the IPE.

The first determinant applies predominately, but not exclusively, to what we have called 'domestic environment of the state'. The second applies predominately, but not exclusively, to the 'external environment of the state'. The internationalization of the US empire-state provided the main 'glue' for these two domains of social action and struggle, often mobilizing anti-Soviet/anti-Communist Cold War rhetoric and ideational schemes. But the US-led IPE was undermined by the neo-capitalist revival of the European and Southeast Asian cores. Global fault-lines began working against the primacy of the US empire-state. We now turn to examine this process.

3

THE FAILURE OF FINANCIAL STATECRAFT (1), 1971–91

There was nothing natural about laissez-faire; free markets could never have come into being merely by allowing things to take their course. Just as cotton manufactures – the leading free trade industry – were created by the help of protective tariffs, export bounties, and indirect wage subsidies, laissez-faire itself was enforced by the state .... Laissez-faire was not a method to achieve a thing; it was the thing to be achieved. While laissez-faire economy was the product of deliberate state action, subsequent restrictions on laissez faire started in a spontaneous way. Laissez-faire was planned; planning was not.

Karl Polanyi, *The Great Transformation* (1944)

A NOTE ON ERNEST MANDEL

Financial statecraft is the name we give to the process initiated by the decision of the Nixon administration in August 1971 to opt out of the gold fetter, thus consciously placing the entire international political economy (IPE) on a pure dollar standard. Free of any constraint, the dollar, it was thought, could be manipulated at will by the executive of the US Fed.

Financial statecraft is not the same as economic statecraft: for example assigning trade privileges, tariffs and quotas, or providing foreign aid in times of drought and disaster. As a Council on Foreign Relations publication suggests, financial statecraft has to do with the US state's role in financialization/globalization.[1] It is the active participation of the US state's monetary institutions in facilitating new forms of global capital flows (securities, asset management, credit default swaps, derivatives and futures, circulation of liquid currencies, portfolio investment) by way of promoting further dollarization, underwriting foreign debt and imposing financial sanctions on undisciplined actors. Financial statecraft has a domestic policy dimension too, which the realists on the Council on Foreign Relations failed to tackle. It is the liquidation, on International Monetary Fund (IMF) orders, by the new subaltern liberal executives of state assets, the liberalization of banking capital, privatizations and manipulation of monetary instruments, such as interest rates, in order to curb inflation or assist bubbles and debt creation in the housing market.[2]

This is what we have called the essence of neoliberalism. Neoliberalism and globalization are the flipsides of the same coin: the dominance of financial and speculative capital over the productive/industrial capital. Nixon's decision in 1971 opened Pandora's box, unleashing the most aggressive and violent aspects of the open door thesis. What we are going to argue here is that this twin policy of neoliberalism/globalization is defensive in form and substance, therefore it is unable to provide an alternative to the long-term historic decline of the Anglo-American imperium that began in earnest in the 1970s. Herein lies our key disagreement with Leo Panitch, Ray Kiely and other scholars, who believe that the 'Volcker revolution' and Clinton's globalization got the US-led global capitalist system on the move again. From this perspective, it is interesting to look at how Mandel's contemporary analysis of the late 1960s approached the first signs of the decline of the United States.

In a short essay published in *New Left Review* in March–April 1969 entitled 'Where is America going?' Mandel began articulating what later came to be called, at least among the Marxists of the period, 'the US decline thesis'.[3] Mandel stated that there were external and internal (to the United States) forces that worked towards destroying the equilibrium established since the Second World War. He identified six of these forces, most of which were to be found in the domestic environment of the US state and society.

Mandel diagnosed that the development of automation increases the number of unskilled workers that are out of work. This hit the black population particularly, which was at this time under the influence of revolutionary ideas and other radical developments across the world. Another factor was the industrial revolution itself and the processes of automation and technological development, which sideline agriculture and marginalize manual labour at the expense of intellectual labour. Characteristically, Mandel said, there were more university students (6 million) than farmers (5.5 million including employees and family help) in the United States. He then went on to tackle an issue dear to John Kenneth Galbraith: technicians and the hierarchical structure of the factory, what Galbraith, as we saw earlier, called 'technostructure'. The real bosses, Mandel said, were not those supervising the production process. What was happening was that there had been a shift of the centre of gravity to the upper echelons of the big corporations, whose main preoccupation was not how to organize production, but how to ensure *reproduction*.[4] Contrary to what Galbraith achieved, Mandel identified a crucial phenomenon: he explained how industrialists may turn into financial speculators en masse, a phenomenon later explained systematically by Brenner, Arrighi, Gowan, Susan Strange and other Marxists and Marxistants.[5] The preoccupation of capitalism with issues of reproduction means that if there is a problem with the very process of accumulation per se and the *valorization* of capital, then capital seeks to diversify its activities away from a single branch of industry and even from industry itself.[6] This, in turn, leads to a mushrooming of financial operations and 'new products', as industrialists themselves want money to finance this strategy and also make more profits out of their invested money in paper assets. Yet, the 'absentee factory-owners are not straw men', explained Mandel: 'they retain ultimate power'.

Another phenomenon that was destroying the social equilibrium in the United States was the erosion of high wages because of an increased rate of inflation. Mandel located the causes of this new inflationary trend not only in the huge military establishment, but also in the acceleration of private debt. The result was a reversal in the growth of the real disposable income of the working class. The highest point of that income, Mandel said, was reached towards the end of 1965 and the beginning of 1966, after which it began to fall, and the increased gap between the incomes of the rich and working people also intensified the contradiction between 'private affluence' and 'public squalor'.

Yet the most important factor disturbing the US-centred imperial economic system, as Mandel underscored, was international competition. Wages in the United States were the highest in the world, a phenomenon that had a historical explanation: US industry suffered from a shortage of labour and could absorb high wages and large waves of migrants because it was relatively isolated from international competition. High wages were also possible because of the higher levels of productivity in the United States compared with

European and Asian capitalist economies. The problem was how this differential could be maintained when US industry was involved in fierce international competition with Western Europe and Japan, and when both Europe and Japan were seeing high levels of technological advance and productivity growth. Thus, Mandel began to see the process of 'uneven and combined development' inscribed in the contours of capitalist development as the root cause of the decline of the United States. This view became more explicit in his subsequent writings, which appeared after the collapse of the Bretton Woods system. Let us quote his rationale at length:

> The law of uneven development led to an increasing decline in the ability of American commodities to compete with those of the USA's most important imperialist rivals .... The foundering of the Bretton Woods system shows that the whole international credit expansion based on the use of the paper dollar as a world currency, could collapse like a house of cards [at this point, Mandel, in a long footnote, explained how US companies, because of credit restrictions in the United States, began to borrow in the short term, at fairly high interest rates, dollars in the possession of European companies, including European branches of American companies, and also of central banks. This 'Euro-dollar' system, however, increased the expansion of credit in the United States, hence the deficit in the US balance of payments – *our note.*] It is a sign of the growing insecurity of national credit expansion. [There is] a contradiction between the role of the dollar as the buffer of the US industrial cycle and its role as a world currency. Its first role implies permanent inflation; its second role maximum stability. It was possible for the system to survive so long as dollar inflation was very mild and American labour productivity unchallenged. But both conditions were gradually eliminated .... The insecurity of the world economy today finds expression in intensified international competition, which in turn corresponds to the relative decline in the preponderance of the USA.[7]

Mandel correctly saw the connection between the increasing US balance of payments deficit since the mid-1960s and the creation of debt through accelerating inflation in the post-war new accumulation regime. Both these factors led to a relative decline of the global position of the US imperial system. He also correctly diagnosed signs of stagnation in industry, as companies were in need of liquidity, and credit expansion threatened to dry up at the very moment when it was needed most. But the historical record since 1971 has shown that he was wrong in predicting that 'none of the other core capitalisms was likely to accept a devalued dollar as the arbiter of the international monetary system'.[8] In the event, this is precisely what happened. The breakdown of Bretton Woods had been engineered by the US elites in order to strengthen the centrality of the US empire-state and of the dollar system: that is, to strengthen the open door system in a period of severe capitalist recession. This is what they wished, but wishes often get tarnished after a short period of accomplishment. One crucial point US policy makers took into consideration was the link between the dollar and 'black gold': oil, and above all Saudi oil. Another was the link with the defence industry and its export capacity, both trends which, we could argue, were manifest in the 1950s, even before the Suez Canal crisis (1956). These were the years of a full-fledged militarization of containment under the policy influence of the famous NSC-68 document, drafted by the head of the policy planning staff, Paul Nitze, in March 1950 (it became declassified in the early 1970s). Some five years after Suez, Dwight Eisenhower, in his farewell address, would talk of a 'military-industrial complex' as an impediment to democracy.

BUSINESS STRATEGIES DEALING WITH STAGFLATION

Because of the inherent contradictions of the capitalist system examined above, the United States came to be exposed to imported inflation from the 1960s. Its Herculean task was to convince the rest of the world to continue to accept devalued dollars in exchange for economic goods and services. It proved very difficult. *Stagflation* was a typical manifestation of an *over-accumulation* crisis inherent in industrial capitalism: great masses of capital could not be invested profitably, as capital owners had no confidence that their investment would generate new, high rates of profit. Thus the mass of industrial workers created during the years of rapid development were now becoming increasingly redundant and obsolete as direct producers/ agents of capital valorization.[9] The tendency of a protracted class situation of over-accumulation and stagnation is to concentrate poverty on one pole and wealth on the other. Both poles are *under-consumed/under-utilized* – which is what distinguishes over-accumulation and stagnation from a virtuous period of capitalist development led by the industrial sector, whether in state or private hands, or both. Over-accumulation and stagnation in industry led the business classes to diversify their class strategies well before the Nixon administration broke away from the gold fetter. For our purposes here, two organically interlinked strategies employed by the bourgeoisie are important. Both, it should be noted, combined with the US Fed and the Nixon administration in initiating the new phase of globalization/financialization and the dismantling of the Keynesian/Fordist/welfarist nexus.

The first strategy was capital's 'flight' to the realm of finance via its transformation into what we called earlier 'new multinational corporations' (involving cross-cutting equity ownership, joint ventures, cross-licensing, diversified portfolio investment and so on). Capital assumed new flexible dimensions, cutting out cumbersome bureaucracies by taking advantage of technological advances. Galbraith's 'technostructure' could no longer hold. Secondary sourcing and the development of subsidiaries knitted together capital from different nations, the aim being to withstand competitive pressures, compensate for inflationary constraints, and find favourable tax regimes and cheap – and ideally skilled – labour.

As Mandel described in his 1969 essay, productive capital was being transformed into financial capital. In other words capitalists were gradually trying to become rentiers in pursuit of hot money. Rentiers are basically money makers who acquire their assets/income by way of extracting royalties from *future* production. As money and dollars could move around the globe unfettered – consider, for instance, the so-called abolition of 'capital controls' by the United States in 1974 – capitalists can invent all sorts of ways to extract profit from future production of values, without guarantees that the assets acquired from speculative activity will be reinvested in all or in part for the creation of new values in material production. This happens because capitalists want always to invest their money-capital in ways that brings them the highest yields with the minimum possible risk. This is how 'stock' and 'security' markets in the Anglo-American world began to develop in a new direction, with their key function being the buying and selling of claims on future economic activity. In this context, the creation of bubbles was unavoidable. Wall Street and the City of London began assuming major global positions as leading financial and banking centres, with investment banks, asset management and consulting companies and a huge shadow banking sector, such as hedge funds, playing a key role. Bonds, shares and later derivatives, mortgage-backed securities, credit default swaps and so on, were all forms of rentier activities with no guarantees of the reinvestment of profits in real value creation.[10]

Yet these capitalist strategies that emerged in the 1960s in the wake of the first signs of stagflation were obstructed by the fixed exchange rates regime of Bretton Woods. This meant that new profiteering outlets for capital in the realm of finance and a renewed financialization via dollarization could only come about in a post-Bretton Woods era. It should also be noted that this type of business activity is something that distinguishes to the present day Anglo-American capitalism from German, French and Japanese capitalisms. From this perspective, the thesis developed by Poulantzas – following Hilferding and Lenin – according to which financial capital is 'the mode of amalgamation of industrial capital and money capital in the reproduction of social capital'[11] as a whole – may be true in a European continental or Japanese context, but it fails to grasp the real development of Anglo-American capitalism. For example, whereas in Germany a bank will become an active and even leading participant in any new business to which it lends money so as to diminish risks on the future extraction of profits, in the United Kingdom a bank will lend money to a new business on the grounds of what assets it possesses that the capitalist can use as collateral. In this context, German capitalism is more cautious and risk-adverse; Anglo-American capitalism is more adventurous and risk-friendly.[12] This is crucial, and should not be confused with the pressure exercised on European continental capitalisms by the United States in order to adopt this new form of open door applied to the financial and banking sectors.

The first business strategy was geared towards committing the US state executive to deregulate the dollar from its gold fetter. The second related strategy pursued by Anglo-American business interests was to engage directly with the state machine in order to adopt a new type of intervention, effecting anti-Keynesian supply-side policies. The main target was presumably inflation. From the late 1960s, Paul Volcker was a key player in the US executive advocating both these strategies in tandem.

With the rates of profitability in tatters, the economic elite began to put pressure on the Keynesian executives to abandon protections for workers.[13] These policies began to make headway first in the United States and the United Kingdom. They involved the purest forms of class exploitation and subordination of labour to capital: the retrenchment of the welfare state, the lowering of wages accompanied by mass lay-offs, waves of privatization of state enterprises and public utilities, and the introduction of flexible labour schemes. All these policies disregarded the need for sustained aggregate demand. Time and again, and contrary to a neo-Smithian and neo-Weberian tradition that sees the state as a bureaucratic machine that stands alone, separate from economic relations, there is clear evidence that the state is, first and foremost, a representative of the socio-economic class (or fraction of a class) that dominates the relations of production and class exploitation. The Anglo-American open door policy and dollar–sterling class interests set the tone for the actions that other, subaltern states had to follow.

In this sense, the post-Second World War capitalist state in Europe and Asia had been an active participant, even a protagonist, in the shaping and reproduction of the global economic system, structured along the line of contradictions and antagonisms between and among various capitals and class interests in the global chain of interests which was rattling under the supremacy of the United States.[14] The US empire-state had dominated the imperial chain of its vassal capitalisms, without being always able to direct and control the class antagonisms manifested across their domestic environments in the way it always wants. The inherent contradictions of the global economic system became manifest in the disintegrative logics of the open door, leading to its historical demise.

Both strategies had to rebuild a functional class regime of *cooperative interpenetration* in order to alter the terrain of class antagonisms, by replacing the bygone era of the fixed exchange rates and a Keynesian regime with that of globalization/neoliberalism. In this context, US business and political elites, working closely with other Organisation for Economic Cooperation and Development (OECD) elites, were aiming at opening up the financial and banking regulation systems in European and Southeast Asian capitalist states. The aim was to transfer streams of value and financial assets from there to the United States. NATO and US power in the European and Pacific theatres would oversee and guarantee this flow of income from the 'periphery' to 'metropolises'. From this perspective, as we argued earlier, the US state is an imperialist state in the classical sense of the word, in that it appropriates international value while this process is accompanied by its guarantor – military power. All in all, globalization and neoliberalism had to merge, in the final instance, for a twin purpose: to restore the (average) rate of profit by defeating the advances of labour-power achieved under the previous accumulation regime, and to undo the constraints imposed on the United States and the United Kingdom by the global competition of Germany and Japan. Let us see how the US empire-state attempted to achieve that. In the process we shall prepare the ground for assessing in subsequent chapters whether its responses were successful in staving off the crisis of profitability that had taken root in the late 1960s – Brenner's key concern. So we will move on examine in detail some key historical processes and policies through which the US executive attempted to implement this new twin strategy promoted by its business classes.

AN UNSTABLE 'PETRODOLLAR'/'WEAPON-DOLLAR' REGIME

There were two inherent contradictions in the Bretton Woods system: first, the privileged position of the dollar as the main global transaction currency, and second, the difficulty the United States had in devaluing its dollar in order to offset balance of payments difficulties and deal with its debt problem. It was contemplated that, had the United States done that, it would have resulted in a parallel devaluation of all other major currencies (the mark, the yen, the British pound and so on) in order to offset the US advantage. But increasing competition from the other capitalist centres (Western Europe and Japan), the escalation of the Vietnam War in the late 1960s, the massive outflow of gold and the Great Society programme pushed US policy makers to print more dollars, inflating the global economy yet without solving an increasing balance of payments deficit and its connection with US debt. The United States also began to accumulate large amounts of foreign dollars coming into the country from the gold buying of France and other countries that followed the French lead. Under these conditions, the gold–dollar equivalence could not hold. By 1970–71 the dollar was completely out of tune with all other major international currencies, a tendency that was articulated in asymmetrical fashion by the rates of inflation across the world creating unsustainable disequilibria in exchange rate regimes. But this did not make US policy makers lose their sleep. When, on August 15, 1971, President Nixon cut the Gordian knot by 'closing the gold window', as Joanne Gowa put it, he knew that this move represented a massive increase of economic freedom and action for the United States, since the entire IPE would have now to turn into a pure dollar standard.[15]

The dollar was becoming the sole standard against which other currencies could be measured. Now, under floating conditions, the US Treasury could devalue the dollar at will, thus reducing foreign debt obligations and boosting exports. And as the United States was the sole power that could print dollars, it could be argued that the move represents a full-fledged transition from *commodity* money to *fiat* money, a situation unique in the monetary history of the last 200 years. Fiat money is a different name for *seigniorage*, which means that the dollar seigniorage can bring royalties to the United States and its business classes by spending or investing money abroad (for instance, in portfolio investment) without the need to earn or produce anything abroad, or without the need to bother very much about changes in the dollar exchange rate. The same goes for setting up a military base abroad: the United States is not constrained by any foreign exchange considerations.

Strictly speaking, the United States was not interested in just shifting the IPE from pegged to floating exchange rates: in essence, the United States was seeking to restore its economic and political leadership in the capitalist world, using multilateral political means and acting under the international political umbrella of *détente*, a foreign policy seeking cooperation and mutual nuclear disarmament with the USSR (see, for instance, the SALT initiatives).[16] Thus, in December 1971, at the Smithsonian Institution in Washington DC, all major industrialist countries agreed to a significant devaluation of the dollar against all major currencies. This was deeply resented by the Japanese and the Europeans alike, but the response by John Connally, as we saw earlier, was sarcastic: 'the dollar is our currency but it's your problem'.

From then on, the road had opened to financialization, as speculators, like post-1971 tourists, could move their money and assets around the world, without major restrictions, capitalizing on favourable exchange rate regimes and playing on the strong/weak currencies ratio. Nixon ensured, despite serious objections from other countries of the capitalist core, that financial relations would progressively be taken out of state control, centred instead on private financial operators and asset managers. Yet, from that point on, the United States had to find a way to convince the world to continue to accept every devalued dollar in exchange for all sorts of services and goods the country needed to get from Asian, European and other producers. A partial solution to this was found in US oil policy, although this should not be seen separately from weapons procurement and the centrality of the Arab–Israeli conflict, what Jonathan Nitzan and Shimshon Bichler called 'weapon-dollar/petro-dollar coalition'. Especially after the Six Day Middle East war in 1967, the United States began simultaneously a massive *commercialization/globalization* of the arms industry and a conspicuous *politicization* of the oil sector.[17] Let us start the story at the beginning.

From 1969 to 1974, Paul Volcker, a former financial economist for Chase Manhattan Bank, had served as under secretary of the

Treasury for international monetary affairs. He had been instrumental in pushing for the decisions leading to the US suspension of gold convertibility in 1971, which ended the Bretton Woods system. Volcker, a Democrat, was nominated by the Carter administration in August 1979 as head of the US Fed, a position he kept under Ronald Reagan until August 1987. When he became chairman of the Fed, inflation was running at 9 per cent, and in 1980 it hit 11 per cent. Since monetarist logic has a natural aversion to inflation and dictates that inflation ruins savings and devalues bond holdings, Volcker's response was to limit the money supply and lead a spectacular rise in the basic interest rate of the Fed: from 8 per cent in 1978 to 19 per cent in 1981.[18] By 1983, the inflation rate decreased to less than 5 per cent, and bond holders and Treasury bill holders, chief among whom were the Japanese and the Saudis, benefited greatly. But the ultimate beneficiary was the US Fed system, as it could divert foreign liquid assets to the financing of the US Cold War military machine. Further, high interest rates sent Latin American debt sky high, decimating growth: the debt crisis hit Argentina in 1981, Brazil in 1983 and Chile and Mexico in 1982. Overall Latin American debt soared to $315 billion in 1983 from $75 billion in 1975. This 'debt dollarization' of Latin American countries resulted in enormous returns of capital for the US Treasury, and dealt a devastating blow to the assets and industrial potential of those countries.[19]

The real response of the US empire-state to stagflation was a financial statecraft along the lines of the new forms of embeddedness of a 'petro-dollar/weapon dollar' regime topped by Volcker's interest rates hike. But, as we shall see, this financial statecraft too failed to reverse the historical and structural decline of Anglo-American world centrality. This is a major oversight in the works by Leo Panitch, Leonard Seabrook, Ray Kiely and others.[20]

Now let us turn back to the role of international energy markets in sustaining the United States' unique role as supplier of the world's reserve currency. As we have maintained elsewhere,[21] the Nixon administration realised that if oil trade and reserves were denominated in dollars, then oil-producing states would obtain more dollars than they could readily spend on domestic projects. One possible solution to this problem would be to invest these oil-produced dollars – hence their nickname 'petrodollars' – in US shares and bonds. This, in turn, could finance the US current account and balance of payments deficits, including US military undertakings, with the United States alone holding the privilege, as we noticed earlier, of being able to print dollars by fiat.[22]

The advantageous position gained by the United States was obvious. Given the dependency of both Europe and Japan on Gulf oil, any disturbance in either the flow of oil from the Gulf to their markets or its price would cause havoc to them, while leaving the United States virtually unaffected. In fact, when OPEC increased the oil price fourfold in the wake of the Yom Kippur war in October 1973, Western European states and Japan felt the heat the most. The increase in the price of oil was not the result of the anger of the Saudi oil producers exhibiting solidarity with their Arab brothers and sisters because of the Yom Kippur war. The oil price rise was the result of Washington's careful financial statecraft in the Gulf states, at least two years before the eruption of the Arab–Israeli war in October 1973. As Peter Gowan argued, petrodollar recycling and a crippling blow to Japanese and European economies were the principal political objectives of the Nixon administration's drive for the OPEC oil price rise.[23]

US hegemony via petro-dollarization in the Gulf was formalized in June 1974, when the US secretary of state, Henry Kissinger, established the US–Saudi Arabian Joint Commission on Economic Co-operation, with the specific purpose of stabilizing oil supplies and prices. The Japanese and the Europeans had no option but to join the bandwagon, albeit grudgingly. As far as Europe is concerned, its plans, under France's lead, to follow up the completion of a customs union in the late 1960s with a monetary union were severely compromised. The Werner Report – named after the prime minister of Luxembourg, Pierre Werner – which described 'a process by which monetary union could be achieved by 1980'[24] was shelved. Europe suffered a massive loss of competitiveness as a result of the dollar fall.

The *de facto* breakdown of the Bretton Woods regime in 1971 was formalized in 1976 during a conference meeting of key IMF members in Kingston, Jamaica.[25] The conference increased the IMF quotas, especially those of OPEC countries, legalized floating exchange rates, reduced the role of gold and let states freely determine which currency they wished to peg their currency against – an essentially pretentious stipulation as most countries would peg their currencies against the dollar anyway, not least because the United States was the dominant power, both politically and militarily. The IMF and the World Bank, both under the paramountcy of the US Treasury, had changed tack too:

Both [the IMF and the World Bank] began to engage in new

forms of lending. The IMF moved from short-term to medium-term lending, and the nature of conditionality changed: instead of insisting primarily on changes in macroeconomic policies aimed at rather rapid external adjustment, it began to insist on changes in microeconomic policies aimed at extensive domestic reforms …. The World Bank moved from project lending with disbursements tied to actual spending on the corresponding project, to various forms of structural adjustment lending, with an urgent emphasis on rapid disbursement.[26]

This is a rather polite way of saying that the two Bretton Woods institutions were changing themselves under the leadership of the United States in order to meet the new requirements of the post-1971 US-led IPE. Among other requirements, this meant the liberalization of the internal accumulation regimes of the subaltern states by way of emphasizing supply-side economics, following the lead of the US empire-state. Conditionality now meant enforcement upon the world of neoliberal restructuring programmes and labour discipline, something that also directly undermined the so-called policies of 'import substitution', a policy generally pursued by Latin American and other periphery states – such as petrostates under the influence of Nasserite Arab nationalism.[27] That is how the beginnings of 'globalization' met the beginnings of 'neoliberalism' in an organic intra-suffusion. But there is more to the affair than meets the eye.

The *politicization* of the oil business went hand in glove with the *commercialization* and *globalization* of the arms industry. As underscored previously, they both had as their backbone the dollar standard. In the 1950s, 95 per cent of US armament exports had been provided as foreign aid, whereas by 1980 the figure had fallen to 45 per cent and by 2000 to 25 per cent. From the early 1970s onwards, US defence production shifted toward having a high degree of privatization and internationalization, followed by an unprecedented degree of mergers, acquisitions and consolidations according to the pattern of 'new multinational corporations'. The so-called 'privatization of the defence industry' that somewhat scared pro-establishment IR scholars and policy makers in the United States in the late 1980s and early 1990s[28] should be seen in the context of a US empire-state whose centrality in the arms industry and procurement does not depend on who has legal ownership of companies, but on the *political direction and control* the empire-state can exercise through security institutions and political agencies, thus determining policy outcomes.

From the early 1970s onwards, the Middle East became the world's chief importer of weaponry, taking the lead from Southeast Asia. Tensions in the Middle East created the necessary requisite for a type of dollar recycling based on weapons sales. Since the 1940s, Nitzan and Bichler argue convincingly, the Middle East's role in world accumulation was intimately linked to oil exports, but from the 1960s onwards, this significance was further augmented by a newer flow of arms imports.[29] These two flows provided a powerful response for the United States to its profitability crisis, inasmuch as the combination of these two flows was associated with the generation of substantial profits for the US defence industry, Anglo-American oil companies and the Treasury Department. Furthermore, it should not be forgotten that the two flows were *dollarized*. Thus, for example, in 1974 Saudi Arabia's arms imports amounted to $2.6 billion, whereas between 1985 and 1992 it spent $25.4 billion. Throughout the 1970s and 1980s the United States increased its arms sales to Middle Eastern states, particularly during the Iraq–Iran war of 1980–88. In 1988, 'the Administration suggested increasing US arms exports by $3.3 billion, to a level exceeding $15 billion – with proposed shipments worth $3.6 billion to Israel, $2.7 billion to Egypt, $950 million to Saudi Arabia, and $1.3 billion to other Middle Eastern countries'.[30] Intensified conflict and rising tensions in the Gulf region, and later in Central Asia and North Africa, which included the Pakistani/Indian orbit, meant greater involvement of the United States in the region, greater militarization of the region and the United States, and greater consolidation of the alliance between US military and energy interests. The transformation of the United States and Israel into 'garrison-prison states' – a concept put forward by Harold Lasswell in 1939–44 and largely ignored by Marxism and critical theory – was in full swing.[31]

Perhaps the best example of the way in which US military and energy interests became locked into US domestic politics and grand strategy is the notorious 'state of the art' US military base of Camp Bondsteel in Kosovo.[32] It was built between July and October 1999 in the wake of Slobodan Milošević's capitulation and financed by Kellogg Brown & Root under a $33.6 million contract. It also needs some $180 million annually to operate. Kellogg Brown & Root was at the time one of the largest oil services corporations, whose managing director was Dick Cheney, later vice-president of the United States under George W. Bush. Meanwhile, the same company – as well as a number of other US-led companies – was interested in getting involved in the trans-Balkan pipeline project from the Bulgarian port of Bourgas to Durres, Albania's Adriatic port. In this context, and taking into account that US strategy in the Balkans and Central Asia was and is to control the complex network of (new and old) oil and gas pipelines so as to eliminate Russian influences, the merging between US politics and its energy interests and military undertakings is obvious.[33] In the event, this weapon-dollar/petro-dollar alliance, coupled with royalties drawn from dollar seigniorage, brought the USSR to its knees in the 1980s, when the Reagan administration could finance its 'Star Wars' project with the recycling of petro/weapon-dollars, whereas the USSR had of course no such arrows in its quiver.

We turn now to neoliberalism, the policy destined to replace the ramifications of Keynesian policy making in the domestic environment of states.

Did any of these policies reverse the long-term relative historical decline of the United States? Did the 'Volcker shock' restore the industrial dynamism of the United States and its global creditor status? Did it produce or initiate a period of monetary and financial stability? Did, in other words, US financial statecraft at both domestic and international levels rebuild US global supremacy? The answer to all those questions is plainly no.

After the collapse of the dollar's powerful role in international finance, the United States entered into a long period of economic instability, including a recession in 1971, an even deeper and longer recession from 1973 to 1975, a period of hyperinflation from 1979 to 1980, followed by a severe recession in 1981–82, a real estate bubble and stock market panic in 1987, and finally another deep recession in 1992–93. Altogether, nine of the years from 1971 to 1993 could be characterized as 'economically troubled', with the years in between reflecting uneasy transitions from one crisis to another. The only constant event that marked this period was an unsteady attempt by the United States to restore the role of the dollar and its own economic power by linking the dollar to two commodities – petroleum and weapons.

The reasons behind the functionality of this petrodollar/weapon-dollar regime were twofold. The first was *economic*, in that the Bretton Woods system never found a way to successfully recycle the huge profits and widespread speculation it generated; the second was *political,* in that the regime shifted the focus of global politics to weapons procurement and build-up, as well as to the Middle East and other areas of petroleum production and conflict.[34] Understanding how that system developed with those contradictions offers important insights into the present crisis, underpinning the thesis developed in our previous work, namely that the wars conducted by the United States after the fall of the USSR have been the wars of an economically weak power. Andre Gunder Frank identified this strategic trend in post-Cold War US foreign policy as follows: 'Washington sees its military might as a trump card that can be employed to prevail over all its rivals in the coming struggle for resources.'[35]

The efforts to recreate the dollar's dominant position in global finance began almost immediately after August 15, 1971 (the day that ended Bretton Woods), based on the emerging role that oil was already playing in the early 1970s as a strategic commodity for industrial production. This made oil a logical choice because, unlike gold, it had a central role in modern economies that could further underpin its value. This advantage was put on dramatic display during the oil embargo that followed the 1973 Arab–Israeli war, when a denial of significant amounts of oil drove the advanced economies of the Bretton Woods system into a panic. Linking the dollar to oil, however, was an example of the art of diplomacy conducted between the United States and Saudi Arabia, which was then the leader of the oil embargo and the principal source of oil for Bretton Woods countries; it was not an effort on behalf of the Bretton Woods system itself.

Since the US–Saudi agreements of 1972–74, Saudi Arabia, which was and remains the world's largest oil producer, has become one of the most reliable of US allies, enjoying a privileged status within OPEC that exempts it from allotted production quotas as the proxy representative of the United States.[36] After the mid-1970s it used its position as OPEC's 'swing producer' to 'manage' oil prices in order to increase or decrease oil production and bring about oil scarcity or glut in the world market according to US interests. The US–Saudi agreements implicitly created a global petrodollar economic system that not only put a floor under the value of the US dollar, but also allowed the United States to once again manage international trade on terms that disadvantaged its European and Japanese competitors. This, coupled with the importance of arms sales and the build up of weaponry, worked by making these commodities a de facto replacement for the pre-1971 gold–dollar standard, thereby guaranteeing a demand for dollars, whose value was ultimately linked to oil and the weapons trade and production. In this scheme, the OECD bloc had to purchase oil, either from OPEC or from one of the smaller oil producers, but they could conduct these purchases only by pricing and buying oil and weapons in dollars, thus restoring the dollar's role as a required reserve currency.[37]

It did not take long for the contradictions within the system to implode. The entire model kept demand for dollars artificially high, and as the price of oil went up following the 1973 Arab–Israeli war, the demand for dollars increased, raising the value of the dollar even further and once again subsidizing US domestic and military spending. This form of dollarization boosted further the inflationary trends in the United States, Europe and Japan, deepening the stagnation of the global economic system.

The creation of the petrodollar system also once again provided a double loan to the United States, first by allowing it to set the terms for the international oil trade, and second by subsidizing the value of the dollar and exempting it from the burden of internal US monetary and economic policies. This allowed the United States to print dollars to pay for its oil imports without giving up goods and services in exchange, as the value of those dollars was supported by the demand created for them by the petrodollar/weapon-dollar regime.[38] The yin and yang of this petrodollar/weapon-dollar economy, however, also meant that US benefits were offset by costs imposed on other capitalist economies – particularly those emerging from post-colonialism and other periphery states – as the United States exported its economic problems. Thus, when the 1973–75 recession began, the United States could shift its effects onto its capitalist partners, which then bore the greater burden as oil prices rose after 1974.

Similarly, the hyperinflation of the late 1970s and the sharp global recession of 1981–82 (which were also linked to the petrodollar economy and caused dollars to pile up once again in an international banking system) became global crises as Bretton Woods institutions struggled to recycle dollars into for-profit investments. This led depositor banks in the advanced capitalist economies to look to less developed countries for profits, because oil-exporting economies were unable to absorb the huge oil revenues that were generated in US dollars.[39]

The tragic results of the crises of the 1970s and early 1980s were, once again, exacerbated by a failure of the United States to exercise leadership within the OECD bloc. Rather than promoting sensible social investments (whether in its own economy or in those of the developing world), the United States chose in the mid-1970s to use the petrodollar/weapon-dollar overhang as an opportunity to promote the purchase of US Treasury bonds and bills, which would act as yet another subsidy for the US economy, especially its increasing current account deficit. The short-term benefits this solution provided, however, were more than offset by its long-term costs, as the United States increasingly came to rely on foreign investors as the primary source of finance for US investments.[40] This had the effect of artificially increasing prices through speculation, leading to an inflationary outburst that undermined the perceived value of the dollar, causing a decline in demand for dollars and a corresponding upward spike in US interest rates that found expression in Volcker's policy.

This in turn forced depositor banks to scramble to find new ways to invest the growing horde of petrodollars, leading to further attempts to dump excess petrodollars in developing economies (for instance, in Latin America), which merely fed the inflationary spiral there, by adding a rapid increase in the price of basic commodities to the mix. But in this case, the vast amount of liquid that flowed into the banking system was accompanied by a disregard for the underlying financial problems that it masked. The banks, which were making huge profits on loans, had little incentive to blow the whistle, and the US executive, which was using the situation to create an illusion of prosperity, had little incentive to self-critically examine a system for which it was ultimately responsible. As Volcker stepped in to radically raise interest rates to cool inflation and protect the dollar, a growing number of the economies of developing countries sank into a deep depression.

These crises might have brought down the entire Bretton Woods institutions, except for massive new spending by the United States as part of a new Cold War initiative. Generally identified as 'Star Wars', this initiative by President Ronald Reagan poured huge amounts of money into military spending, presumably in an effort to drive the Soviet Union into bankruptcy. But the reasons were not systemic, as mainstream IR, and especially its old-fashioned realist IR branch, want us to believe. The reasons lie in the domestic stagflation of the US economy: that is, the over-accumulation crisis of the core, which employed all policy means possible to fight over-accumulation and regain the global initiative. But capitalism is a beast that imperial policy, whether monetary/neoliberal or Keynesian, cannot tame. For example, the Star Wars project, never really carried out, helped to temporarily dry up the petrodollar surplus by channelling it into military development, but it also touched off another burst of speculation within the United States which centred on commercial and residential real estate. While much smaller than the present

Table 3.1 Average profit rates (%) in three sectors

	1948–69	1969–79	1979–90
Manufacturing	24.8	15.05	13.0
Non-farm non-manufacturing	11.1	10.3	9.1
Non-farm private	20.5	17.1	15.0

Source: adapted from Brenner (2003a, p. 21).

speculative bubble, the collapse of this real estate speculation was at the time the most serious financial crisis to hit the United States since the Great Depression, sparking the largest single-day decline in US stock prices and shaking confidence in the economy that continued through the 1992–93 economic recession.[41]

Volcker's neoliberal financial statecraft provided no solution to the issue of stagnation and low rates of growth, and it did not solve the problem of unemployment across the core, despite the introduction of flexible labour schemes (part-time work, fractional contracts and so on) and other devastating measures for labour. Importantly, neoliberal policies and the dismantling of the Keynesian state apparatus, personified by Margaret Thatcher and Ronald Reagan, did not restore the rate of profit, especially in manufacturing. And this happened despite a substantial fall in real wages (see Tables 3.1 and 3.2).

During the decade 1979–89, average Japanese annual real GDP growth fell by half (it was 10 per cent) and growth in the OECD-Europe to 2.3 per cent. Denmark, the Netherlands, Greece, Sweden and West Germany were the countries most hit by the long downturn. Between 1950 and 1973 the average world GDP growth

Table 3.2 Comparing average profit and unemployment rates, and average annual rates of change for real wages in private business, in selected OECD countries

| | Net profit rate | | Real wage | | Unempl't rate | |
	1950–70	1970–93	1950–73	1973–93	1950–73	1973–93
United States	2.9	9.9	2.7	0.2	4.2	6.7
Germany	23.2	13.8	5.7	1.9	2.3	5.7
Japan	21.6	17.2	6.3	2.7	1.6	2.1
G-7	17.6	13.3	–	–	3.1	6.2

Source: adapted from Brenner (2003a, p. 8).

was at 4 per cent, whereas between 1973 and 1996 it fell to 2.9 per cent. Between 1965 and 1980 the average annual growth rate in the Middle East and North Africa was 6.7 per cent, but it fell to 0.5 per cent between 1980 and 1990 (for Latin America and the Caribbean the numbers were 6 per cent and 0.5 per cent respectively). Post-1971 neoliberal financial statecraft failed spectacularly to deliver growth, welfare and prosperity.[42]

4

THE FAILURE OF FINANCIAL STATECRAFT (2), 1991–2011

> In the way that even an accumulation of debts can appear as an accumulation of capital, we see the distortion involved in the credit system reach its culmination.
>
> Karl Marx, *Capital* (1867)

TOWARDS A PERIODIZATION OF IMPERIAL ORDERS

Political economists have offered important insights in understanding capitalist crises in conjunction with the strategies employed by political agencies. Colin Hay, for instance, has launched an interesting concept, that of 'crisis displacement strategies'.[1] In a rather constructivist statement, he defines these strategies as stemming 'from a new trajectory imposed upon the state' and when 'the intense and condensed temporality of crisis emerges as a strategic moment in the structural transformation of the state'. From this perspective, 'crises are revealed as "epoch-making" moments marking the transition between phases of historical-political time'. This is an interesting approach, which draws heavily from a rather constructivist elaboration of the international, building on Anthony Giddens' notion of 'structuration'. It was on the basis of this that Alexander Wendt articulated his description in 1987.[2] This approach, in our view, obscures the agency/structure binary in social sciences and falls within old Hegelian schemata of an 'identity' between the 'subject' and the 'object', an approach not dissimilar to Georg Lukács' early work, *History and Class Consciousness* (completed in 1921–22).[3] From this perspective, we would like to insist on the utility of the concept of *financial statecraft* in interpreting the reality of US economic strategy as US policy makers themselves perceive it, and act upon it. We can now move on to deal with the issue of periodization.

Our periodization of Anglo-American political economy does not conform to a simple 'Cold War' (1945–89) and 'post-Cold War' classification. We argue that this distinction is flawed for a number of reasons, of which the most important are:

- As we have discussed in our previous work, the notion of 'Cold War' corresponded to a deliberate militarization of containment for reasons related to US domestic requirements and the economic-strategic need to polarize Western Europe against the USSR. The interpretation of the notion of containment by Dean Acheson and Paul Nitze met with opposition in the person who first proposed the containment thesis, George Kennan.[4] In other words, the so-called 'Cold War' was an artificial/ideational construction serving political and economic purposes within the Western core, rather than a 'natural' confrontation stemming from the antagonistic relationship of the two social systems.

- If the militarization of containment and the Cold War 'communism-free world' binary are rather fictitious constructions of US elites for purposes other than the *real* need for the West to securitize against a perceived Soviet threat, then a Cold War never *really* existed, or to the extent that it did, then it continues to the present day under different binary forms. For example, and as NATO's Kosovo campaign has shown, Russia continues to be considered as a threat by the United States. Arguably, and as a number of US public documents demonstrate – see, for instance, the various reports of the Pentagon's Quadrennial Defence Review over the last five years – China is also a security threat for the United States today.

- Our focus being the Anglo-American-led global capitalist system, the phases of growth and crises of capitalist modernity reviewed here do not correspond to a political periodization, however conceived, with or without 'Cold War' as a variable. Undoubtedly, this is an oversight that many authors commit when attempting to put together an all-encompassing analytical historical framework, including both international economics and politics.[5]

- The literature on the phases of economic development and the crises that ensued indicates that a different periodization is needed in order to grasp the asymmetrical, uneven and combined growth of the international political economy (IPE) over the last 150 years. We have also seen that the economic crisis of the West in the 1970s is linked to the contradictions of and the shifts within the global capitalist system, not to any antagonism or competition between the Soviet bloc and the United States. Furthermore, the literature indicates that the world economy in the 1990s, a most fascinating decade marked by a chaotic situation in Eastern and Central Europe and the brief revival of the US economy under the Clinton administration, experienced a period of economic growth, with the revival of profit rates to some extent, which appeared as a triumph of neoliberalism and financialization. In this chapter, the argument we put forward is that this is a false picture and that the crisis of over-accumulation in the 1970s is being solved via a deepening of the crisis in the West and a simultaneous power shift to the global East. This is a key part of our global fault-lines argument.

Concluding his widely popular 1988 study of global political economy, *The Rise and Fall of the Great Powers*, English born and Oxford-trained Yale historian Paul Kennedy observed that:

the task facing American statesmen over the next decades ... is to recognize that broad trends are under way, and that there is a need to 'manage' affairs so that the *relative* erosion of the United States' position takes place slowly and smoothly.[6]

Kennedy claimed that empires rise and decline as a result of their ability to stay abreast of economic and technological change and so to achieve relative prosperity and dynamism. In chronicling the decline of the United States as a global power, Kennedy compared measures of the economic robustness of the United States, such as levels of industrialization and the growth of real gross national product (GDP), with those of Europe, Russia and Japan. What appeared from his analysis was a shift in the global political economy over the last 50 years which followed from underlying structural changes in the organization of the global financial and trading systems. As this book has argued, these shifts reflect fault-lines in relationships between social formations and economies that have been growing as a consequence of deep historical trends, with China, India and Brazil now emerging as new centres of power that are replacing the concentrations of power that developed in the post-Second World War era. These shifts frame the present crisis as something more than an episodic and incidental spasm in the onward expansion of global capitalism, and we would like to argue that economic power is much more driven by long-term and dynamic factors than is generally acknowledged.[7]

Kennedy has been joined in his arguments about the structural decline of US power in the global political economy by several other authors who similarly see global political economy through a historical lens, among them Andre Gunder Frank and Emmanuel Todd.[8] However, until recently their arguments had been greeted with little enthusiasm by mainstream US and European political economy and economics theorists, because they contradict what these scholars believe to be a global political economy driven by unassailable US power.[9] But mainstream views are precisely such, because they underwrite a positivist and an ahistorical view that reinforces existing structures of power and policy making. A more critical view of the global political economy abandons the comforts offered by positivist and ahistorical explanations, and in so doing pledges itself to an encounter with the long march of historical processes and the theories it supports.

A critical historical analysis requires a definition of how it is critical and an identification of the spatial and temporal movements in historical perspective. In this case, a critical analysis of the global political economy and its present crisis begins with understanding that this subject is structurally bounded with the political acts of governments, because governments arguably influence, although they do not determine, the structural relationships within the global economy.[10] This does not imply that ideology and culture are not important – they are – but emphasizes that government, acting as the institutional instrument of political elites, facilitates the way that ideology and culture function through the structures that it authorizes. This varies from country to country according to the peculiar history and internal politics of a particular country, with internal political shifts inevitably rippling out to become shifts in the global political economy. In many cases, these internal shifts are prompted by national political elites, but occasionally, as in the present crisis, internal shifts appear quite beyond the control of national political elites, causing shifts in the global political economy that are similarly beyond the control of structures created by national governments. In the later case, these global shifts illuminate fault-lines in relationships between and among nations and societies that have long historical trails.

In particular, Frank's 1998 thesis in *Re-Orient: Global political economy in the Asian age* offers broad analytical tools that have proved their value in anticipating what is now increasingly acknowledged as a primary shift in the global political economy toward China and India as emerging international powers. One of the central purposes of this book is to test the tools of Frank's thesis and extrapolate their application to the present crisis in an effort to determine their continued relevance. This discussion attempts to identify both the visible shifts and less visible fault-lines that underlie the global political economy in crisis. This broader focus argues against a Eurocentric view of IPE, as does Frank and other scholars, which distinguishes our work from texts that follow modern liberal, realist, mainstream Marxist and constructivist approaches.[11] In other words, a periodization of imperial orders in history requires a non-Western and a truly global understanding of global economic history, its social processes and the contradictions that moved it forward in time and space. The starting point cannot be the industrial revolution in Britain, which should be seen only as a moment, albeit crucial, in the history of humanity and world civilizations.

The history of IPE from 1944 to date is the consequence of deep historical currents that reach back centuries, if not millennia. This deep history reveals that China and India have historical claims to economic and political leadership that are re-emerging, and that global financial systems have always been extensions of national politics into the economic arena. These basic historical observations act as a starting point for understanding how and why the economic structures built at Bretton Woods were designed as retrospective tools to ensure the emergence of strong central powers that could act to police the IPE. As the two most powerful war survivors, the United States and the Soviet Union stepped into their respective policing roles, but with clearly defined spheres of influence. But as subsequent events demonstrated, their dominant positions were largely temporary, as the parallel economic and political systems that they dominated were strained by continuing shifts in global economic relationships. These fault-lines produced critically important crises in the global political economy:

- the collapse of Bretton Woods system, which was undermined by European and Japanese reconstruction and the Cold War
- the global credit crisis of the early 1980s, which was induced by the creation of a US-dominated petrodollar economy in the 1970s

- the global monetary crisis of the late 1990s, which grew from an extension of neoliberalism into the global financial system after the collapse of the Soviet bloc countries
- the present global credit/financial/economic crisis, which reflects an accumulation of speculative debt generated partly to conceal and/or delay the decline of the 'old' core European–American–Japanese global political economy centres.

Typically, dominant responses to each crisis represented a menu of policy choices that were designed to address past rather than present problems in a way that would preserve the relative power of existing economic and political elites. Thus, all relied on conventional political and economic theory to explain the crisis and on existing institutions to solve it. No doubt, in each case conventional ideas gave way to political realities, and solutions were imposed that tilted towards preserving power rather than solving problems. It is also the case that each crisis followed a script of denial: the problems were not openly acknowledged until they broke out into the public sphere. Leaders preferred to put a bland face on policy choices that made them appear to maintain continuity, whether they did or not, and blame was laid on individuals, rather than on structural and/or ideological deficiencies. Only long after each crisis had passed was there any thorough and objective discussion about its nature.

We now turn to examine the IPE of the last 20 years. In particular, we consider whether the policies implemented under Clinton in the 1990s reversed the long downturn of Anglo-American capitalism and, as a consequence, the long downturn of Western capitalism as a whole. We then move on to examine briefly US financial statecraft in Eastern Europe in order to show that the 'shock therapy' neoliberal policy put forth by Harvard University economist Jeffrey Sachs did not benefit post-Soviet societies, and did not deliver growth and prosperity. All in all, we argue that the policies of financialization/globalization and neoliberalism pursued by executives from the United States and the United Kingdom did not reverse the declining trajectory of Western capitalism. If anything, they underpinned the rise of new rivals, such as China, Russia and India. At the same time, the United States proved incapable of relaunching itself as a major creditor power offering developmental perspectives to weak and depressed economies, as it did after the Second World War. Arguably, these processes are strictly interconnected.

THE EXPLOSION OF FINANCIALIZATION AND HOW IT UNDERMINED GROWTH

Capitalism, as a social and global system, rests on the search for profit and the accumulation of capital. What stimulates investment is, however, not just the absolute level of profits, but the 'rate of profit', which is the ratio of profits to investment. Most observers of capitalism consider the rate of profit as one of the most important indicators of the 'robustness' of the economic system. Classical economists, especially Adam Smith, David Ricardo and Karl Marx, believed that the rate of profit in a capitalist economic system would tend to fall over time. The rate of profit is an essential indicator that determines, as well as exposes, conditions of accumulation: in other words, the 'health' of a particular economic body. In the world economy, the rate of profit stayed more or less steady, and even rising, all through the late 1940s, the 1950s and the early 1960s. As a result, these years witnessed a steady rise in the levels of investment, and a continual boom. But from the late 1960s onwards, profit rates fell continuously, especially in manufacturing, with the global economy witnessing a real decline in the rate of global GDP growth: as we saw earlier, growth slowed, profits dropped, inflation and unemployment rose, and a fiscal crisis of the state stepped in.

We also outlined the responses: governments, under the lead of the United States and its central bank, introduced a series of measures, which later came to be known as neoliberalism. Neoliberal response(s) to the recession took the form of 'Reaganism' in the United States and 'Thatcherism' in the United Kingdom, with their policies spreading through most of the developed economies of the West. Under pressure from the leading capitalist agencies (primarily the United States) and the US Treasury – via the IMF and the World Bank – core European and Asian economies have adopted structural adjustment programmes along the same lines. As a result, global growth averaged 1.4 per cent in the 1980s and 1.1 per cent in the 1990s. But it was 3.5 per cent in the 1960s and 2.4 per cent in the 1970s.[12] Strong global growth was no more.[13]

Let us now look at profits. Net profit rates in manufacturing in the United States were 10 per cent in 1980 – the lowest point ever – and went up to 15 per cent in 1989, the best Reaganite year, then hit 19 per cent in 1997–98, the best years under Clinton, before they started to fall again.[14] What caused this partial recovery in US manufacturing? The argument put forth here by Brenner is very convincing:

What mattered most was the value of the currency. Between 1985
and 1990, and then between 1990 and 1995, the exchange rate of
the yen and mark appreciated against the dollar at the extraordinary average annual rates of 10.5% and 12.7%, respectively, and
then 9.1% and 2.5% respectively. The way was thus prepared for
an enormous gain in US manufacturing competitiveness. Between
1985 and 1995 US nominal wages expressed in dollars rose at an
average annual rate of 4.65%, while those of Japan and Germany
rose respectively at an average annual rates of 15.1% and 13.7%.
Over the same ten-year period, manufacturing unit labour costs
expressed in dollars rose at an average annual rate of 0.75% in
the US, compared to 11.7% and 11.3% in Japan and Germany
respectively. By 1995, therefore, hourly wages for manufacturing
production workers were $17.19 in the US, $23.66 in Japan,
and $31.85 in Germany. On the basis of such extraordinary
advances in relative costs, US producers could make major gains
in overseas sales.[15]

In short, the essential features in this partial recovery of the rate
of profit in the United States were currency devaluation and the
increase of the share of total profits in the total national income at
the expense of wages. This meant increased pressure for people to
work harder, especially migrant and unskilled labour, and all kinds
of attacks and cuts on welfare services. It meant a fall in the real
wages and a massive increase in working hours. Almost everywhere
in the world, the proportion of the wealth produced that went
back to workers had decreased since the 1970s.[16] However, and
despite the fact that this approach is methodologically flawed as an
aggregate factor, we should also add the role of the US consumer
debt – examined below – in stimulating the partial recovery of the
1990s.

But still, as seen in the figures above, the profit rates never
recovered more than about half their previous decline. The US
Federal Reserve and the Bank of England began to cut interest
rates and encourage lending in order to deal with periodic mini-
recessions and encourage investment. At the same time, money
became very cheap for the average consumer, who was encouraged
to borrow. An active state-led process of 'deregulation' began. This
included, among other aspects, the elimination of robust oversight
on financial institutions, investment banks, hedge funds and all sorts
of operators and new financial instruments. Such measures were
able to encourage spending to some extent and thus to extend the

boom, but we can now firmly conclude that these practices simply delayed the bursting of the bubble for a few years, inasmuch as the growth registered was fictitious and debt-led. This was a clever way on the part of the Anglo-American elites to pass the debt from the state to society, yet this proved to be a temporary measure offering only a short breathing space for the already declining US hegemonic system.

The Carter administration initiated industrial deregulation in airlines, trucking and state-owned enterprises, the landmark being the bailout of Chrysler in 1980. This set the tone for what was to follow. Tax reform acts reduced taxes on individuals, placing a disproportionate burden on the weak and the deprived, as the social security tax – the equivalent of national insurance contributions in the United Kingdom – increased by 25 per cent. As far as the transformation of industrialists into financial operators and rentiers was concerned, this took on an entirely exceptional form: huge amounts of liquid were financialized into shares, bonds and other instruments, including participation in the interest-bearing schemes of non-manufacturing firms, the aim being easy profiteering in any business environment conducive to it. 'Manufacturing corporations' interest payment as a proportion of profits', Brenner observed, 'having grown to 15% during the years 1973–79 compared to just 3.8% for the years 1950–73, increased to 35% between 1982 and 1990 and 24% between 1990 and 1996.'[17] Mergers and acquisitions continued apace (during the Reagan years in the 1980s, their total value was circa $1.40 trillion, the result of some 31,200 mergers and acquisitions). With active government encouragement, and during the period 1975–90, 'the proportion of the total investment on plant and equipment in the private business economy annually devoted to finance, insurance and real estate (FIRE), doubled from about 12–13% to about 25–23%.'[18]

All this resulted in a substantial increase in the share of financial services in the GDP of the United States, which surpassed that of industry in the mid-1990s. From 1973 to 2008 the portion of manufacturing in GDP fell from 25 per cent to 12 per cent. The share represented by financial services rose from 12 per cent to 21 per cent. In parallel to this, borrowing at all levels was encouraged by new financial structures, which were reshaped and relaxed to allow high levels of risky borrowing.[19] That is how General Motors was displaced by Walmart and Goldman Sachs as the United States' 'business template'.[20] Meanwhile, defence spending continued. US military share as a percentage of the world total in 1996 increased by 20 per cent over the peak Reaganite year, 1985. Whereas in 1985 the United States was spending only 65 per cent as much on defence as did the Soviet bloc, China and Cuba, just few months before 9/11 it was spending more than twice as much as did all these former Communist threats. Clearly, this spending was partly financed by the US debt Saudi, Japanese, and later Chinese and other Asian producers were buying.[21] It is important to pay attention to the debt dimension of the US economy in the 1990s and after, because it is directly linked to deindustrialization, the position of the dollar, and eventually to financialization and neoliberal policy making.

The over-accumulation crisis of the 1970s led the United States and other core economies to escape to financialization and neoliberalism. But this hindered the growth of the real economy while increasing the growth of debt relative to GDP. The outstanding consumer debt as a percentage of disposable income in the United States rose from $1,450 billion in 1981 to $6,960.6 billion in 2000 and $11,496.6 billion in 2005.[22] In the end, total debt in the US economy – that is, debt owed by households, investment and commercial banks, non-financial business as well as government – amounted to 'three and a half times the nation's GDP', and was not far from the $44 trillion GDP for the entire world'.[23] This has also contributed to growth, as measured by national accounting practices with which we methodologically disagree, as they give a false and rather misleading image of economic development, welfare and modernization. Thus, the truth of the matter remains as noted by Robert Brenner: whereas financial profits rose from 15 per cent in 1960 to 40 per cent in 2005, profits in manufacturing fell from about 50 per cent in 1960 down to 13 per cent in 2003. But we need to go a step further: to point to the outsourcing to the global East, especially of manufacturing and labour-power, processes that should be seen as a result of the failure of financialization and neoliberalism to put the political economies of the United States and the United Kingdom back on a developmental track.

Before we look at the present crisis as such in the United States and the United Kingdom, let us consider how the United States attempted to take advantage of the collapse of state-socialist economies of the Soviet arc, thus temporarily displacing the problems of post-1971 IPE to the dilapidated economies of former Council for Mutual Economic Assistance (COMECON) states. The operation was spearheaded by the IMF and the Word Bank, two key vehicles through which the US Treasury internationalized its operations worldwide.

THE INTERNATIONALIZATION OF THE US TREASURY

General comments

The deregulation and internationalization of Bretton Woods institutions in the 1990s occurred in the context of the collapse of the USSR and the embedded power of neoliberalism – achieved in the 1980s – as the driving policy form of a new political-economy dynamics in the United States and the United Kingdom. With no socialist system available and with Europe unable to provide any feasible alternative (see below), the former members of COMECON and other states emerging from the Soviet collapse had no choice but to join the Bretton Woods institutions and accept Jeffrey Sachs' shock-therapy policy recipe. The effect of this was to expand the powers of the US Treasury. As an ideology, neoliberalism was making headway with the writings of such intellectuals as Friedrich Hayek and Milton Friedman.[24] Neoliberal ideologues were able to articulate a hegemonic discourse presenting the failure of state socialism in the East and the breakdown of Keynesianism in the West as identical projects and the source of all evils. The key claim was that capitalism as a social system was failing to thrive under state-led policies and socioeconomic practices. These arguments particularly targeted the Bretton Woods assumptions about liberal institutionalism and government regulation, favouring instead a free-market system left to the management of private enterprise. Neoliberalism, however, also came with a political price in undermining the basic liberal concept of a social contract between citizens and their government for the provision of essential social services, and concentrating economic power in the hands of private capital: more accurately, of financial capital.

While the collapse of socialist systems in the early 1990s opened the door to an extension of Bretton Woods institutions and their reconstruction around neoliberalism, it also removed an important safety valve that had acted to protect Bretton Woods during its many crises: the state-socialist economies of COMECON had offered a relatively stable, long-term market for the excess production of Bretton Woods member-states from 1949 to 1991, thereby partially buffering them against capitalist crises of over-accumulation. At the same time, this socialist alternative market provided a counterweight to the Cold War practices of the United States and its Bretton Woods allies, which restricted the free exchange of ideas and justified militarism and intervention in the post-colonial world. Once this safety net and counterweight were gone, the comfortable balance of a bipolar world disappeared with it. Its absence after 1991 increasingly exposed the Bretton Woods regime to capitalism's own contradictions, such as its tendencies toward speculation and over-accumulation, its reliance on the US Treasury, and its disregard for the connection between unpopular neoliberal economic policies and their political consequences. This is one good example showing how global fault-lines operate in the international system.

With the Bretton Woods system evolving into a fully integrated global financial system by the late 1990s, the role of the US Treasury in neoliberal reconstruction became more visible. In fact, the US Treasury became a direct organiser of political hegemony within OECD countries via the control of Bretton Woods institutions, some of which had been transformed, such as the GATT into the World Trade Organization (WTO) (1994). The institutional power that the United States enjoyed in governing the IMF and World Bank before 1991 was thereafter joined by an even greater power of persuasion that drew public as well as private institutions to neoliberalism and financialization around the world.[25]

Thus, when the United States dismantled its own Depression-era restraint on speculative investments by banks – the Glass–Steagall Act – and replaced it with the Gramm–Leach–Bliley Act, labelled the Financial Services Modernization Act of 1999, it effectively institutionalized and formalized *casino capitalism* on a world scale.[26] Once introduced, casino capitalism rippled through the global economy, promoting massive concentrations and exchanges of capital among global speculators, the transfer of speculative funds to international banks and other financial institutions, and the development of an array of new speculative investment tools to generate quick and easy profits. This whole process of extreme financialization has completely lost sight of the fact that without real production there is no value. Production has become increasingly incidental to the much more lucrative business of 'balance-sheet restructuring'.

It should come as no surprise that the neoliberal transformation of the global economy ended badly. Warning signs of its destructive capacity had been in evidence during the US Savings & Loan fiasco of 1987. Then, with the added power of the internet and its global communications revolution, the neoliberal promotion of unregulated currency trading ricocheted like a bullet inside the global banking system, first creating the Asian financial crisis, which led the US government to make a frantic multibillion dollar midnight rescue of Long-Term Capital Management, and later generating a stock market bubble and the 'dot.com' bubble, which when it collapsed in late 1999 added further evidence of the dangers that came from unregulated speculation.

What is remarkable is not the many failures of neoliberalism over the past 15 years, including the pyramided investments on speculative debt which came to balloon overall global paper capital from a relatively modest sum of $70 trillion in the late 1990s to more than $700 trillion by 2007, but the inability of capitalist governments to extract themselves from its grip. Thus, rather than acting to restrain capitalist excess, these governments stood aside to encourage the even greater speculation that eventually produced the collapse of 2007–08.[27]

But like its history, the dynamics of the present crisis lie below the surface of events. Certainly, subprime lending was a precipitating factor, but it also represents a series of policy choices that were driven by changing circumstances in the global political economy. Some of these were within the control of capitalist governments, such as the dismantling of Depression-era regulations of financial markets. But others, including the rapid evolution of global systems of trade and communications and the regeneration of China and India as major global economic centres, were historically beyond Anglo-American policy control. Clearly separating the 'inside' from the 'outside' is critical to understanding why and how this crisis unfolded, and where it might take the global political economy. Time and again, this crisis is the result of contradictions of essentially new forms of combined and uneven capitalist development, including resource depletion and environmental degradation, all of which, in their merger with social struggle, reactivate the causal configuration of the global fault-lines. Financialization, resource depletion and environmental degradation first became acute in the 1970s, and today operate as severe constraints not only upon US power, but also upon any power or coalition/ensemble of powers that will succeed the US imperium. These three vulnerabilities of the US-led global hegemonic system are also vulnerabilities of China and all E-7 powers.[28]

All in all, the two elements that we feel are most important in understanding the present crisis are its ideational origins in neoliberalism (which has produced some distinctive tools for crisis management, such as new modes of financial statecraft, as we saw earlier) and the rapid evolution of extra-governmental dynamics in the US-led global system (which has substantially undermined the ability of Anglo-American executives to contain the very effects of the policies they unleashed). It is therefore apparent that

Anglo-American liberal state executives act dictatorially, imposing neoliberal recipes around the world. For that very reason, governments, including the US executive, may fit today, more than ever, with the 'vulgar' orthodox Marxist definition of the state: 'the capitalist state is an instrument of the bourgeoisie manipulated at will', although we should qualify the term bourgeoisie with the adjective 'financial'. As neoliberalism and financialization come under scrutiny, their management tools should also be examined to ensure that they do not survive its demise, and as the global system continues to evolve new relationships and dynamics, these must be taken into account when considering how the global political economy can and might also move beyond the 'growth at all costs' economic model to a model that recognizes the real costs and benefits of growth.

Shock therapy for the East

Recent literature on subprime lending generally argues that its widespread adoption was possible because of the repeal of the Glass–Steagall Act. This Act had been adopted in 1933 in an effort to restrain the unregulated speculation that contributed to the length and severity of the Great Depression.[29] The argument goes that its repeal in 1999 added instability to the financial system by allowing investment banks to access a wide range of previously denied speculative investments and operate high-risk instruments. Yet the repeal of Glass–Steagall itself reflected the institutionalization of neoliberalism at the heart of the US financial system as a means of finding new ways to 'modernize' the financial services industry to profitably recycle huge amounts of paper and liquid that had become concentrated in the banks.[30] Seeing the repeal of Glass–Steagall as a response to contradictions stemming from within liberal Keynesianism – what Robert Brenner called 'asset-price Keynesianism' – raises more substantive issues about how capitalist reforms are generated out of crises as efforts to secure the interests of financial capital, rather than to serve broader class interests in capitalism as a whole.

If we use this wider, structural lens, it is apparent how both the repeal of Glass–Steagall and the subsequent expansion of subprime lending were arguably forms of financial statecraft adopted by capitalist governments to avoid the consequences of earlier policy accommodations, all of which contained the seeds of an eventual systemic crisis. As we explained in Chapter 3, financial statecraft is not new. For example, when the United States 'closed the gold window' and devalued the dollar in 1968–71, it did so in order to deal with the accumulation of US international debt during the Vietnam war, which exposed tensions with other capitalist governments that would no longer subsidize US economic and political profligacy. In its place, as we saw, the United States pursued a 'petro-dollar/weapon-dollar' policy that continued to promote the interests of the US Treasury and the dollar as the key international payments currency. But as with the present crisis and its links to neoliberal reforms, the petrodollar/weapon-dollar system quickly became the source of a new and more severe international economic crisis, as huge amounts of new capital flooded into the capitalist banking system, and demanded opportunities for profitable investment. Thus, both forms of financial statecraft achieved short-term reprieves that only introduced new contradictions and tensions within the global political economy in general, and the US and UK economies in particular, which demanded new financial interventions inasmuch as the logic of the system in itself could provide no other alternative.[31] Time and again, this is essentially a function of global fault-lines.

One of the most interesting cases of financial statecraft was the so-called shock therapy policy approach, developed by Harvard University professor Jeffrey Sachs. We will confine ourselves here to a brief presentation of the issue, because it has already been dealt with adequately in the relevant critical scholarship. However, this short presentation is important: in the context of our overall revisionist global fault-lines argument, it shows how shock therapy failed to deliver what it promised: in other words, modernization, prosperity and growth for East-Central Europe and the Balkans.

A good starting point is the involvement of Bretton Woods agencies in the creation of Yugoslavia's debt since the 1970s. This is a devastating affair because, intentionally or not, and as Susan Woodward's groundbreaking work has shown, this involvement initiated the bloody break-up of the country. It is only Western mythology that attributes it to the ethnic nationalism and mutual hatred of the peoples of Yugoslavia.

Mainstream explanations of the violent break-up of Yugoslavia argue that the main culprit was the highly politicized ethnic hatred between the peoples and the elites of the constituent states of Yugoslavia, which blew out of all proportion after the country's charismatic leader, Marshall Tito, died in 1980. More sophisticated accounts add as a cause to the collapse of the country the very impact of the disintegration of the Soviet empire. Being a non-aligned country, Yugoslavia needed the support of both the West and the USSR to maintain a balance between its borrowing requirements and defence needs. With the USSR gone, Yugoslavia could no longer keep its state cohesion. But these are not the real causes that led to the violent disintegration of Yugoslavia. If they count at all, these variables should be seen in conjunction with the interference of concrete exogenous agencies and even state actors, such as Germany and the Vatican, and above all the IMF and the World Bank.

Yugoslavia's socialist economic experiment, which followed Edvard Kardelj's theories of 'self-management', coupled with its 'non-aligned' stance in foreign affairs, proved workable during the 'Golden Age'. Yugoslavia could borrow money from both the Soviet Union and Bretton Woods institutions, it could buy from and sell to both capitalist and socialist countries, and overall, it was able to maintain a stable current account. In addition, this stable international environment contained Yugoslavia's regional economic disequilibria, such as the disparity between the rich Northern federal states of Slovenia and Croatia, and the poor South (Macedonia and parts of Serbia).[32] However, when the Western economies entered into a long period of recession and stagflation in the 1970s, the result was the blocking of Yugoslav exports. This initiated a vicious cycle of borrowing and debt creation from abroad, especially from the IMF (which might be equated with the US Treasury).

When the IMF began imposing conditionality on its handouts in the early 1980s, it met with fierce opposition from Slovenia and Croatia. IMF conditionality implied an end to Yugoslavia's nearly co-federal state structure, and entailed that the richest of the republics would have to foot the bill for the neoliberal-led reforms: privatizations of state assets, liberalization of the banking and financial system, retrenchment of welfare apparatuses and severe reduction in wages, and all that in order presumably to tame inflation. It was precisely this policy that deepened the ethnic divisions and pushed the political elites of each republic to adopt a nationalist agenda in order to appeal to their electoral base – which, after all, would have had to pay for the federal debt. The Yugoslav state was a classic case of a structured inequality among regions, in which ethnic tensions were exacerbated by a neoliberal package of economic reforms imposed from outside. Susan Woodward aptly summarized the break-up of the country as follows:

> The [Yugoslav] conflict is not the result of historical animosities and it is not a return to the pre-communist past; it is the result of the politics of transforming a socialist society to a market

economy and democracy. A critical element of this failure was economic decline, caused largely by a programme intended to resolve a foreign debt crisis …. Normal political conflicts over economic resources between central and regional governments and over the economic and political reforms of the debt-repayment package became constitutional conflicts and then a crisis of the state itself among politicians who were unwilling to compromise …. Nationalism became a political force when leaders in the republics sought popular support as bargaining chips in federal disputes.[33]

The Vatican and Germany, having their own agendas in the Balkans, supported the secession efforts of Slovenia and Croatia.[34] Especially worth noting is the deal crafted between the German and UK elites in the run up to the Maastricht Treaty (December 1991), when the United Kingdom convinced Germany to agree to its opt-out from the EU Social Charter and the Common Foreign and Security Policy (CFSP) in return for letting Germany to go ahead with the recognition of Croatia. This initiated the bloodshed. The European Commission's publicly declared common position at the time was to keep Yugoslavia together. That is how the road to ethnic war opened.

In the old good tradition of the open door, whether intentionally or not, US-led neoliberal financial statecraft in Yugoslavia, coupled with Germany's and other European powers' agendas, brought about war and the disintegration of the country. It also did very little to deliver growth and prosperity in the war-torn successor states. In fact, quite the opposite: the process of liberalization and the rapid introduction of a free market created a new type of crony capitalism and corrupt practices, obstructing any meaningful endogenous entrepreneurial undertaking that could have led to job creation and new economies of scale.[35] Interestingly, this practice was 'theorized' by economist Jeffrey Sachs in his so-called shock therapy model of 1990. The context in which shock therapy was put forth is quite revealing.

The 1980s revived Europe's effort to dissociate itself from the dollar's strategic grip. Delors' agenda encompassed an increasingly integrated European market and the launching of a common currency, a project that, as we saw earlier, failed to materialize in the late 1960s. A reunified Germany was driving European monetary policy, and East European markets were very important for German industry and exports. A new *Ostpolitik* was revived under Germany's chancellor, Helmut Kohl. The project comprised two interrelated policy dimensions.[36] The first was a reform package for the economic reconstruction of Eastern Europe and the Balkans which, similarly to the post-Second World War Marshall Plan, was to be administered by endogenous forces on the basis of a post-Keynesian type of economic recovery, stabilization and growth. The COMECON region would remain united and Cold War barriers to East–West trade would be removed. The second was the gradual integration of the former communist countries into the European Union, and the institutionalization of a powerful geostrategic axis aiming at a common foreign and defence policy. But Clinton had a different idea. In the political field, he argued, 'Europe may have a separable, but not separate' defence identity from NATO.[37] In the economic field, he embraced Sachs' version of the open door.

The declared wish of shock therapy was the economic reorganization of the state–market nexus in the East in order to achieve 'a recovery of human freedom and a democratically based rise in living standards'.[38] But as we shall see, none of this was delivered. Sachs rejected any form of Keynesianism and a gradual transition to free market, opting instead for a rapid sell-off of state assets and the immediate integration of East-Central Europe into the West European market. Open trade, currency convertibility, reliance on the private sector, membership of Bretton Woods institutions and openness to foreign investment were Sachs' developmental articles of faith that each former Communist country should subscribe to. As Peter Gowan convincingly showed as early as 1994–95,[39] shock therapy practice for Eastern-Central Europe failed miserably to deliver on all of its promises.

Because East European markets were individually too small to provide the economies of scale that would have made their companies internationally competitive, free trade badly hit all East-Central European companies, even in those sectors where the countries of the region were strong: steel, detergents, pulp, iron, chemicals, agriculture and apparel. Overall, imports from the West increased, and this created a permanent current account imbalance and dependency on the IMF and other Bretton Woods institutions. All this quickly implanted severe fiscal crises into virtually all former communist countries. Given the anti-inflationary bias of the West, public spending was excluded as a policy to address the deficits. The door for IMF borrowing had been opened. Throughout the 1990s living standards deteriorated sharply across East-Central Europe, growth turned negative and unemployment skyrocketed (see Tables 4.1 and 4.2).

Table 4.1 Unemployment rates in six post-Communist states, 1995–98

Country	1995	1996	1997	1998
Czech Republic	2.9	3.5	5.0	6.0
Hungary	10.4	10.5	10.0	9.0
Bulgaria	11.0	12.5	16.5	19.0
Poland	14.9	13.6	11.9	11.5
Romania	8.9	6.1	9.2	9.0
Russia	8.8	9.3	9.7	11.8

Source: Rukavishnikov (1999).

The shock therapy version of the open door did not deliver on its promises. If anything, it plunged the political economies of the former Soviet and Ottoman countries into abject misery, underdevelopment and debt. Privatizations meant, first and foremost, the unfolding of the Stalinist secret apparatuses, which had developed expertise in cash, arms and drugs smuggling under authoritarian socialism. Thus, as Misha Glenny's elegant narrative shows, crime networks in the former Soviet space flourished and became transnational.[40] For example, when communism fell, there were suddenly thousands of unemployed cops and spooks in Bulgaria with first-hand experience of international crime. And, Glenny's account goes, there were also many wrestlers and weightlifters, pumped-up on state-issued steroids, who would make for ideal muscle in the protection rackets that quickly sprung up. Drugs, prostitution, money laundering and other underground activities began operating on a large scale. The Bulgarians were soon in competition with others: Moldovans, Albanians, Kazakhs, Georgians, Yugoslavs and Russians, all seeking turf in the new gangsterland of Eastern Europe. That is the real achievement of shock therapy. Only when those political economies began pursuing an internally stimulated growth strategy from the late 1990s and early 2000s onwards did the economic and social conditions of their societies and states begin to change. None of this should have come as a surprise to a careful and unbiased student of international politics: 'the IMF "stabilisation" regimes for East-Central Europe have been the familiar ones of the 1980s Latin American experience', Gowan wrote.[41]

The US Treasury, via the Bretton Woods institutions and the appropriation of debt mechanism, attempts to deplete and liquidate the resources of weak societies and states in order to transfer much-needed cash to fund its own borrowing requirements and international debts. But this is not a strategy for growth; nor is it

Table 4.2 Average annual GDP growth in East-Central Europe, the Caucasus and Central Asia, 1989-98

Country	Growth %
Albania	0.29
Armenia	-4.93
Azerbaijan	-7.68
Belarus	-1.49
Bulgaria	-3.95
Croatia	-2.16
Czech Republic	-0.22
Estonia	-2.94
Macedonia	-5.11
Georgia	-9.26
Hungary	-0.31
Kazakhstan	-4.67
Kyrgyzstan	-3.91
Latvia	-3.72
Lithuania	-3.8
Moldova	-9.12
Poland	1.8
Romania	-3.04
Russia	-6.26
Slovakia	0.34
Slovenia	0.24
Tajikistan	-8.17
Turkmenistan	-8.17
Ukraine	-8.9
Uzbekistan	-7.7
Mean	-3.8

Source: Frye (2002).

a strategy pursued by a creditor power, as was the case after the Second World War. This is a strategy pursued by a power in continuous relative economic decline since the epoch of Vietnam War, and emphatically so since 1968–71.

THE IMPLOSION OF FINANCIALIZATION AND THE CASE OF THE UNITED KINGDOM

After the bust of the 'dot.com' bubble and the recession of 2001–02, the US government cut taxes again, and the Federal Reserve slashed interest rates even further. All this encouraged even greater levels of more risky borrowing than before, which drove the housing bubble. Mortgage companies lowered their lending standards and introduced new products, such as adjustable mortgages, interest-only mortgages and promotional teaser rates. All this encouraged speculation in residential housing and a new 'buy to let' industry began flourishing. Demand for assets such as homes increased, without a corresponding increase in new real value being produced in the system. Walden Bello observes:

> The subprime mortgage crisis was not a case of supply outrunning real demand. The 'demand' was largely fabricated by speculative mania on the part of developers and financiers that wanted to make great profits from their access to foreign money – most of it Asian and Chinese in origin – that flooded the US in the last decade.[42]

The demand was largely fabricated by speculative mania on the part of the building developers and financial institutions and operators, including estate agents (some of which were transformed into building societies and banks). This caused the prices of these assets to rise even further. On paper, people's and businesses' wealth increased, so it seemed they now had the means to borrow more, and they became 'irrationally exuberant'. All of this led to a further increase in demand, and so on.[43] Many people were provided with mortgages – by relaxing income documentation requirements, such as the self-certified mortgages in the United Kingdom – to buy overpriced properties that they could not, in reality, afford. John Bellamy Foster argued:

> The housing bubble associated with rising house prices and the attendant increases in home refinancing and spending, which has been developing for decades, was a major factor in allowing the economy to recover from the 2000 stock market meltdown and the recession in the following year.[44]

Under the euphemistic heading of 'financial innovation', a number of changes in institutional arrangements enabled banks and mortgage lenders to escape regulatory restrictions and expand their activities even further.[45]

It seemed, at the time, that the economy was being dragged out of recession, yet we can claim in retrospect that the same measures (that is, the role finance played in resolving the recessions of the last decade with a 'cheap money, easy credit' strategy) laid the ground for the much more serious problems the system faces today. Greater levels of risky borrowing led to speculative bubbles and temporary prosperity, and these ultimately ended with corporate collapse and in recession in the real economy.[46]

The rise of profit in the spheres of financial and banking capital, being mostly collateral paper asset and leveraging, was not enough to raise investment to its previous levels. At the same time, neoliberal policies were lowering real wages, undercutting the capacity of workers to buy consumer goods, especially houses.[47] Because the drain on wages was not used to invest more, extra profits could only be accumulated in the financial sector. As a result, a large amount of increased business profits was invested in various financial schemes. The value of financial wealth has grown considerably, and the relations between productive capital and financial capital were profoundly modified, subordinating all other economic activities to the financial sector. The road to wealth accumulation was no longer manufacturing industry or the provision of financial services associated with manufacturing, but the buying and selling of paper assets.

Certain old forms of wealth creation via financialization were revived. These, for example, took the form of creating insurance schemes on future claims, and the use of risky instruments such as credit default swaps (CDS), which are basically forms of insurance to protect lenders in the event of loan default. This, in turn, created a diversified shadow market of leveraging using borrowed funds for making profits. Shadow banks are financial intermediaries that conduct financial operations without access to central bank liquidity or public sector credit guarantees. As such, they are also entirely unregulated by any public authority. Hedge funds and investments banks, such as Fannie Mae (founded in 1938) and Freddie Mac (founded in 1970) took the lead as shadow banking global operators, their bases being Wall Street and the City of London.[48] They operated with structured investment vehicles (SIVs), mutual funds, limited-purpose finance companies and so on. In this context, certain old forms of securitization revived, such as mortgage-backed securities. The idea behind these is simple: pooling debts, such as home mortgages, car loans, credit card borrowing and so on, and packaging them into 'tranches', is argued to reduce the overall risk. A side-effect is that lenders and borrowers become dissociated from each other. Then credit rating agencies, such as Standard & Poor's,

Moody's and Fitch, rate the credit-worthiness of these packages (as A, B, C or junk). The logic of financial speculation dictated that the higher a 'packaged product' was rated, the more money would end up in the pockets of speculators and bond-dealers. This kept the whole financial architecture operational and alive. The credit agencies tended to exaggerate the quality of the packages, and once a package was sold, the risk was spread across the world. That was the latest 'new political economy' of globalization/financialization. It collapsed when the poor from New Orleans started the process of pulling the rug from under the system, defaulting on the monthly payments on their subprime mortgages.

We want to emphasize that these instruments and practices did not come out of the blue. They were in full operation in the 1920s, but were eased out after the 1929 crash, and under the fixed exchange rate rules of Bretton Woods, only to come to the fore again after 1971. The first currency futures market was opened in 1972 in Chicago, the home of Milton Friedman and his 'Chicago boys'.[49] Until the recent crisis, there was a constant search for even further investment opportunities for this sort of financial wealth acquisition. Let us repeat here again that this process, widely referred to as *financialization*, is related to the increasing role of financial motives, financial markets, financial actors and financial institutions in the operations of domestic and international economies. The truth of the matter is, however, that the whole system remained extremely vulnerable.

The computerization of finance in the 1990s and the ability to employ complex mathematical formulas dramatically improved the system's ability to innovate, and a number of long-standing barriers to the reach and range of permissible activities were gradually undermined by various changes in the US financial services industry. Legislation assisted too. As we saw earlier, the Financial Services Modernization Act of 1999, known as the Gramm–Leach–Bliley Act, repealed the banking activity restrictions of the Depression-era Glass–Steagall Act, which had separated commercial and investment banking in order to control speculation and protect bank deposits. As a result the financial system became increasingly volatile and unpredictable. By the end of the century, the level of personal borrowing in the United States rose to the record level of 9 per cent of GDP. Especially mortgage refinancings – what in the United Kingdom is referred to as remortgaging – and home-equity loans (on the bubble-inflated values of their houses) allowed US households to cash in on the capital gains from rising housing prices without having to sell off their homes. As if financialization was producing its own exclusive over-accumulation crisis, it tried to find exit strategies inasmuch as there was no other way all the goods and services produced within the system could be sold.[50]

Levels of debt, subprime lending and banks

The gap between stagnant or even declining wages and fast-increasing consumer expenditure was closed by the accumulation of consumer debt. Consumer debt, coupled with all sorts of cheap commodities manufactured in China and other Asian states pouring into the US market, allowed many working families to maintain their standard of living to some extent. In 2007 US households spent more of their disposable income to pay off debts (14 per cent) than to buy food (13 per cent). Household indebtedness in the United States rose from 50 per cent of GDP in 1980 to 71 per cent in 2000 and 100 per cent in 2007. This was devastating. The financial sector's indebtedness was 21 per cent of GDP in 1980, 83 per cent in 2000 and 116 per cent by 2007.[51] Thus, when interest rates began to rise in 2006–07, the result was catastrophic: the poor and the deprived could not pay their monthly dues to their mortgage lenders and home insurers, and had to default. This reverberated across the global debt and securitization chain, contaminating all papers and futures, as well as all their collateral buyers, insurers, private bondholders, pension funds, investment and commercial banks: the list is endless. This is a very peculiar form of 'class struggle': it shows the deep contradictions of the global capitalist system and its negative dynamics, as well as the way in which the poor can take revenge over the rentiers who created their debt.

In the United Kingdom borrowing levels were proportionately even greater. Until the current crisis, the house boom was even crazier, with average house prices quadrupling in twelve years. The reason why the United Kingdom is in so much trouble is that both its corporate debts and its household debts are huge. It is this combination that makes the UK economy such a credit liability. Michael Saunders from CitiGroup has calculated UK 'external debt' – what the country owes the rest of the world – to be as high as 400 per cent of GDP, the highest in the G7 by some margin. The next down, France, is 176 per cent. The US external debt is just 100 per cent. Japan has half the United States' debt level.[52]

Between mid-2000 and 2004, US households took on $3 trillion in mortgages.[53] Where did this money come from? During the same period, the US government, as well as the private sector, borrowed

$3 trillion from the rest of the world. Between a third and a half of mortgages were financed with foreign money. The total US debt (that is, the combined debt of individual households, private business and government) had doubled as a proportion of GDP since 1980, and was 350 per cent of GDP even before the recent dramatic takeovers of new debt by the government. This is one result of 'financialization': an enormous increase in debt of all kinds.[54] Another result, equally serious, is the inability of the project to contribute to any real growth for the United States, as Figure 4.1 indicates. (Please note our due reservations over the methodology used to calculate GDP growth.)

Subprime lending offers important lessons that show why this present crisis is a fundamental, systemic crisis of the capitalist process, and not just a garden-variety recession caused by the 'bad' behaviour of a handful of greedy speculators. What capitalism as an economic system does most efficiently, especially when left to itself, is to create and increase social and political inequalities. And what it does most inefficiently is account for social needs and systemic change. The money merry-go-round that accompanied subprime lending before the present crisis offers insights into how the contradictory tensions within modern capitalism ensured that it would come to crisis.

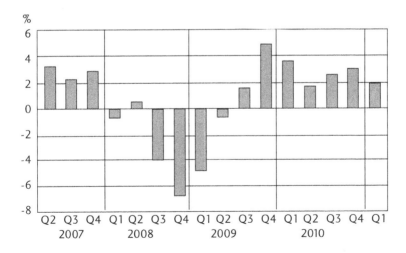

Figure 4.1 Quarter-to-quarter growth in real GDP

Note: Real GDP is measured at seasonally adjusted annual rates.
Source: adapted from US Bureau of Economic Analysis.

Subprime lending has commonly been attributed to the dismantling of the Depression-era government regulation of the banking industry, which opened the door for investment banks to enter and eventually dominate real estate markets. Yet, the repeal of Glass–Steagall was itself prompted by a two-decades-long movement toward deregulation designed to increase opportunities for profit by financial capitalists. It was proposed by neoliberal economists.[55] This clearly indicates that the origins of the crisis lay not in the speculation that acted as its trigger, but in the way the financial system was designed to encourage that speculation. The 'money merry-go-round' – an expression dear to Mandel and Susan Strange[56] – that became visible after the collapse of the speculative frenzy must be seen as fundamental and systemic, rather than as merely the bad behaviour of those within it.

If the origins of subprime lending were in the 1980s,[57] then the mechanisms that charged up the money merry-go-round in the 2000s can also be traced to that same period, and linked to the problem of recycling the vast amounts of capital produced as profits in the system. The primary difference between the 1980s and the 2000s was the source of this profit. In the first case it was primarily the petrodollars that gathered in US banks, and in the second case it was the vast profits from the speculative frenzy that followed the collapse of the Soviet Union. The second case was far more global in origin and effect, and was greatly enhanced by the transformation of the global economy through emerging communications technologies.

What is remarkable is how closely these two crises – separated by almost two decades – match up in the way that they formed, threatened the system, and then planted the seeds of further crises. For example, in both cases borrowers who could not have qualified for a home purchase under standard mortgage processes were qualified under 'special' provisions for the purpose of enhancing lender profits, which in the case of subprime loans went mostly to investors.[58] Additionally, in both cases the borrower rather than the lender was saddled with the risks of default, with capitalist banks on both occasions enjoying government support and protection from any failure.

The greatest differences between the two crises were in the scale of the lending and the potential for disaster. For example, the amount of global capital devoted during the latest period to subprime lending was staggering, amounting at one point to $12 trillion in the United States alone,[59] whereas the excess petrodollars that required recycling during the earlier crisis amounted only to $111 billion in the peak year of 1980.[60] With the Cold War in full bloom during the first crisis, US power remained largely what it had been during the post-war period, which made it much easier for the United States to coerce cooperation from other Bretton Woods members, while the current crisis has been exacerbated by a measurable decline in US power, which has limited its ability to act unilaterally in setting the global policy agenda.[61] Finally, the 1980s crisis occurred at a time when governments generally had a much larger measure of control over their national economies and the United States had a stronger hand in managing global economic institutions. The present crisis has clearly demonstrated the limits of economic control enjoyed by governments generally.

The details of the money merry-go-round and its aftermath are also a guide to how banks have been failing during the crisis. Unlike the central banks of other countries, the US Federal Reserve is entirely controlled by the private sector, with representatives from business, banking and finance acting as its governors. This arrangement meant that this crisis was managed by capitalists who were largely beyond the control of the putative 'democratic' US Congress, and they left the worst effects of the crisis to be borne by the middle and working classes.[62] The crisis has not affected all banks equally, and individual bank failures mark points in the fault-lines within US capitalism. In the broad sense, these fault-lines represent conflicts of interest in national capital, with the neoliberal reconstruction that began in the 1970s favouring financial capital over industrial capital. The multi-layered pyramid of economic power that has followed in its wake is driving the United States further toward a dependence on international banking and finance to secure its own economy and its global economic influence. However, this pyramid also continues to widen the conflicts in US capitalism, undermining its long-term viability as leader of the Bretton Woods system.

It also should be understood that only small and middle-sized banks were actually allowed to fail, and in those cases their assets were absorbed by larger banks at fire sale prices. During the third quarter of 2009 alone, more than 140 banks failed, were closed or merged, and all but a handful of these were small and/or regional banks whose primary customers were local businesses, homeowners, and other members of the middle and working classes.[63] Among investment banks, only Bear Stearns, which was forcibly merged by the Federal Reserve into the Bank of America in March 2008, and

Lehman Brothers suffered a similar fate. The disparate treatment of big and small banks illustrates not so much that the US government plays a key role in managing finance, but that it allows this management to be done by financial capitalists who are largely immune from government influence.[64] Thus, when big investment banks began to generate new speculative instruments, on top of the ones that they had previously invented, they were already 'too big to fail' because they constituted the political as well as the economic core of US society and the state.

The remaining events in the banking crisis of 2008 add some finer points on how this marriage of financial capital and government functions. For example, the crisis arose first as the underlying value of bank assets, including subprime mortgages, came into question. The doubt about value then limited the ability of banks to provide credit, based on restrictions imposed by the Federal Reserve.[65] This eventually caused new credit to dry up, as lenders could not assess the risk that new lending might entail. This 'credit crunch' quickly spread throughout the United States, and then the world, through the interconnections that had been developed in the global banking system, and the web of borrowing and lending that followed, including the packaging and repackaging of debt in various 'products'. Thus, the 'Toxic Asset Relief Program' (TARP) that was designed in a midnight bargaining session could not provide any material relief to creditors, be they private homeowners, small businesses, or state or local governments, because its focus was on relieving the speculative pressures that had enveloped US banks. Thereafter, the economic stimulus package that was developed by the incoming Obama administration continued to focus its efforts on stabilizing banks, even as the broader economy continued to decline. This focus had a particularly pernicious effect on the working class, whose job losses and home foreclosures were compounded by an evaporating social safety net and the loss of essential state and local government services.

Three years after the collapse of Lehman Brothers sparked the greatest financial crisis and economic downturn since the Great Depression, none of the underlying contradictions of the world system have been resolved. As 2011 drew to a close, none of the conditions that caused the meltdown of September 2008 had been dealt with properly. Global imbalances and deep-rooted tensions have deepened even further. The financial and economic crisis continues with no end in sight. We are now well into the fifth year of the global crisis, and the outlook remains far from settled. Hundreds of billions of dollars have been made available to save banks and financial houses around the world.

The plight of the Eurozone is beyond belief. In 2003, as it was preparing for the Olympic Games which it hosted the following year, Greece's borrowing boosted its GDP (measured in a way that created the fictitious appearance of growth) by 5.9 per cent. In 2010 it dropped down to -4.5 per cent.[66] Portugal's GDP was 4.1 per cent in 1999, but -2.5 per cent in 2009. Basically, all of Europe's peripheral lame ducks (Greece, Portugal, Spain, Ireland, Italy) threaten the viability of the Eurozone. Governments and central banks took off the books of the banks the worthless or so-called toxic assets, which were transferred onto state balance sheets. Greece, already bankrupt, receives one bailout after another because this is the only way for the private bondholders of the Greek debt to transfer it to public institutions and the European Central Bank (ECB), so it is the European and Greek taxpayers who are paying that debt. The bailout operation, and similar measures such as 'quantitative easing' (printing money to bail out private bondholders and banks), have cost more than 25 per cent of global GDP, which is tantamount to the globe's 'black' or 'invisible' economic sector. This large-scale bailout, however, did not solve the problem.

The false claim that the governments have broken the back of the recession is running out of steam. Recent figures point to a marked decline in economic activity in all of the 16 countries of the Eurozone. Leading countries outside the Eurozone also recorded negative growth figures, and where the figures appear positive it is because of quantitative easing and other monetary measures that only bring temporary relief. There is a sharp worsening of the economic situation in all Western economies. The concerns about the US economic outlook and the continued debt crisis in Europe also hit risk markets hard. Unemployment has not stopped growing, and the housing market remains depressed at historically low levels. Economists warn of a 'lost generation' as youth unemployment soars as high as 40 per cent in some European countries. The United States and the other leading developed countries all face the prospect of low economic growth and high unemployment, whereas the challenge of deleveraging remains.

Far from easing the dire crisis conditions, governments of the advanced economies, in line with the international financial institutions, are now implementing sharp austerity programmes on a scale not seen since the 1930s. Everywhere in the Western world there is unemployment, foreclosures, bankruptcies, depressed housing markets, and no recovery in sight. Already, in many advanced economies the highest number of people since the 1930s are now jobless or unable to find full-time work. But unlike the 1930s, when the credit crunch was tackled by governments with a turn to Keynesianism, especially after the war, the governments of the West today seem to have opted to deal with the crisis by way of deepening neoliberalism and globalization. No doubt they are wrong, and they are digging the hole even deeper.

Austerity in the United Kingdom

Let us briefly examine the situation in the United Kingdom – a country in which we both reside – in the aftermath of the financial crisis.

Over the last three to four years (2007–2010) the UK government has pumped more than £375 billion into the banking system through bailouts and a series of 'unconventional measures' – a rather political term, basically meaning 'desperate attempts' – but very little of this has flowed back into the real economy. This figure is almost half of the declared total public deficit.[67] None of this has made the situation better; the immense concentration of wealth in the hands of a small financial elite has become more extreme. Economic imbalances and tensions have deepened.

The agreement between the Conservatives and the Liberal Democrats, the first coalition government in the United Kingdom since 1931, gives the government carte blanche to balance the budget with massive cuts in public services, jobs and wages. The coalition's intended austerity measures are on a scale never seen in the modern United Kingdom. The coalition is currently planning to impose cuts between £85 billion and £100 billion over the next four years. What is planned here will dwarf anything that was undertaken by Margaret Thatcher in the 1980s. If the coalition starts to introduce huge budget cuts, there will be massive unemployment in the public sector. As a conservative estimate, 750,000 public sector job losses do not look far off the mark. About 100,000 of the jobs would be lost in Scotland because of its disproportionate bigger public sector. And those still in work will face wage freezes and cuts. Job insecurity will rise for nearly everyone. The Chartered Institute of Personnel and Development (CIPD) and KPMG have issued a report warning that redundancies are poised to rise significantly.[68] On the other hand, corporation tax is to be cut from its present level of 28 per cent to 24 per cent, which will give the United Kingdom the lowest level of any developed country. Massive unemployment and lower wages imply lower tax receipts, and even bigger budget deficits and debt loads.

Austerity and high unemployment also risks social unrest. Greece is already losing control of its streets, and a number of other Eurozone countries are moving in that direction. The London riots of summer 2011 should be seen as part of a Europe-wide concatenation of uprisings linked to widespread discontent about government austerity policies. It is very unlikely that introducing savage austerity measures while the economy is still on a downward spiral will resolve any problems – the crisis will simply be displaced from one sphere to another. The austerity measures of the coalition government are therefore at risk of damaging short-term growth prospects, and will increase the possibility of a double dip recession.[69] All in all, the reforms that the coalition government is experimenting with will deepen the Thatcherite programmes of the 1980s and 1990s and, as elsewhere in Europe and the West, increase the cleavage between the rich and the poor. This, we argue, is accelerating the process of the decline of the West, as the majority of people are left out of the political and economic processes that determine growth, welfare and environmentalist socialist perspectives.

Many people are not happy about the cuts, but think that there is no choice but to sacrifice to save the economy. The UK public and media appear to have accepted the line presented by the coalition government that the total package of cuts worth £128 billion by 2015–16 is 'unavoidable' because of Labour's careless spending, and almost self-made huge deficits. Until the financial crash of 2008, however, the Labour governments had succeeded in keeping national debt below a 40 per cent of GDP target. In 2006–07, public sector net debt was 36 per cent of GDP. In 2008, it rose rapidly primarily because of 'financial interventions' to bail out Northern Rock, RBS and other banks, because of lower tax receipts, and because of higher spending on unemployment benefits, all caused by the recession. So the current deficit was caused primarily by the recession, not by the previous administration's pre-crash spending plans. In 2010 it stood at 63.7 per cent of national GDP, and was projected to peak at 74.9 per cent in 2014–15.[70]

UK Prime Minister David Cameron's 'Big Society' programme offers an ideological justification for the intended massive cuts. It is obvious that the cuts of this scale are about much more than just deficit reduction. Critics have argued that the cuts are part of an agenda to transfer services from the public sector to the private sector. The pretence of 'there is no alternative' is a means for the

Conservative project to radically transform the state towards an ever more neoliberal direction.

In general, Keynesian deficit financing to achieve a constructive result requires a very careful approach to spending cuts and overall fiscal policy. Reducing the overall debt/GDP ratio is difficult by simple fiscal measures, and not always necessary. Sometimes a large fiscal deficit can be useful to actually reduce the ratio if the fiscal deficit creates a larger GDP. The economy must also be on a growth path in order to achieve required economic and financial benefits. But if the country suffers from not only low or no growth, but also no growth in the working-age population, reducing the debt/GDP ratio seems unrealistic and is also highly risky. Therefore in order to achieve a balanced annual budget, careful fiscal measures should be accompanied by other measures such as tax rises and growth-led investment. But the UK government does not even follow these tested pre-socialist recipes. It currently seems to be obsessed about the need for belt-tightening and continuous financial statecraft, but the real problem is inadequate productive spending: in other words, the lack of real economic activity. Cutting government spending too soon may make the situation more drastic, and the recession more severe and lengthy. There is a real danger that spending cuts could reduce economic growth and therefore hinder attempts to improve tax revenues. If the course of the Great Slump is a useful example, the current policy of the coalition government could have the unintended consequence of exacerbating the crisis rather than beginning to address it.

The current coalition, which at the time of writing (June–July 2011) was shaken by the emerging details of News International's phone hacking scandals, is citing the experience of Canada during the late 1980s and the 1990s as a success story for massive spending cuts bringing down huge budget deficits. Canada had a budget deficit of 9 per cent of GDP in 1992. By 1997 it was showing a surplus. At first sight this looks like a good comparison: two countries with large budget deficits trying to deal with the crisis by introducing fast and massive spending cuts. However there are huge differences, mainly in terms of the context and the global environment. Canada in the 1990s was aided by the pick-up in the global economy, and especially relatively strong US expansion. In the middle of this US-centred growth spurt, Canada bought itself a significant slice of that growth. This is evident especially in the rapid growth of investment in energy and mining.[71] The United Kingdom, however, does not have an expanding and relatively buoyant economy for a neighbour. It has the Eurozone, which itself is struggling with the same financial and economic crisis. In the 1990s, the United States still exercised economic hegemony, and the US consumer was still the world's engine of growth. All this helped to boost revenue growth significantly without a huge squeeze on taxes. The US market was there for Canadian companies, and also many jobless Canadians could get jobs over the border. Today, the United States is in severe, albeit relative, economic decline, with the socioeconomic centre of gravity moving away from the Western economies.[72]

In the United Kingdom, in the near future the bad news for manufacturing is likely to continue. New jobs are more likely to be part-time and temporary, and mainly in service sectors such as call centres, internet services, retail outlets, and more ephemeral trades like advertising and the media. This trend has already been clear for the last three decades. In 1970, some 9 million people worked in manufacturing. Today the number is less than 4 million. There is no sign that this trend is about to be reversed. According to a recent survey, most UK workers are better suited for a job selling hamburgers than designing microchips. More than one-third of those between 25 and 34 in the United Kingdom have no GSCE-level qualifications.[73]

The current deficit is the result not of mistakes which can be attributed to previous administrators or an individual blunder, as claimed by the coalition, but of deep-rooted structural changes within the US-centred global economy, in which the United Kingdom figures as the United States' most important partner. The Office for Budget Responsibility forecasts that unemployment will remain well above 7 per cent for the next two years, and above 6 per cent for the following two. Structural deficits are usually based on the notion that once there is a return to full employment (clearly that does not mean 6 per cent or more unemployment), revenues should be balanced against expenditure. It makes little or no sense to seek to achieve a balance before full employment is reached, and to do it on the basis of an unemployment trend that is already well above acceptable levels.[74]

The right task is to find a fair and sustainable path out of crisis. To formulate policy alternatives, it is important to emphasize what caused the crisis. Budget deficits more or less automatically heal with economic recovery. Trying to cut the deficit quickly, in the midst of a serious recession, is likely to damage the economy drastically and extend the crisis. The government instead should concentrate on environmentally sustainable growth, and let this type of growth reduce the deficit. This is a tall order. During the Second World War, the UK national debt reached very high figures of up to 150 per cent of GDP. It is normal practice that countries borrow more during the time of serious national and international crises, like wars, or economic upheavals such as the one currently affecting the world, and pay back the debt over a period of time. In this sense, a budget deficit can be an effective way to deal with such crises. If anything, the problem of low economic activity is the real issue, and it is more urgent to deal with this than to focus on fiscal stability.

When the coalition of Conservatives and Liberals that succeeded the Labour government introduced an emergency budget in September 1931, Keynes stood out against the chorus of approval. The budget was, he wrote, 'replete with folly and injustice'. Cuts will not reduce a deficit, but productive investment and demand-led policies, as pre-socialist measures, will. The Confederation of British Industry (CBI) has announced that it expects economic growth in 2012 to be much slower than previously predicted, thanks to the coalition government's emergency budget. Much weaker consumer spending (resulting from the large-scale unemployment and lower wages also predicted by the CBI) is the main reason for this. Ian McCafferty, CBI chief economic adviser, said:

> The recovery continues to be choppy and lacking in vigour. Expansion in certain sectors is being offset by weaker performance in others. What remains striking is how little we expect the pace of growth to accelerate in 2012, and that it will be far less robust than we would normally expect in the second and third years of a recovery.

Cutting too far and too fast will mean more people out of work, fewer jobs in the economy, a lower level of taxation from workers and businesses, and more people on unemployment benefit, which will cost the government more. As we are writing this, the governor of the Bank of England continues to keep the basic interest rate of the Bank very low, at 0.5 per cent, which is unprecedented. Yet this has failed to stimulate demand simply because the manipulation of monetary instruments alone cannot deliver growth, let alone environmentally friendly growth. For growth to be achieved, the ruling classes that have been managing UK capitalism since the 1970s have to concede defeat, or be defeated by the working classes, the real victims of the financial crisis.[75]

5

THE POWER SHIFT TO
THE GLOBAL EAST

Our industry has been concentrated in the coastal areas ....
Nearly 70% of light and heavy industrial production is to be
found in the coastal areas and only 30% in the country's interior.
This is an absurd situation inherited from history. Some of the
industries in the coastal areas should be moved into the interior
so as to make the economic situation more balanced and also to
prepare the country better for dealing with war. But that does not
mean that all industries will have to leave the coast. In fact, we
can build there factories and mines of very large size and scale.

Mao Zedong, 'On the relationship between the industry of
coastal areas and the industry in the interior of the country',
April 26, 1956[1]

We have had a couple of hundred bad years, but now we're
back.

Clyde Prestowitz quotes a Chinese friend
(www.economist.com/node/7961926)

As we set out in Chapter 1, China, Russia, Brazil and other fast-
growing emerging economies are fully fledged members of an
international division of labour and capital. This fact, and the way
in which global fault-lines have been operating since the late 1960s,
tend to shift power away from its traditional Anglo-Saxon core
and its international monetary medium, the US dollar. Let us recap
briefly the story so far.

By the 1970s, West European and Japanese capital had recovered
from the devastation of the Second World War and begun outcompeting US corporations, and US economic primacy, both in the
United States and abroad. By the 1980s, it was the turn of Southeast

Asian capital to outcompete both US and West European capital through, among others, the formation of a new kind of transnational business structure – a structure that was deeply rooted in the region's history and geography, and that combined the advantages of a massive, young, dynamic population with flexible business networks. This was a very significant development in a context in which all the major indicators pointed out to the economic power of the United States being in stagnation and relative economic decline since the late 1960s. Its share of world trade and manufacturing was substantially less than it had been just prior to the end of the Cold War, and its relative economic strength measured against the European Union and the East Asian economic group of Japan, China and other Southeast Asian countries was similarly in retreat.

In other words, the real roots of the current crisis lie in downward pressure on profitability under the conditions of sharply increased competition stemming from West European capital in the 1970s and Southeast Asian economies since the late 1980s. A closer look at the extraordinary economic expansion of the Southeast Asian region over the last 20 years can give some insights into the remarkable new kind of global economic order that is emerging at the edges of the current systemic crisis.

Napoleon famously said 'Let China sleep, for when China wakes up, she will shake the world.' Since the mid-1980s China has woken up.[2] The late Andre Gunder Frank argued that the centres of gravity in the world economy are dramatically shifting towards the Asia-Pacific region, and that the days of 'Eurocentrism' are numbered. *ReOrient* (1998) calls into question virtually every set of assumptions that has dominated macrohistorical sociology since the inception of the discipline.[3] The thesis is quite straightforward: a truly global perspective is needed in studying macrohistorical changes in the world – the rise and fall of empires, the industrial revolution, the decline of the East and the corresponding rise of the West, colonialism in India and the American revolution, and so on. In a rather neo-Hegelian/Lukácsian perspective, Frank argues again and again that the whole is greater than the sum of its parts, and the parts can only be understood in relation to the whole. In this respect, class analysis is only one part of the story: a holistic class analysis in global time and space, capturing the entire dynamics of societies, cultures and political economies in their antagonism, is what is needed.

The more than 8 per cent average annual economic growth set by a number of East Asian economies for the last 20 years is outstanding in the 140 years of recorded economic history. This is all the more so as it has been recorded at a time of total stagnation or near stagnation in most of the developed economies of the West. As Scott L. Kastner noted, 'the rise of China represents one of the most fundamental shifts in world politics over the past few decades'.[4] Never has a country so large changed so much in such a short period of time.[5] The opening up of China's economy to global forces was part of US Cold War policy, with the intention of reaching a rapprochement with Mao Zedong in the 1970s against the Soviet bloc.

The economic modernization programme activated by Deng Xiaoping in 1978 – ironically, the name given to this policy by Deng was 'Open Door' – accomplished consistent growth rates of 9–10 per cent throughout the 1980s and 1990s. Deng established pragmatic economic reforms that transformed China into a market-oriented economy. Under Deng, the whole approach to economic growth took a new direction: 'the main task of socialism is to develop the productive forces, steadily improve the life of the people, and keep increasing the material wealth of society .... So to keep rich is no sin'.[6] For more than two decades, China has marched to the banner of 'reform and opening to the outside world'.[7] Deng's economic programme was regarded by many observers as one of the historical turning points of the twentieth century. How ironic it is that now, three decades later, the United States increasingly regards a fast-expanding market economy in China as a serious threat to its own global hegemony. This is exactly an expression of the tragedy of the US open door policy and its current form, that of globalization.

ISSUES BETWEEN THE UNITED STATES AND CHINA

The US political elite is not only more aware of the limits of its own power, it is also much more concerned about the strengths of potential rivals. The US National Intelligence Council's 2008 report – the Council supports the director of national intelligence and is the centre for long-range analysis in the US intelligence community – presents a detailed and comprehensive report on global trends to 2025. Most press coverage focused on the report's key message of the 'sun setting on US power' (there were almost identical headlines in the *Guardian* and *The Times*). It is explicitly mentioned in the report that by 2025, the United States will be less dominant, and 'China will have the world's second largest economy and will be a leading military power'. Furthermore, the report identified China, India and the United States, as 'three of the largest' economies.[8]

It seems that the unprecedented transfer of wealth roughly from West to East that is now under way will continue for the foreseeable future. This unprecedented economic growth, coupled with 1.5 billion more people, will undoubtedly put pressure on world's key resources –particularly energy, food and water – raising the spectre of scarcities emerging as demand outstrips supply.[9]

One flashpoint with the United States is China's fast-growing demand for oil. China became the world's second-largest consumer of petroleum products in 2004, having surpassed Japan for the first time in 2003, with a total demand of 6.5 million barrels per day (bbl/d). China's oil demand is projected by the US Energy Information Administration (EIA) to reach 14.2 million bbl/d by 2025, with net imports of 10.9 million bbl/d.[10]

All the existing evidence indicates that even without a total collapse of the US global supremacy, there seems to be satisfactory evidence for a great and rapid shift of wealth and power to China and India, and other emerging economies.[11] The transfer of power from the West to the East has been gathering pace since the late 1990s, and Washington think tanks have been publishing thick white papers charting Asia's, and China's in particular, rapid progress in microelectronics, nanotech, and aerospace, and printing gloomy scenarios about what it means for the global leadership of the United States. China, India and other emerging economies have so far boasted growth rates that could outstrip those of major Western countries for decades to come. Importantly, and unlike the case with the West, a key component of this growth is not debt or financial sophistry, but manufacturing and material production.

THE GROWTH OF EMERGING ECONOMIES

China is currently the world's second largest economy, with an annual economic growth of more than 8 per cent – it overtook Japan in February 2011. India's annual growth rate is also 8 per cent, and has just begun to undermine the US 'weapon-dollar' regime: the Indian government's decision in July 2011 to reject offers from two US firms to supply fighter jets worth an estimated $12 billion has put into question the future of US–India defence collaboration and military sales. By mid-century, India is expected to have 1.6 billion people, and 220 million more workers than China. No doubt, this could be a source for instability. But it is also a great advantage for growth if the government can provide education and opportunity for India's masses.[12] Brazil is the world's seventh largest economy, and the second largest in the Western hemisphere after the United States. Brazil's GDP growth is over 5 per cent, and the country is predicted to become one of the five largest economies in the world in the future.

China has become the engine driving the recovery of other Asian economies from the recessions of the 1990s. Japan, for example, has become the largest beneficiary of China's economic growth, and its leading economic indicators have improved as a result. Thanks to increased exports to China, Japan has finally emerged from a decade-long economic crisis. After China, India is emerging as an economic superpower. With economic growth topping 9 per cent in 2007, an acknowledged nuclear capability, and a growing role in international relations, it has attained the status of a leading emerging power.

India is today playing an invaluable role in the global innovation chain. Motorola, Hewlett-Packard, Cisco Systems and many other high-tech giants now rely on their teams in India to devise software platforms and dazzling multimedia features for next-generation devices. Intel has 2000 electrical engineers with PhDs in Bangalore designing state-of-the-art ships. Indian engineering houses use 3-D computer simulations to produce sophisticated designs of everything from car engines and forklifts to aircraft wings, for clients like General Motors and Boeing Corp.[13]

The post-war era witnessed economic miracles in Japan and South Korea. But neither was big enough to power worldwide growth, or change the direction of the global economy across a complete spectrum of industries. China and India, by contrast, possess the weight and dynamism to transform the twenty-first-century global economy. The closest parallel to their emergence is the saga of the nineteenth-century United States: a huge continental economy with a young population, providing a driving force that enabled it to grab the lead in agriculture, apparel and the high technologies of the era, such as steam engines, the telegraph and electric lights. But in a way, even the rise of the United States falls short in comparison with what has been happening in China and India for the last two decades. Never has the world seen the simultaneous and sustained take-offs of two countries which together account for one-third of the world's population.

What makes the two Asian giants especially powerful is that they complement each other's strengths. All indications suggest that China will stay dominant in mass manufacturing, and it is one of the few countries building multibillion-dollar electronics and heavy industrial plants. The Chinese not only produce textiles and cheap toys, they also make semiconductors and very advanced technology. Indeed, the world semiconductor fabrication capacity is dominated by the Asia-Pacific region.[14] India is a rising power in software, design, services and precision industry. If Chinese and Indian industries truly collaborated, they would take over the world high-tech industry. These immense workforces are already converging. Because the global deployment of high-speed internet communications renders geography almost irrelevant, now multinationals are able to have their goods built in China with software and circuitry designed in India. Together they are combining Indian software technology with Chinese hardware technology to achieve world leadership in the global information technology industry. In 2005, India and China formed a 'strategic partnership'. More recently (October 2008) they agreed to hold their first-ever joint military exercise.[15] The refusal by India to go ahead with the buying of US military hardware in July 2011 may well be connected to the China link.

One obvious reason for this shift in the balance of power in many technologies is that China and India produce a combined total of more than half a million engineering and science graduates per annum. The total number of graduates in the United States is only 60,000. In three years' time, the total number of young researchers will go up to 1.6 million in India and China together. Because these two countries can throw more brains at technical problems,

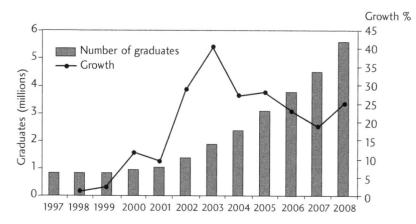

Figure 5.1 The number of the graduates in China from 1997 to 2008

Source: adapted from Chinese Ministry of Education.[16]

their contribution to research and innovation is increasing very quickly.[16]

Western business is not just shifting research work to Asia because Indian and Chinese brains are young, cheap and plentiful. Thanks to the comprehensive and intense technological education available in China and India, in many cases, Asian engineers are better educated than Western engineers, and they combine complex skills: mastery of latest software tools, a knack for complex mathematical algorithms, and fluency in new multimedia technologies. It is true that many Western companies came to India and China for the low cost, but they are staying for the quality, and they are investing for the innovation. China and India are rapidly moving from providing low-cost manufacturing and services to being innovation powerhouses. Now it is becoming increasingly clear that China and India (and some other emerging economies) are taking centre stage in the global competition for innovation and talent. China and India now boast some of the world's top science and research universities, including the seven-campus Indian Institutes of Technology as well as Beijing's Tsinghua University.[18] Arrighi is quite right when he argues, and repeats again and again, in *Adam Smith in Beijing* that the Chinese labour force is not just cheap but also highly skilled. 'One of the most striking features of the Chinese labour market', Raphael Kaplinsky endorses further, 'is its growing level of education and skilling'.[19]

CONTROL OVER RESOURCES

Over the last decade, China has quietly cornered the market on rare earth elements (REE) – europium, gadolinium, dysprosium, terbium and others – and now supplies about 95 per cent of the world's consumption, a dominance that industry experts say could give Beijing control over the future of consumer electronics and green technology.[20] REEs are a class of minerals with properties that make them essential for applications including miniaturized electronics, computer disk drives, display screens, missile guidance, pollution control catalysts and advanced materials. In 1994, China's share of the market was 46 per cent, according to industry statistics. The REE market, estimated to be worth up to $1 billion a year, is dwarfed by the global trade in bulk commodities like iron ore, but controlling the supply of these minerals gives China a strategic advantage as it seeks to build powerful high-technology industries and modernize its armed forces. The military requires REEs in a significant way as it has become increasingly reliant on their widespread use, particularly in building advanced aircraft materials, guided missiles and blast protection.

Environmental applications of REEs have increased markedly over the past three decades. In many applications, REEs are advantageous because of their relatively low toxicity. For example, the most common types of rechargeable batteries (known as Ni-Cd) contain either cadmium (Cd) or lead. Rechargeable lanthanum-nickel (La-Ni-H) batteries are now used in computer and communications applications, and could eventually replace lead-acid batteries in automobiles. Although more expensive, La-Ni-H batteries offer greater energy density, better charge-discharge characteristics, and fewer environmental problems upon disposal or recycling, so they are gradually replacing Ni-Cd. As the Chinese REE industry grows, many of the processors and end users of these minerals are moving their advanced manufacturing and research and development

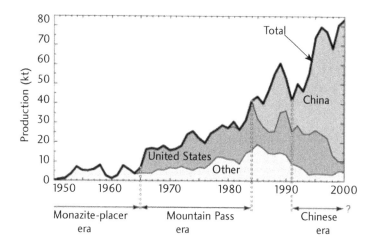

Figure 5.2 Global production of rare earth oxides, 1950–2000

Source: adapted from US Geological Survey (2002).

Note: Global rare earth element production (1 kt=106 kg) is shown in four categories: United States, almost entirely from Mountain Pass, California; China, from several deposits; all other countries combined, largely from monazite-bearing placers; and global total. Four periods of production are evident: the monazite-placer era, starting in the late 1800s and ending abruptly in 1964; the Mountain Pass era, starting in 1965 and ending about 1984; a transitional period from about 1984 to 1991; and the Chinese era, beginning about 1991.

facilities to China, increasing the growth of critical industries, particularly in electronics. Companies such as Intel, Nokia, Motorola, Microsoft and Cisco Systems have all invested heavily in manufacturing and research in China, which now accounts for more than 30 per cent of consumption of REEs.[21] REEs are now considered to be an absolutely essential component in shaping modern and future technology.

THE GROWING CONSUMER CLASSES

What is driving innovation in Asia, however, is not only the Western demand, but increasingly a fast-rising home-grown consumer class. China is currently the world's third largest travel market, with 120 million air passengers in 2004 alone. It is currently the world's second largest market for automobiles, after the United States. For instance, Volkswagen is producing more cars in China than in Germany.[22] China has the world's biggest base of mobile phone subscribers – 700 million. The fastest growth in demand for semiconductors is overwhelmingly concentrated in China. Much of this growth is in the expansion of the mobile phone market. China has currently overtaken the United States in numbers of homes connected to broadband. The rapid growth of the Chinese internet market has turned the country into a promised land for many internet giants, like Yahoo, Google, MSN and e-Bay.[23] Recent studies show that the attitudes and aspirations of today's Chinese and Indians resemble those of Americans a few decades ago. Surveys of thousands of young adults in both countries found that they are overwhelmingly optimistic about the future, and believe success is in their hands.[24]

In terms of size, speed and directional flow, the global shift in relative wealth and economic power now under way – roughly from West to East – is without precedent in modern history.[25] The last 10 to 15 years have witnessed 3 billion people entering into the global *capitalist* economy. In many past examples, newcomers generally carried out unskilled, labour-intensive tasks. What is interesting about today's Chinese and Indian population is that while on average they are poor, and most of them are unskilled, a small percentage (around 300 million) are highly skilled and well educated. A small percentage of 3 billion is a lot of people. These skilled, educated workers are ready to produce everything with the latest scientific methods. These 300 million highly skilled newcomers – a number as large as the US population, larger than that of Japan or any European country – will make a big impact on the global economy. And what is important for our purposes here is that they are engaged in *material production* and *commerce*, two aspects of the real economy that US-led globalization/ financialization could not care less about.

Both India and China will become major power centres by 2020 even if they remain middle-income countries, on account of their having the highest populations in the world. Their fast integration into the world economy during the last 20 years has already dramatically changed the pattern of the world economy, something that has been described as 'the most significant global shift in the geography of the world economy during the past 40 years'.[26] As the global crisis churns, China and India are emerging as more vital players in limiting the economic damage from the worst global financial crisis in almost 80 years. Together, India and China, two of the largest economies in the world, clearly have the wherewithal to take a leading role and reshape the world imperial order.[27] Their chances for doing so will increase dramatically if an effort to further stimulate internal demand takes root, rebalancing their dependence on exports.

In the coming decades, how these Asian giants integrate with the rest of the world will largely shape the twenty-first-century global order. All these powerful trends may soon be followed by increasing Asia's geopolitical strength. To explain the current financial crisis and economic downturn in the context of an epochal shift in the world-system away from North American/West European dominance and towards Asia would provide us with a longer-term and deeper understanding of the global economy in the current century. The twenty-first century looks set to be fashioned by the rise of China and India at the social and state levels, and the formidable rise of Pacific–Asia–India as the foremost economic zones at the regional level. Along with these, a number of other regional powers, such as Brazil, Russia, South Africa and Turkey, will seek realignments and different economic and political alliances.

All this should not really be surprising. Asia, and especially East Asia, was dominant for most of human history, and remained so until very recently (less than 200 years ago). China and the area that is now India then accounted for about 75 per cent of global GDP. Even in 1820, China and India together were worth more than 50 per cent of world trade. Europe's share was relatively insignificant, and the United States had been discovered but was still not important beyond the Western hemisphere. For a number of reasons Asian economies lost their position to the West and slipped into increasing economic insignificance, but it seems only temporarily.[28] That shift happened in the nineteenth century, and another shift appears to be happening again at the beginning of the twenty-first century, as the centre of the world economy shifts back to the East. Measured by purchasing power, China had 13 per cent of the world's GDP in 2007. By 2050 it is expected to reach 20 per cent. India will grow from 6 per cent to 12 per cent, the United States will slip from 21 per cent to 14 per cent, and Europe from 21 per cent to 10 per cent.[29] Peter Dicken describes this ongoing process as 'the changing global economic map', arguing that 'old geographies of production, distribution and consumption are continuously being disrupted and that new geographies are continuously being created. In that sense, the global economic map is always in a state of becoming'.[30]

BRAZIL'S EXPERIENCE

Brazil also appears a strong contender to be well on the path to world power status. With consistent and rapid growth since 2003, driven by record low unemployment and a confident new middle class of free-spending consumers, Brazil has the eighth largest GDP in the world. It is the world's fifth largest country in both population and land area. The Brazilian population has grown 1.5 per cent annually on average over the past few decades to 189 million inhabitants in 2008, most of whom reside in cities. Brazil's case has been strengthened by its government's role in promoting infrastructure, industry and agricultural commodities, as well as in investing in the ethanol and oil production that have made the country energy self-sufficient. The Latin American powerhouse, Brazil is the largest producer of many soft commodities, such as sugar, coffee and oranges, the second largest producer of soybeans and ethanol, and the number one exporter of all these products. The country is also the second largest producer of beef, and ranks third for chicken and fourth for pork. It exports more beef and poultry than any other country. The cost of production in the Brazilian agricultural sector is currently lower than for most producer countries.

Brazil has also huge mineral reserves – especially iron ore, aluminium, copper, chromium, gold, tin, nickel, manganese, zinc and potassium – and a clear advantage in all major sectors associated with these commodities. The recent huge discoveries of oil reserves in the pre-salt layer has made Brazil a major player in the world market and it is projected to become a net exporter of fuel in the next decade. But it is not just commodities that are driving the economic boom in Brazil. The country has also a substantial manu-facturing base and a sizeable automobile industry. Brazilian aviation giant Embraer is the world's third-largest jet aircraft maker, behind Boeing and Airbus, and a main supplier of regional jets to the US market. When Brazilian President Dilma Rousseff visited China in early 2011, one of her biggest achievements was to sign a contract with Beijing for 20 commercial jets from Embraer.[31]

The growth cycle was interrupted briefly by the global crisis of 2008, but the Brazilian economy has proved much more resilient to crises than many other leading economies. Brazil's GDP grew more than analysts forecast, pulling the economy out of recession thanks to rising domestic demand. Consistent job growth, coupled with tax breaks and record low borrowing costs, have been driving consumer spending, helping the Brazilian economy rebound from the global financial crisis faster than was previously expected. All key economic indicators suggest that the country is likely to experi-ence higher and – even more importantly – less volatile economic growth in the next 10 to 20 years.[32]

Research by PricewaterhouseCoopers (PwC) predicts that soon the collective size of E7 (emerging seven economies: Brazil, China, India, Indonesia, Mexico, Russia and Turkey) will be about 25 per cent larger than the collective size of the current G-7 'rich' economies. 'By 2020', according to the same research, 'China, India, Brazil, Indonesia and Russia will between them account for 30% of global GDP. The change will bring an important shift in the global balance of economic power.'[33] A more recent (January 2011) survey by PwC predicts that 'the E7 economies will by 2050 be around 64% larger than the current G7'. The report reads:

> In the following decade from 2020 to 2030, however, the process of overtaking is likely to be reinforced, with total E7 GDP projected to be around 44% higher by 2030 than total G7 GDP in PPP terms. The gap would widen further beyond that, with the E7 almost twice as large as the G7 by 2050 in PPP terms(...). The key drivers of the E7 growth are China and India, although the former's growth will slow down progressively due to its significantly lower labour force growth arising from its one child policy. India's growth will remain fairly strong even in the last decade of our projections. Despite China's slowdown in growth, it is expected to overtake the US as the world's largest economy (measured by GDP at PPPs) sometime before 2020.[34]

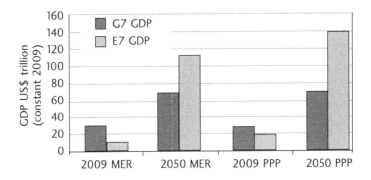

Figure 5.3 The relative size of G7 and E7 economies (2009 and estimates for 2050)

Source: adapted from PricewaterhouseCoopers (2011).

Similarly, a Carnegie Endowment research report points out that:

The world's economic balance of power is shifting rapidly, and the trend has only been accelerated by the global recession. China remains on a path to overtake the United States as the world's largest economic power within a generation, and India will join both as a global leader by mid-century .... The weight of global economic activity is already shifting substantially from the G7 countries toward emerging economies in Asia and Latin America. Over the next 40 years, this trend is expected to accelerate .... After nearly a century as the world's pre-eminent economic power, the United States is projected to relinquish this title to China in 2032. Rapid annual growth of 5.6% and a strengthening currency – the renminbi's real exchange rate against the dollar is predicted to appreciate by more than 1% per year – will drive China's U.S. dollar GDP up from $3.3 trillion in 2009 to $46.3 trillion in 2050, 20% larger than that of the United States in real dollar terms and 90% larger in PPP terms.[35]

Observers now talk of the emergence of a new 'Seven Sisters' (a term used to describe the seven major Anglo-American companies that controlled the world's oil after the Second World War). Today it is not ExxonMobil, Royal Dutch Shell and the other Western companies, but Russia's Gazprom, China's CNPC, Venezuela's PDVSA, Brazil's Petrobras, the Saudi Aramco and Malaysia's Petronas that are the

Table 5.1 When could the E7 economies overtake the G7 in GDP at PPP and MER rankings?

2010	China overtakes Japan, India overtakes Canada
2011	India overtakes Japan, Brazil overtakes France India overtakes Spain, Russia overtakes Canada
2012	Russia overtakes Spain, Mexico overtakes Australia
2013	Brazil overtakes the United Kingdom
2014	Russia overtakes Germany, India overtakes Brazil
2015	Indonesia overtakes Turkey, India overtakes Italy
2016	India overtakes the United Kingdom
2017	Brazil overtakes Italy, Indonesia overtakes Turkey
2018	China overtakes the United States, Indonesia overtakes Canada, India overtakes France
2019	Mexico overtakes Italy
2020	Turkey overtakes Canada
2021	Indonesia overtakes Spain
2022	India overtakes Germany, Russia overtakes Italy
2023	Brazil overtakes the United Kingdom, Indonesia overtakes Australia
2024	Indonesia overtakes South Korea, Turkey overtakes Spain, Mexico overtakes Canada, Turkey overtakes Australia
2025	Brazil overtakes Germany, Mexico overtakes Spain
2027	Brazil overtakes France
2028	Mexico overtakes France, Turkey overtakes South Korea India overtakes Japan
2029	Russia overtakes the United Kingdom, Indonesia overtakes South Korea
2030	Indonesia overtakes Italy
2031	Mexico overtakes the United Kingdom, Turkey overtakes South Korea
2032	China overtakes the United States, Brazil overtakes Germany, Indonesia overtakes Canada
2033	Turkey overtakes Italy, Russia overtakes France Indonesia overtakes Spain
2034	Mexico overtakes Italy
2035	Turkey overtakes Spain
2037	Brazil overtakes Russia
2039	Brazil overtakes Japan, Mexico overtakes Germany Indonesia overtakes Italy
2040	Indonesia overtakes France
2042	Russia overtakes Germany
2044	Indonesia overtakes the United Kingdom, Brazil overtakes Japan
2045	India overtakes the United States
2047	Indonesia overtakes Germany
2048	Mexico overtakes the United Kingdom
2050	Mexico overtakes Germany, Indonesia overtakes France

Source: PricewaterhouseCoopers (2011, p.16).

giant producers.[36] This is what global fault-lines do, and this is how they operate in the international system: whereas capitalists, with the assistance of the state, can outflank workers organized in trade unions (for instance, neoliberal policy making outflanked labour-power in the West), capitalist companies, through free market competition, can be outflanked by other capitalist companies (for example, Southeast Asian and Chinese capitalist companies are outflanking Western capitalist companies).

PROJECTED RESULTS OF THE SHIFT IN ECONOMIC POWER

Whatever we think of the details, methodologies and differences of such projections, there is no doubt that momentous changes are happening in the global economy. With the rapid rise of alternative economic power caucuses, the relative weight of the United States in the global economy is plainly declining. The balance of economic power is shifting to China, India and other emerging economies, placing the Asian region, under Chinese leadership, in a much more competitive position in relation to the United States. Russia and Iran, with the first and second largest natural gas resources in the world, have the potential to undercut NATO's expansion in Eurasia by, among other things, blackmailing Europe over the supply of much-needed raw materials. The increase in output in the emerging economies means the departure of numerous industries from the old industrialized countries, as a result of which real wages in the United States and Western Europe are steadily declining, strengthening the trend to chronic unemployment (which is also one of the main reasons behind the current financial crisis).

As a result of this still continuing trend, the purchasing power of the populations in the advanced economies will diminish even further. One factor that could start to prop up the Western economies in relative terms is the purchasing power of Asian consumers in Western countries proper: purchasing assets, real estate, retailing, hotels and so on. But this might come at a cost: it would mean the reversal of the dependency relationship between West and East, North and South, whereby formerly poor regions, societies and states will now be in a position not only to overcome their economic and political dependency on the industrial/imperial West, but actually to have the West serve their own capitalist and imperial ambitions.

The unconstrained development of global economy in new regions brings devaluation to previously leading centres through

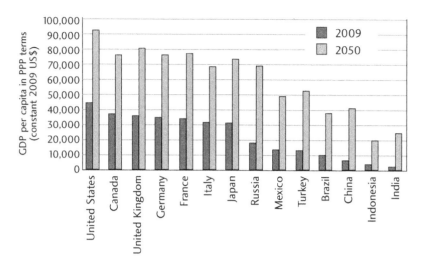

Figure 5.4 GDP per capita levels in PPP terms for the G7 and E7 economies

Source: adapted from PricewaterhouseCoopers (2011, p. 23).

intensified international competition. If industrialism and influence go hand in hand, then the wealth accumulation in China, India and other emerging economies will eventually change the geopolitical landscape, first of Eurasia and later of the world. If manufacturing and economies of scale are the linchpins of global economic supremacy, then Anglo-American economies can bounce back, even if temporarily, only via wars hemmed in by ideational schemes ('humanitarian interventions', the 'war on terror', 'the survival of Israel' and so forth). In this respect, the central question that arises is what the implications of China's (and India's) rapid rise are for the political-economic trajectory of a global capitalist system in which the United States finds it increasingly difficult to act effectively as the hegemonic power.[38]

All the available indications are that the current financial crisis, and economic downturn will confirm and possibly accelerate the shift in economic power to Asia, in particular to China. It seems that many producers in emerging market economies are not suffering as much as their counterparts in the developed world economies in the current global crisis. It is obvious that their exports have been hit, but many of them have found that domestic demand is relatively buoyant. That is because their own economies are on an upward growth path that is not so cyclical, so they can turn to the domestic market and exploit pent-up domestic demand. This is now happening, first and foremost in China. Of course not all emerging market economies are the same, and the recent troubles have confirmed that a separation is occurring between the more and less robust emerging economies. The gap in growth rates between the emerging and advanced world is widening fast. Emerging economies accounted for about 60 per cent of the global expansion for 2010 and 2011. This is up from about 25 per cent ten years ago. Since the beginning of the crisis in 2008, the United States has fallen behind Brazil, China and India as the preferred place to invest.

Emerging market countries are naturally feeling the effects of the global financial crisis and economic downturn. 'The data so far', Paul Kennedy argues, 'suggest the economies of China and India are growing (not as fast as in the past but still growing), while the US's economy shrinks in absolute terms'.[39] Thanks to its capital controls, its huge saving surplus and its publicly owned and state-controlled banking system, China seems to be well shielded from the Western financial and economic difficulties.[40] Mortgage assets and the housing market in China shows much greater stability and strength than the shaky and risky mortgage and lending structures in the United States and other Western economies. China's banks are now the strongest in the world, with capital ratios far above almost all other large banks in the world and debt levels that are far lower.[41] This is not to say that risks for a financial meltdown do not exist in China – far from it. The challenge for the Chinese rulers, however, is to address the looming crisis of over-accumulation of capital by avoiding a resort to financialization and an increase in debt levels.

China has already become a major actor in world currency and financial markets. The country holds $3 trillion in foreign exchange reserves. In particular, China's dollar holdings are a source of considerable financial leverage in the global financial markets. China has an especially effective financial system, which seems to be well positioned to finance the next phase in its economic expansion. Many observers also agree that the Chinese economy has a much bigger margin for manoeuvre, because its exposure to the speculative toxic assets that lay at the root of the recent financial crisis is much lower than that of the US and West European economies. Furthermore, China's yuan remains basically stable at a reasonable equilibrium level, which helps to prevent the international financial and currency market from further turbulence.

The president of the World Bank published a column in the *Financial Times* in November 2010 calling for a fundamental revamping of the global currency system involving a lesser role for the US dollar. Robert Zoellick urged the G20 to build a cooperative monetary system that reflects emerging economic conditions. This new system, he says, is likely to need to involve the dollar, the euro, the yen, the pound and the Chinese renminbi.[42] It seems that China faces the global crisis from a position of strength.[43] This is how Roger Altman, a US investment banker, put it:

> In financial terms, China is little affected by the crisis in the West. Its entire financial system plays a relatively small role in its economy, and it apparently has no exposure to the toxic assets that have brought the U.S. and European banking systems to their knees. China also runs a budget surplus and a very large current account surplus, and it carries little government debt.[44]

Thus, while the rest of the world is grappling with the global slowdown, China is figuring out ways to exploit it. Squeezed between falling profits and the credit crunch, a growing number of troubled corporations and countries are turning to cash-rich China for a bailout. Momentarily, even Greece considered receiving help from Russia and China in 2010, but it was and is too dependent on transatlantic power structures to have gone ahead with such a dramatic change of policy. China now appears to be in a much stronger bargaining position than it has been in the last few years. Flush with cash at a time when most countries and global corporations are struggling to access capital, China spent nearly US$60 billion in less than a week in February 2009 in a series of deals that will secure a long-term supply of iron ore, copper, zinc and oil. Recently it started buying debt of peripheral Eurozone countries, such as Italy.[45] Brazil signed a deal to supply China with 100,000 to 160,000 barrels of oil a day in exchange for billions of dollars of investment. Under the agreement signed in Brasilia, the state-owned China Development Bank will provide finance to Brazil's state-run energy company Petrobras to develop its oil reserves. In 2008, trade between China and Brazil totalled $36 billion, making China Brazil's second largest trading partner.[46]

The China Development Bank is also lending money to Russian oil companies as part of a loans-for-shares deal. This would oblige Russia to supply 15 million tons of oil a year to China from 2011 to 2030 in exchange for $25 billion in loans to the state-controlled Rosneft oil company and Transneft pipeline operator.[47] In exchange for finance, Russia will provide China with an additional 300,000 barrels of oil a day over 20 years through a dedicated pipeline. Other recent multibillion dollar deals include the purchase by China Petrochemical Corp., the country's second-largest oil producer, of Canada's Tanganyika Oil, which works in Syria, and the bid that China Minmetals has made for OZ Minerals, an Australian zinc producer on the verge of bankruptcy.

The current financial crisis has opened the door to a wider range of takeover possibilities for Chinese state and private companies. So far, Australia has been the country most often targeted by China for strategic investments. It seems cash-rich China has a clear advantage over Western countries in the current worldwide downturn, and will be able to continue to make significant acquisitions and deals at good prices in Africa, Latin America, Russia and beyond thanks to its strong financial balance sheet. It seems likely that China will exploit the current economic crisis in a manner that enables it to emerge as the dominant economic power in the world in the foreseeable future.[48]

A free trade agreement (FTA) between the Association of South East Asian Nations (ASEAN) and China came into effect on January 1, 2010, creating the world's third largest free trade bloc behind the European Union and the North American Free Trade Association (NAFTA). The FTA is a continuation of processes that have been developing over the past decade. Trade with China played a significant role for many ASEAN countries in their recovery from the devastating impact of the 1997–98 Asian financial crisis. Two-way trade between ASEAN and China amounted to US$19.5 billion in 1995, rose to $57.6 billion in 2003 and hit $231 billion in 2008. China has supplanted the United States as ASEAN's third largest trading partner after Japan and the European Union. The combined population of the free trade bloc is 1.9 billion people and its combined GDP is $6 trillion. This is the latest indication that Asian economies are beginning to vote with their feet as the relative decline of US capitalism continues.

ANALYSIS AND INTERPRETATION

In *The Rise and Fall of the Great Powers* (1988), Paul Kennedy shows how economic data provided clear signals about which powers were rising and which ones falling back between 1500 and the 1980s. In his survey, Kennedy detects a pattern repeated over and over: 'Wealth is usually needed to underpin military power, and military power is usually needed to acquire and protect wealth.'

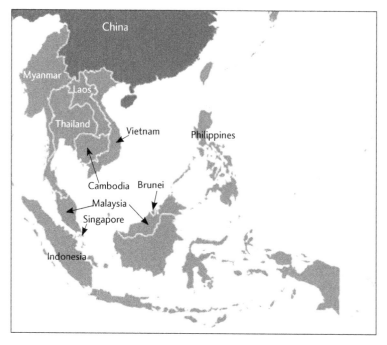

Figure 5.5 China and the Association of Southeast Asian Nations

Source: adapted from the CIA World Factbook.

Kennedy argues that the strength of a great power can only be properly measured relative to other powers, and he argues that great power ascendancy (over the long term or in specific conflicts) correlates strongly with available resources and economic durability. Military over-stretch and a concomitant relative decline is the consistent threat facing powers whose ambitions and security requirements are greater than their resource base can provide for. He argues that military superiority by itself is often deceptive, since it may be weakening a state's ability to compete economically and fund future conflicts. Kennedy demonstrates that while it is true that in the year 1900 Britain stood as the world's greatest power, the writing was already on the wall. The figures for shipbuilding, military spending, amount of coal produced, GDP and other relevant categories clearly showed that Britain was being overtaken by Germany and the United States.[49]

Less sophisticated accounts on the rise of China (or 'the rest of the world') are offered by John Mearsheimer in his *The Tragedy* of *Great Power Politics* (2001) and Fareed Zakaria in *The Post-American World* (2008).[50] According to Mearsheimer, great powers rise and fall as a result of an 'offensive realism' doctrine of a systemic state power maximization, which helps balance the system out at any moment in history, undermining unipolarity and other alliance systems. The 'tragedy of great power' reflects precisely the innate propensity of the global system, which is miraculously pushing all great powers to maximize the power they already possess, causing wars and making ways for other powers to rise. Here, the international system is visualized as a 'society' composed of the sum of its individuals, whereby each state in the political market behaves angrily and on the basis of their own interests, just as an individual does in a bazaar when the seller refuses to lower the price of a commodity. For all these reasons China is bound to be the next hegemon, and in addition, its economic wealth will eventually translate into military might. Zakaria, as all good journalists do, plays with words: 'it would be a mistake', he says, 'to talk of the rise of Asia and China', simply because the United States is not really declining, whereas many other parts of the world are registering fast growth rates. What happens, he explains, is that 'as the rest of the world is growing fast', then the world becomes 'post-American rather than anti-American'. He then tries to pinpoint opportunities for the United States in this new 'post-American world'.

In these analyses, domestic politics, class considerations and other concerns, such as the environment, are wholly absent. The methodological foundations of these and similar arguments are also flawed. Mearsheimer, for example, wanting to recast some 250 years of modern history in order to prove his theoretical point of 'offensive realism' and 'off-shore balancing', cherry picks historical cases that fit his preconceived theoretical scheme.[51] What saves Mearsheimer, and indeed every realist in IR, is the centrality they attribute to the concepts of conflict and competition, albeit for the wrong reasons (the nature of the state to compete with other states for security reasons and so on). But this all is beside the point. No state is a class-free agent, and conflict (the sacred metaphysical principle of realists) and cooperation (the sacred metaphysical principle of liberals) are in the service of social classes. If their interests converge, then there is cooperation; if their interests diverge, then there is conflict. The obvious cannot be elevated into theory. At best, it can be a description. At worst a prescription for the imperial narrative to correct its course.

China is potentially uplifting the whole of Asia, and indeed the

world, as global fault-lines evolve unevenly and discursively across
the world, and in all the economic caucuses that were previously
subordinated by 'sterling-dollar diplomacy', including the Middle
East. (Events in the Middle East will depend on how class power is
exercised after the revolts of 2011–12 across the region.) Moreover,
China's success is conditional upon certain domestic reforms it has
to carry out. These are concerned with the extent to which the
Chinese state addresses the problem of boosting aggregate demand,
taking the country away from its dependence on US and European
consumers. If China eventually moves ahead to implement a policy
of internal demand stimulation, then Mao's insight about an industrial rebalancing of the coastal areas with the interior will come true,
while signalling the death rattle for Western supremacy. But there is
more to the story.

Our global fault-lines argument suggests that China's rise is
contingent upon the way it uses and transforms resource depletion
and environmental degradation to its own long-term advantage.
China could relaunch an industrious revolution, as Arrighi put it,
that will be quite different from the West's industrial revolution,
but it will do so only if it manages to overcome the three vulnerabilities all global powers have been subjected to since the 1970s.
To repeat, these are financialization – examined thoroughly in the
previous chapters focusing on the Anglo-American model – resource
depletion and environmental degradation.

6

RESOURCE DEPLETION AND ENVIRONMENTAL DEGRADATION[1]

As individual capitalists are engaged in production and exchange for the sake of the immediate profit, only the nearest, most immediate results must first be taken into account. As long as the individual manufacturer or merchant sells a manufactured or purchased commodity with the usual coveted profit, he is satisfied and does not concern himself with what afterwards becomes of the commodity and its purchasers. The same thing applies to the natural effects of the same actions. What cared the Spanish planters in Cuba, who burned down forests on the slopes of the mountains and obtained from the ashes sufficient fertiliser for one generation of very highly profitable coffee trees – what cared they that the heavy tropical rainfall afterwards washed away the unprotected upper stratum of the soil, leaving behind only bare rock! In relation to nature, as to society, the present mode of production is predominantly concerned only about the immediate, the most tangible result; and then surprise is expressed that the more remote effects of actions directed to this end turn out to be quite different, are mostly quite the opposite in character; that the harmony of supply and demand is transformed into the very reverse opposite, as shown by the course of each ten years' industrial cycle.

Frederick Engels (1876)

The final and perhaps greatest vulnerabilities of the world system in the first decade of the twenty-first century concern the availability and distribution of critical resources such as oil, food and water, and the ecological crisis.

The very logic of accumulation under the current economic system necessitates that the material elements (resources) of nature

133

are transformed into commodities at an ever-increasing rate. In the long history of human excessiveness in production and consumption, the stability of the economic order, as an unrestrained structure, has been dependent on continued accumulation in a cycle of never-ending expansion. It appears to be so more than ever today. This means that more and more materials from nature must be consumed in the process of production. So the world's most valuable energy supplies and minerals are being extracted and consumed at breakneck speed.

OIL

In the contemporary world, hardly any issue causes more stress, either directly or indirectly, than the exploration, production and consumption of the world's energy resources, and in particular oil. From the war in Iraq to rising food and fuel prices, energy consumption has been a crucial topic. A direct consequence of the consumption of oil is air pollution in the form of sulphur dioxide, nitrous oxides and carbon dioxide, which are a burden on society because of current health issues and future costs related to global warming.

Oil is the most strategic raw material. It can hardly be overstated how crucial petroleum is to our modern industrial society. Virtually every aspect of modern industrial life requires oil, gas and electricity (largely created from these fossil fuels). Modern life depends on petroleum as the main energy source. Every day we rely on fossil fuels in one way or another – to transport us to work, to cook our food, to light, heat, and cool our homes, and even to grow our food. Our lives are so dependent on petroleum that it is impossible to imagine a world without it. There is very little we consume or use in our lives that does not use petroleum in its manufacture.

Oil fuels the economy. It is the largest single traded product in the world. It provides about 95 per cent of all transportation fuels and 40 per cent of global energy. Oil is also a key determinant of national security. Today's modern armies are entirely dependent on oil-powered ships, planes, helicopters and armoured vehicles. Oil also supplies feedstock for thousands of manufactured products and is vital for food manufacturing: 17 per cent of our energy is used for producing food. Modern agriculture makes heavy use of oil in a variety of ways. We use oil for fertilisers, pesticides, and for the packaging and distribution of food.[2]

Since 1900, global trade and a global economy have developed, and the world's population has been enabled to grow in size from

1.65 billion to 6.9 billion by drawing down a massive natural gift of energy in the form of cheap crude oil. Up until early modern times, miners, scientists, natural philosophers and other 'experts' believed that gold, silver and other minerals were vegetable-like in that, when mined, they would literally grow back like mown grass. This belief was not wrong in principle in the case of coal and its hydrocarbon cousins in gaseous and liquid form, because they are the remains of ancient organisms. As a practical maxim, however, it was completely mistaken, because the time it would take normal geological processes to transform organic matter into coal, natural gas and petroleum is of the order of millions of years. Therefore, for all practical purposes, these fuels are finite, nonrenewable energy sources. In any given region there is a fixed amount of oil before exploitation begins, and after every drop of oil taken out there will be that amount of less oil left under the ground. Therefore, it is not a controversial statement to say that oil is in fact in limited supply.

Just as with any fixed nonrenewable resource, the supply of oil is limited, and its consumption will rise, peak (the point beyond which oil production will irreversibly start declining) and decline. Oil production follows a bell curve, and after the production reaches its peak (meaning when half the oil is taken out), oil production will inevitably fall.[3] On the upslope of the curve, there is the first oil, the oil closer to the surface, which is also called 'cheap oil' or 'easy oil', because it is easier and cheaper to take that oil out and also it is better quality (it is 'light', low-sulphur oil, therefore cheaper to refine). On the upslope of the curve, oil production costs are lower than on the down slope, when extra effort (and cost) is needed to extract the remaining poorer-quality oil from deeper in the reservoirs, and extra cost needed to refine this 'heavy oil' (which is high-sulphur, very viscous and does not flow easily). Thus, once oil production reaches its peak, global demand for oil is most likely to exceed the capacity to produce it, prices will rise, and oil-dependent economies will face serious problems.[4] 'An increasing body of evidence suggests that the era of "easy oil" is over and that we have entered a new period of "tough oil"'.[5]

Today, oil and gas experts around the world are increasingly alarmed at the current and future scarcity of the 'black gold'. As demand for energy explodes worldwide, there is less of it available and, it seems, less exploration for it. Crude oil prices have doubled since 2001, and this is not simply the result of speculation on the part of rentier interests. There may still be times when oil prices fall temporarily as a result of a sharp decline in consumer demand in periods of economic crisis, but the general long-term trend is unquestionably upward in the price of crude oil. US refineries are working close to capacity, yet no new refinery has been constructed since 1976. And oil tankers are fully booked, but outdated ships are being decommissioned faster than new ones are being built. In May and June 2011 the West released oil from its strategic reserves in order to ease a price hike, which was only in part the result of financial speculation in oil and gas markets.

According to many estimates, the world is depleting oil reserves at an annual rate of 6 per cent. The United States consumes a quarter of the current global demand. At the same time, growth in demand is rising at an annual rate of 2.2 per cent. All this means that the world's oil industry would have to find the equivalent of more than 8 per cent a year in newly discovered oil reserves to maintain an orderly oil market. Unfortunately, discoveries are lagging behind, primarily because new large oil deposits are not being found, but also because even if they were, there is a considerable time lag between a discovery and turning the oil into a usable energy product. Many observers have drawn attention to the extraordinary technological accomplishments of the industry over the past few decades. Of course, advanced technologies will buy a little more time before production commences to fall, but it is also important to appreciate that spending more money on oil exploration will not really change this situation. There is only so much crude oil in the world, and the industry is estimated to have found about 90 per cent of it.[6]

There are some indications that, in the years to come, the search for new sources of oil may be transformed into a quest for entirely new sources of energy. The replacement of fossil fuels by alternatives such as solar, wind, geothermal, biomass, hydrogen and nuclear fission does not yet seem to be a viable alternative. So far, the available energy alternatives, mostly solar and wind power, offer only diluted energy substitutes, since they not as powerful as fuel sources as oil. For solar and wind energy to come close to providing the same amount of energy as oil currently does would require a truly massive scaling-up in production and deployment of these technologies, and still they would come nowhere near to matching the convenience and density of oil. Therefore, while conservation and renewable energy are much in the news, the reality is that neither of these factors is likely to have any significant impact on the steadily growing demand for oil products.

OIL SCARCITY AND ITS IMPACT

Many analysts, looking at the current discovery and production levels of oil fields around the world suggest that within the next decade, the supply of conventional oil will be unable to keep up with demand. We are also witnessing the impact in the increasing scarcity and cost of food and other critical resources that rely on oil. There are some reports that there has been a surge of motorists running out of fuel because they could not afford to fill their tanks. Airlines are cutting back on flights, and some are beginning to charge extra for checked baggage. During the last couple of years, in some parts of the world, rising fuel prices have led to massive protests and strikes. Many leading economists and oil experts claim that the price of oil generally reflects the fast-rising demand from China and India, and stagnant produc-tion as reserves of accessible oil become less plentiful. According to some experts, even a shortfall between demand and supply of as little as 10–15 per cent would be enough to shatter an oil-dependent economy. There were serious oil-related crises in the 1970s, but these 'oil shocks' were caused by political factors rather than the decreasing amount of oil. Unlike the oil shocks of the 1970s, this time there seems to be a permanent decline. It is becoming clear that cheap fuel is no longer something that we can take for granted. The economy is already suffering because of this. The end of cheap oil indicates a potentially spectacular reshaping of the globalized trade flows that have emerged in the last two decades.[7] Matthew Simmons, a member of Dick Cheney's Energy Task Force, put it as follows:

> Without volume energy we have no sustainable water, we have no sustainable food, we now have no sustainable healthcare. And since five-sixths of the world still barely uses any energy it really is an important issue. And since five-sixths of the world is still growing fast or too fast it's even a more important issue. What peaking does mean, in energy terms, is that once you've peaked, further growth in supply, is over. Peaking is generally, also, a relatively quick transition to a relatively serious decline at least on a basin-by-basin basis. And the issue then, is the world's biggest serious question.[8]

Energy (and food) prices might decline, but this will be only because of the severity of the recession. Recent trends – and as entrepreneurs, among others, are trying to make up the shortfall in their profits by raising market prices – may be inflationary, but these ups and downs in the market should not impede sober assessment. A report by the International Energy Agency (IEA), 2008 World Energy Outlook (WEO), paints a depressing picture of an oil industry having to run faster and faster, like a hamster trapped on a wheel, just to keep pace with burgeoning oil demand over the next 20 years.[9] The first paragraph of the IEA report reads: 'The world's energy system is at a crossroads. Current global trends in energy supply and consumption are patently unsustainable – environmentally, economically, socially.' The report, released in November 2008, estimates that the industry will need to find 64 million barrels per day (bpd) of new oil production capacity to meet the expected growth in demand by 21 million bpd by 2030 and offset 43 million bpd of expected declines from existing fields. The total cost is put at around $5 trillion at today's prices. The study, based on detailed data for the world's 580 largest oilfields and an extrapolation to the remaining 70,000 smaller fields, estimates output from existing and future fields will decline by 6.7–8.6 per cent a year. When the recession finally comes to an end, all of the factors that drove oil to its record high in recent years will once again be exposed, and crude will soar to record highs. In the meantime, however, low oil prices are crippling investment in new capacity, a reality that will lead to much higher prices down the road.[10]

In its report *Global Trends 2025: The National Intelligence Council's 2025 Project*, the National Intelligence Council speculates that:

Countries capable of significantly expanding production will dwindle; oil and gas production will be concentrated in unstable areas .... As a result of this and other factors, the world will be in the midst of a fundamental energy transition away from oil toward natural gas and coal and other alternatives.[11]

This implies that the United States might after all no longer bother with Middle East oil, although there are still a number of powerful incentives for the United States to have a substantial military presence in the region (to deprive China and India of cheap oil, for the defence and security of Israel, to balance out Russian competition and so on).

THE ENVIRONMENT IN CRISIS

The world economy was able to enjoy impressive growth in the twentieth century, largely because it benefited from cheap and abundant oil, and could afford to ignore environmental costs. The severe effects of global environmental damage have now risen to the point that the very survival of the humanity is at stake. This challenges the dark heart of capitalism as a system that by necessity exploits people and the Earth. This has been particularly true during the neoliberal era because its efforts to privatize global economic governance have undermined the limited liberal attempts to achieve improvements in the human condition and environmental sustainability through international institutions.

By far the most controversial feature of environmental damage is potential atmospheric damage: that is, damage to the gaseous membrane that maintains all life on Earth. Especially the combustion products of fossil fuels is the major source of danger to the Earth's atmosphere. The problems arise because some of the key gaseous components of the atmosphere are becoming excessively concentrated, and many experts believe that this situation is dangerously upsetting the delicate balance between the various gaseous components of the Earth's atmosphere.[12] The result is what is by now a clearly documented process of climate change.

Human-induced global warming is only one among many serious environmental consequences caused by the never-ending drive of accumulation under the existing economic system. A quarter of all deaths in the world today have some links to environmental factors.

[T]he environmental crisis we now confront is quantitatively and qualitatively different from anything before, simply because so many people have been inflicting damage on the world's ecosystem during the present century [20th] that the system as a whole – not simply its various parts – may be in danger.[13]

The environmental problems associated with all aspects of production, distribution and consumption trigger crucial questions about the future sustainability of economy and society in the way it is currently organized. Demand for food and energy will jump 50 per cent by 2030 and for fresh water by 30 per cent, as the population tops 8.3 billion. The world population is expected to grow by 1.2 billion over the next 20 years, and all of these people will want food, shelter and energy, further straining the planet's already stretched resources.[14] This is the secret ticking time bomb under the global economic system in the twenty-first century. The only long-term solution is to significantly reduce our energy usage. This does not just mean using energy-efficient light bulbs, taking the bus to work or cycling. In order to reduce our energy consumption, we must consume fewer products. The only rational response to the impending end of the cheap oil age is to redesign all aspects of our lives. Those outside of Europe and the United States will recognize that this trend has been under way for some time now among critical political ecologists, with some of its most serious spokespersons emerging from the developing world.[15]

RESPONSES TO ENVIRONMENTAL CHALLENGES

The central point in environmental sustainability is preserving a balance between human needs and nature's balance. As was pointed out by Karl Marx long ago in introducing the term 'reification', the natural tendency of capitalism is to reduce all human relationships to objectified and quantified values for the marketplace. This universal aspect of capitalism continuously attempts to reduce nature to a set of market values that can be bartered in the capitalist market place. Thus, it is no accident that the present campaign to craft an international agreement regarding climate change, most of which has occurred at the height of neoliberal era and within a globally organized capitalist system, has focused on market mechanisms such as emissions trading. As informed critics have pointed out, none of these market-based proposals hold any real promise of slowing, let alone stopping, global warming.[16]

In reality, since capitalist governments depend on economic growth for the sake of growth for their political legitimacy, they also depend on ready access to and the use of natural resources, which clashes with any serious effort to rein in resource consumption for the sake of ecological sustainability. Unfortunately, capitalist ideology also pervades liberal environmental organizations, making it sometimes difficult to separate out ecologically sustainable choices from those that are economically viable or profitable. This situation is expressed in many of the central ecological debates of our time, such as the challenges of a changing climate. Slowly, a non-market response to the ecological crisis is beginning to form, asking, 'Will climate change enforce global justice? Will capitalism, East and West, North and South, survive the climate crisis?' The work of articulating how democratic and genuine human-centred approaches can offer a meaningful alternative to the capitalist marketplace, exemplified by those in the eco-socialist movement and critical political ecologists, emphasizes that humans have the capacity – outside of the competitive relationships fostered by capitalism – to collaborate for long-term ecological sustainability. In fact, sustainability itself requires something more than mere environmental management: it requires a rethinking of the nature of property as well as the possibilities for collective action.[17]

No doubt, the ultimate argument in favour of meaningful alternatives is that it begins with efforts to ameliorate conflict and achieve a working, non-exploitative consensus. Keynesian liberals claim to want the same ends, yet they do not want to abandon competitive and exploitative capitalism. The contradiction is obvious but the journey from liberalism to real meaningful alternatives must address the basic question: how then do you continue economics? Some radical political economists have attempted an answer through what they term ecologically sustainable 'steady-state' economics, which blends the idea of democratic socialism with a reduction in the material base of society. The biggest challenge to this approach has been a residual attachment to the idea, held by both capitalists and state socialists, that growth is essential to the political legitimacy of any economic system. However, this resistance is also the result of something of a Eurocentric 'modernist' approach, which is losing currency among ordinary people and has always been questioned by many traditional and industrious societies.[18]

CONCLUSION

To articulate the past historically does not mean to recognize it 'the way it really was' (Ranke). It means to seize hold of a memory as it flashes up at a moment of danger. Historical materialism wishes to retain that image of the past which unexpectedly appears to man singled out by history at a moment of danger. The danger affects both the content of the tradition and its receivers. The same threat hangs over both: that of becoming a tool of the ruling classes. In every era the attempt must be made anew to wrest tradition away from a conformism that is about to overpower it. The Messiah comes not only as the redeemer; he comes as the subduer of Antichrist. Only that historian will have the gift of fanning the spark of hope in the past who is firmly convinced that *even the dead* will not be safe from the enemy if he wins. And this enemy has not ceased to be victorious.

Walter Benjamin, *Theses on the Philosophy of History* (1939)

SUMMING UP THE ARGUMENT

This book has argued that the international political economy (IPE) of the US empire has been in a continuous decline since the late 1960s, and that its new policies of globalization/financialization and neoliberalism – what we have labelled as 'financial statecraft I (1971–91) and II (1991–2011)' – have failed to arrest this decline. In the 1960s and 1970s the sterling–dollar bloc was outcompeted by Japan and West Germany; in the 1990s and 2000s by China and other emerging political economies. At the roots of this problem stands the tendency of the rate of profit to fall,[1] resulting in the outsourcing of manufacturing and labour-power, as well as the migration from industry to '*haute finance*'. Thus, as we have shown, financialization and neoliberalism are great vulnerabilities, especially in the context of US and UK financial systems and political economies: they have proved to have little contact with the real economy and development, let alone green development and growth.

Apparently, Western capitalism has found no empirical/political ways to escape its structural crises of over-accumulation, theoretically analysed by Marx in *Capital*. Further, as we have maintained, US neo-imperialism, via its 'shock therapy' East European policy, failed to appropriate enough international value from the collapsing socialist markets to restore its profitability and industrial might. What we have called 'the internationalization of the US Treasury' proved to be a way of making easy money in global currency markets and paper asset speculation, rather than laying the ground for solid growth in the former socialist economies and the United States proper.

As the industrial might of the United States and the United Kingdom had already been undermined by the German and Japanese caucuses, and as the responses the stagflation of the 1970s were financialization and neoliberalism, the fall of the USSR and its client states brought about no substantial benefits to the Anglo-Americans. Power had already begun to shift, creating new fault-lines in the global system. Because of these shifts, the US-centred global system has encountered repeated and more severe crises, making the system ever more dependent on short-term speculation and financial manipulation (extreme financialization), which in turn led to an increased dependence on debt, especially consumer debt, and speculative bubbles (what Robert Brenner calls 'asset price Keynesianism') to generate the level of quick profits necessary for the system to continue.

Mainstream international relations (IR), whether of realist, constructivist or liberal stock, has spectacularly failed to address these issues. But Marxisant and critical scholars did not. Even when Marxist scholars – such as Leo Panitch and Ray Kiely – argue that contemporary US neo-imperial relations (financialization and neoliberalism) strengthen rather than weaken the state executives of Western capitalisms, the fact remains that their analyses fare much better than mainstream discourse on the crisis. For a crucial expression of the systemic crisis of capitalism is the observable reality of an increasingly predator state, whose main disciplinarian functions – policing, surveillance, violence – become all the more visible in suppressing the working masses. The most striking example of the ruthlessness of the new police-cum-predator state in Europe is observed today in the countries of the periphery (Greece, Italy, Portugal, Spain), which face enormous debt problems that undermine the very existence of the euro as a monetary project with the ambition to become a global reserve currency. If, for example,

Greece defaults on its debt obligations, the entire euro structure will come under question.

The world economy witnessed a number of crises in the period from the 1970s onwards, most of them being signal crises, in the sense that they were signalling something much more significant and deeper than their immediate reasons and consequences (high inflation, fiscal crisis of the state, stagnation, endemic unemployment and so on). With the recent bursting of the housing bubble, what we are observing now is the terminal crisis of the US financial centrality and industrial hegemony. We say this without suggesting or insinuating that the United States might not bounce back, albeit temporarily, via the initiation of wars and/or a descend to chaos, as Arrighi has outlined in his later writings as a possible future scenario. But however it takes shape, this imperial transition will be arduous, painful and protracted.

Our work has analysed in depth the current financial crisis and how it has trickled down to the real economy, becoming a global systemic crisis. This crisis has shown how fragile are the foundations of the US system of power, a fragility that mainstream IR theory has spectacularly failed (and fails) to see and address: without any major confrontation by an organized labour movement, the system collapsed like a pack of cards. But beyond that, this crisis has shown how the constantly shifting tectonic plates of historical and social development – what we have termed here global fault-lines – can generate massive movements drawing new fault-lines in the geographies of the global political economy, time and space. Because the real systemic/structural reasons for the present crisis are not the technical aspects of financialization, but the reasons why financialization was and is promoted (that is, the declining role and dynamism of the US economy in the face of the strong challenge from the emerging economic giants), simple technical (financial/monetary) measures cannot solve the problem. Saskia Sassen has already pointed this out dramatically. At the root of the problems is a long-term fall and failure to recover the rate of profit, and the outsourcing of employment and industrial investment to the global East. Indeed, there is no real solution because what we are witnessing is the declining vitality of the advanced economies (the United States, Western Europe and Japan), and a massive shift of economic power and activities to the East, in the real Gunder Frankian sense.

One of the successes of US vice president Joe Biden's visit to China in August 2011 was the announcement by Coca-Cola of a further $4 billion investment in 2012, topping its 16 plants already there. Apple, the world's largest corporation by market capitalization, outstripping even Exxon Mobil, followed suit.[2] In the long run, this works in favour of China: it accentuates industrial outsourcing and the transfer of know-how from the West to the East, while uplifting purchasing power of Chinese and Asian consumers, especially if China opts to stimulate growth via a democratic and progressive management of aggregate demand, something that is no more than a dim prospect for the United States. It is in this sense that we have argued that the most important developments over the last two to three decades have not been the collapse of the USSR or 9/11. Rather, the key variable affecting long-term trends in the international system has been the transition of China and Russia to capitalism and free trade. The theoretical notion of 'uneven and combined development' explains this very well, without the need to resort to the concept of 'global fault-lines'. Our argument, however, has been that *global fault-lines* is more heuristic and all-encompassing than the notion of *combined and uneven development*, which in addition suffers from a certain Eurocentrism.

PROSPECTS FOR THE FUTURE

We have argued that financialization is not the only vulnerability of the United States, a declining power: it is also a vulnerability of all rising powers, not least because they are capitalist powers. Yet this is not the only vulnerability of the international system. Finite oil and the looming ecological crisis are equally serious problems that humanity is facing. After contracting during the initial stages of the present crisis, energy consumption has resumed its typical pattern of growth. The global revival will need cheap energy, produced in greater quantities than before. The reliance on hydrocarbons, however, will probably decline markedly, simply because the amount of remaining oil resources will not be sufficient. Therefore, it is to be expected that under the impact of the crisis there might be greater emphasis on the development of alternative fuels, and eventually some major breakthroughs in this area.

However it remains very likely that the current crisis will rebalance world economic growth further away from the United States and United Kingdom towards the emerging economies of Asia and elsewhere, especially China and India. The depth and severity of the current crisis is likely to lead to major changes in global political economy, and these will result in a major geopolitical shift. It is clear to us that the direction of 'globalization' has already changed, assuming a truly global dimension, although the dangers of the disintegration of the Atlantic economies – consider, for example, the plight of the Eurozone and the de facto Greek default – may lead to new types of authoritarianism and protectionism.[3]

The world today resembles the uncertainty and the vengeance of the 1930s or even the 1900s. A likely outcome of the crisis will be a severely declining role for the US dollar and the euro (as the world's reserve currencies) in the international financial and trade system. But, as we have seen in this book, there were similar uncertainties in the inter-war period, and at that time they led to authoritarianism and racism. One possibility is that the dollar will be replaced by a basket of the world's main currencies. Because of the protracted recession and stagnation and the relative strength of the banking sector of the Asian states, it is quite possible that the emerging economies will increasingly shape the future of global finance just as they are already shaping the direction of global trade.

Another, very disturbing, possibility is that states will adopt protectionism and mercantilism under dictatorial rule. This is very likely to be the case should the Eurozone economies collapse. Whatever the case, the crisis is destined to bring about fundamental changes in the global economic, political, social and ideational structures of capitalism. The world will be different when the carnage stops.

In order to develop further, the world economy needs qualitative changes in the direction of an environmentally friendly socialist project. Because of the severe constraints imposed by resource depletion and environmental problems, there are limits to the narrow pursuit of profit maximization. Yet at no other time in the last 50 years have those limits seemed more flexible. Global fault-lines do not work only in favour of imperial forces, shifting the boundaries of capitalist hegemony from one imperial power to another; they also work in favour of socialism and green politics, emancipating new radical forces and social subjects demanding social power and ecologically sustainable development. After Edward Bernstein, Donald Sassoon has reminded us that socialism has always been the permanent shadow of capitalism.[4]

We are writing this being fully conscientious what it means to want to predict events: it is always impossible to do so with any certainty. Yet there is no reason to expect that the current crisis that began in 2007 will end quickly. There is no quick way out of this crisis, and the political classes in charge are incapable of addressing its causes. It is not yet easy to predict the true extent of

US hegemonic decline. It is more likely that what we are witnessing will prove to be the start of a long slump lasting many years rather than a quick and sustainable recovery. The last systemic crisis of the world economy in the 1930s lasted about a decade and a half. Given the power that the US economy still can amass with a GDP of nearly $15 trillion, as well as its sheer military superiority over all its rivals taken alone or in combination, the hegemonic transition, as this book has argued, will be very long and extremely painful.

Our intention is not to anticipate events; rather, we want to highlight trends. Predictions about complex and dynamic structures, such as the global political economy, are always risky. From this perspective, the task of scholarship remains unaltered since Marx: 'to discover the rational kernel within the mystical shell'. This is what we have tried to do here, taking as a starting point the current financial-cum-political economy crisis and the various interpretations of it. Thus, as we pointed out in the Introduction, we have reinterpreted the past in the light of the event – the financial crisis and its consequences. Only in this global historical sense it is possible to glimpse the future: as an extension of these long-term trends and shifts occurring beneath the 'mystical' and smooth skin of social and economic phenomena. Let us consider one such phenomenon.

Soon after the downgrade by Standard & Poor's of the US debt in August 2011, US vice president Joe Biden, flew to Beijing. In a major speech he gave at Sichuan University on August 21, 2011, Biden said among other things that the United States has a major interest in protecting China's investment in US debt. (China holds some $1.16 trillion of US debt.) He added, 'The US has never defaulted, and never will.'[5] This statement, and obviously the visit itself, revealed the increasing economic weakness of the United States and the ineffective monetary method by which it is trying to balance its bilateral deficit with China. There has been long-term pressure on the Chinese authorities to substantially revalue the yuan, making US exports more competitive, but they have continued to procrastinate. Desperate in the face of this intransigence, the United States began to print more dollars (a process now known as quantitative easing) in order, among other objectives, to devalue the dollar, inflate the global economy and force a revaluation of the yuan, making Chinese exports more expensive. This is a desperate measure that will not work and the United States knows that very well. But 'selling protection' and flexing muscles works better than diplomacy and efforts towards the consensual achievement of policy objectives.

In the same speech, Biden underscored that the United States has been and will always be a Pacific power, and claimed that this fact actually benefited China as it allowed her to 'focus on domestic development' and growth. This echoes Arrighi's prophetic comment in his 'Postscript to the second edition of *The Long Twentieth Century*' (March 21, 2009), that the United States and its European allies could attempt to use their military superiority to extract a 'protection payment' from the emerging caucuses of East Asia. (In essence, the argument is that China should continue to buy US debt in exchange for the protection offered to it by US power in the Pacific rim.) But there is more to the affair than meets the eye. Knowing that China is completely dependent on oil, gas and other hydrocarbons for its industrial expansion, the United States attempts, at times successfully, to shut out China from Middle Eastern, North African and Central Asian producers. For instance, China has been left out of the Libyan oil market – as we are writing this, the NATO coalition is installing a client regime which is annulling all the Chinese investments that were made under Gaddafi's rule. Meanwhile US naval power is daily challenging China's presence in the South and East China Seas, especially in the Malacca Straits. Thus at almost every level of the US–China relationship we see both tension or conflict and the economic cooperation that is necessary due to their mutual interdependence and the US' decline. Yet the picture is broader.

The world economic landscape is changing rapidly, and a very different world is emerging. It is perhaps too early to tell whether the United States and its European allies on the one hand, and the new emerging economic superpowers of China, India, Brazil and Russia on the other, will head down the path to geopolitical rivalry, but the warning signs are certainly present. The rise of China and other large emerging powers, and their resulting competition with the declining US hegemon, will have geopolitical consequences. In the near future, the United States and the emerging powers are likely to engage in more intense competition over global trade and finance. A more assertive and dynamic China and a less competitive US economy make it likely that trade disputes will become more politicized.

We have argued in this book that the current protracted and severe financial-cum-economic crisis has not come out of the blue. It is the outcome of deep-seated contradictions within the asymmetrical social and political/ideational structures of the global economic system. It is not a 'failure' of the system, but it is central to the mode of functioning of the system itself. It is not the result of 'mistakes' or 'deviations', but rather it is inherent to the disintegrative logics of the capitalist system. The current crisis is only one aspect of a larger multidimensional set of simultaneous and interacting crises on a global scale. This is a discussion of shifting tectonic plates in the world economy, longer-term movements together with some more sudden and unexpected eruptions. At this moment of acute systemic crisis, great shifts are taking place in the balance of economic hegemony among the global powers. New fault-lines can be discerned in the global system. Just like the movements of the tectonic plates that originate in the Earth's radioactive, solid iron inner core, the vast shifts in the structures of the global political/economic system are the outcome of changes that have been taking place beneath the surface of economic life over years, if not decades.

What does this crisis mean for the global imperial system? Is this the end of the capitalist organization of the world economy? A downturn, or a crisis, does not necessarily mean that the current system comes to a halt. There is nothing to suggest that the present crisis is paving the way for the collapse of the capitalist system. It signifies the opening of a new epoch in history, in which some of the old structures give way and new forms may develop to radically affect the global structures of power and imperialism. However, if the current pattern of global imbalances and vulnerabilities persists, so will recurrent financial and economic crises of the kind we have seen recently. And the more the crises persist, the more the power will be shifting to the global East, increasing the chances of new imperial wars, but also of new socialist and green alternatives. Seen in broader historical terms, this crisis is only one of a string of crises that have all had the same effect of further concentrating economic and political power in the hands of capitalists, who invariably have used past crises as an opportunity to adapt the basic capitalist institutions so they can be used to generate new ways to profit. Historically, the rising economic success of the emerging economies and the slowing down in the core economies of the developed world are generating an entirely new state of affairs in the twenty-first century. As a result, the first decade of the new millennium raised a fundamental question: will the United States adapt and recapture its leadership in the world system, albeit temporarily, or will it follow late-nineteenth-century Great Britain into a long and painful economic/political/military decline until it is eventually bailed out or bought out by its former vassals?

Whatever the future developments will bring, one thing is perfectly clear to us: as it transpires that the imperial order is shifting from the

West to the East, the world today is too complicated for any single power to dominate it. The United States is likely to continue trying to maintain its supremacy by relying on diminishing assets and desperate financial and neoliberal policies to patch up its deficiencies and structural problems. Hegemonic powers come and then eventually go, but the whole process of growth and decline is lengthy and painful, and it will be even more painful than previously, we argue, in the case of the United States. History demonstrates that all global powers experience a long period of growth, followed by an equally long period of contraction. At this latter stage, they tend to become progressively more aggressive and unstable: the wounded animal is the most dangerous of all.

British imperial hegemony was already in decline by the end of the nineteenth century, but it still remained an important military and economic power to be reckoned with. US power has been in decline since the late 1960s, essentially because it lost some economic power in relation to others who have gained significant influence. This has been particularly obvious over the last 20 years. The fact, however, remains that the United States is still by far the most powerful country in a military/political sense, and will continue to be so for some years to come. From its globe-girdling military bases and its world-circling spy satellites, the United States keeps an eye on everything; it is everywhere and ready to intervene always. Equipped with advanced precision-guided munitions, high-performance aircraft and intercontinental-range missiles, the US armed forces can unquestionably deliver death and destruction to any target on Earth and expect little in the way of retaliation.[6] Yet 'US reliance on this, the … only remaining, strategy of military political blackmail can also lead the US to [economic] bankruptcy as the failing dollar pillar fails to support it as well'.[7] The 'American Century' is ending, if it ever existed, and clinging to it as an icon is both unnecessary and dangerous: confrontation in the name of empire only encourages conflict. Bill Bonner and Addison Wiggin had a different way of putting it: 'A great empire is to the world of geo-politics what a great bubble is to the world of economics. It is attractive at the outset but a catastrophe eventually. We know of no exceptions.'[8]

The future, as ever, is open to all kind of choices and agential strategies, and crises such as this should be seen as incubators for new choices for all social classes and political subjects. But these choices must be articulated. We need more than just a critical assessment of the capitalist system as it is. It is necessary to spell out a vision of an alternative future that is at once more efficient, more humane and more ecologically sustainable. A socialist alternative, as a relatively new way of organizing societies, must account for its past failures by addressing the problems of management and concentrations of power that plagued and eventually undermined COMECON and the Soviet system. In its pure form, its most powerful weapon is that it begins by assuming that society is an inclusive social compact that builds structures around the human needs of the many, rather than the profits and privileges of the few. It would also have the potential to deal meaningfully with the world environmental crisis, because it relies on neither the growth imperative, nor the externalization of the costs of pollution that is practised by capitalism. But as we have tried to explain here, that task must begin by carefully examining the present structures, inherent trends and fault-lines of the global economy, and how they have been, and continue to be, reshaped by historical change. We must be vigilant because as Walter Benjamin insinuates, capitalism in all of the authoritarian forms it can take has not ceased to be victorious.

NOTES

1 GLOBAL FAULT-LINES

1   See Kenneth Waltz's classic *Man, the State and War* (1954).
2   See Vassilis K. Fouskas and Bülent Gökay, *The New American Imperialism: Bush's War on Terror and Blood for Oil* (2005, ch. 2).
3   Among others, see Peter Gowan (1999b, pp. 19 ff.).
4   On this issue, see Fouskas and Gökay (2005, ch. 1).
5   Gardner (1956).
6   One of the first works in the 1990s to remind us of this, was Paul Hirst and Grahame Thompson's *Globalisation in Question* (1996). Hirst and Thompson argued that by comparison with the period 1870–1914, the post-Cold War world was much less globalized, especially economically, and that the trend was towards regionalization rather than globalization. They also saw, quite correctly, that globalization is a state-driven policy, and not a spontaneous market process.
7   Important in this respect is the work by Costas Lapavitsas, who leads the RMF (Research on Money and Finance) team at SOAS in London; see Lapavitsas (2010). This type of interpenetration of international finance dominated by Anglo-American venture capital created the impression among US mainstream liberal political economists and IR experts that the post-Bretton Woods world was becoming increasingly interdependent and cooperative; see, among others, the works by Joseph Nye and Robert Keohane that began appearing in the 1970s.
8   We argue that 'open door' is a structural/historical feature of US imperial policy since the development of the frontier thesis in the 1880s and 1890s, according to which the expansion of democracy and the free market economics of the US social system abroad is consubstantial with security and prosperity for all involved in that internationalized sociopolitical system, including political security and economic prosperity for the United States itself. The classic work on the 'open door' is Williams (1959). Many authors have since adopted Williams' perspective, including such contemporary scholars as Andrew Bacevich (e.g. 2002) and Christopher Layne (2006). Ray Kiely argues that 'open door' is a conjunctural rather than a structural/permanent feature of US expansionism. Our disagreement with Kiely is laid out in our review of his important work *Rethinking Imperialism* (2010), in *Political*

Quarterly (Fouskas, 2012). We argue that 'open door' is a structural feature of US grand strategy because, among other reasons, it reflects the structural needs of US capitalism to either stave off crises of over-accumulation or manipulate foreign monetary regimes for domestic purposes of consumption and international projection of power.

9   Hilferding (1981).

10 The literature on these issues is very extensive; see, among others, Allen and Gale (2001) and Champonnois (2006).

11 In his analysis of the credit crunch (2009), the late Peter Gowan wrote that it would be a mistake to locate the financial crisis in the 'real economy', as it is indeed the 'financial structure-cum-agents that has been the driving force behind the present crisis'. In his text, Gowan qualifies further his analyses of the dollar–Wall Street regime (DWSR) which he developed ten years earlier in *The Global Gamble* (1999b).

12 At a Johnson Controls plant in Michigan in April 2011, Obama gave a major speech trying to regenerate industrial activity in the United States – in this particular case the industry that makes lithium-ion batteries for electric cars. But as we show in Chapter 2, the US car industry is already being outcompeted by its global rivals; see Thaler (2011, p. 11).

13 Gowan (2008, p. 354).

14 The inability of the United States to set itself on a path for growth via boosting demand is outlined by Robert Reich, professor of public policy at the University of California (2011, p. 13). Lawrence Summer, who led Obama's National Economic Council until late 2010, noted that between 2006 and 2011, US economic growth averaged less than 1 per cent a year, similar to that of Japan 'in the period its bubble burst' (*Washington Post*, June 13, 2011).

15 See Spiegel and Blitz (2011, pp. 1, 7). For our analysis of the Libyan crisis and an explanation why France took the lead in it, see Fouskas (2011).

16 *China Times*, June 21, 2011.

17 Neoliberalism refers to a renewed form of an ideology that goes back to the late eighteenth and nineteenth centuries, long before 'liberal' meant 'progressive'. The classic expression of the liberal ideology of the time is Adam Smith's 1776 book *The Wealth of Nations*. The core idea there is an insistence on the separation of the political sphere from the economic sphere. An autonomous economic sphere is envisioned in which the market is supreme. The market is conceived as made up of individual actors who freely engage in exchanges based on self-interest. Whether buyer or seller, each seeks to maximize their individual gain, and enters into contractual agreements only if it is perceived to be to one's own advantage. The market is then the mechanism for summing up individual goods, producing the maximum good for the greatest number. This utilitarian calculus is performed through the invisible hand of the market, as Smith put it. There is no common good, there is only the sum of individual goods (DuRand, nd).

18 Among others, Parthasarathy (2011, pp. 21–2).

19 On the concept of 'uneven and combined development', see the most recent and theoretically important contributions by Justin Rosenberg and Alex Callinicos in their exchange of letters in *Cambridge Review of International Affairs*, 21(1), March 2008, pp. 77–112. See also Van Der Linden (2007). The concept was first used by Trotsky, and later further elaborated by Ernest Mandel and George Novack.

20 In this respect, the contributions by Giovanni Arrighi, Michel Aglietta and others – reviewed below – are of paramount significance.

21 For the concept of US neo-imperialism, see our previous joint work (Fouskas and Gökay, 2005), especially the Conclusion.

22 A similar position is developed by Michel Aglietta (2008).

23 There has been no international order in history that is not at the same time an imperial order: that is, an order dominated by imperial powers. We prefer the term 'imperial order', as we believe it depicts historical reality more accurately.

24 These views were expressed, among others, by columnists of the *Financial Times, Wall Street Journal, Wall Street Journal Europe, The Economist, The Times Magazine* and other mainstream media and online sources and during the period stretching from summer 2007 to the time of writing. One of the few notable exceptions to this chorus was Martin Wolf of the *Financial Times*.

25 The manipulation of interest rates by Paul Volcker, head of the American Fed from the late 1970s to 1987, is typical of a policy aiming at smashing working-class power. This process, on which we dwell later, is well examined in Panitch and Gindin (2005).

26 Marazzi (nd, p. 48).

27 Keynes (1936, p. 159). Similar conclusions can be drawn from the works of Hyman Minsky, Michal Kallecki and Joseph Schumpeter.

28 Important and influential economists, such as James Crotty, Paul Krugman and Joseph Stiglitz, adopt this perspective. See in particular the articles in the special issue of *Cambridge Journal of Economics* on the financial crisis (no. 33, 2009), especially Crotty's contribution, who deals with the crisis as if it was caused by what he calls 'New Financial Architecture'. See also Krugman (2008).

29 In *Capital*, Marx defines the relation M–M' as representing a sum of money lent out at interest to obtain more money, or one currency or financial claim traded for another. The relation C–M–C' represents a commodity sold for money and buying another, different commodity with an equal or higher value, whereas the relation M–C–M' means money used to buy a commodity which is resold to obtain a larger sum of money.

30 See among others Sassen (2008).

31 Pettifor (2008).

32 In this respect, it is interesting to read an interview with Madoff in the *Financial Times* (Madoff, 2011).

33 See in particular Harvey (2010).
34 What is currently in vogue is the so-called theory of 'imbalances'. This interpretation sees that large imbalances in the 'real economy' or the 'financial sector', or both, are bound to disrupt the functioning of economic systems. Interestingly, this approach ends up proposing a rather neo-Kautskian framework of more globalized institutional regulation, beyond the 'nation-state'. See especially the papers presented to the conference 'Lessons from the Euro-zone Crisis', UCL, University of London, London June 2, 2011 (speakers included Edmond Alphandery, Giles Merritt, Yiannos Papantoniou, Wendy Carlin and Sir John Gieve).
35 This is the case with Niall Ferguson. Although he sees aspects of economic decline of the United States in his *The Ascent of Money* (2009a) and elsewhere (e.g. Ferguson, 2005), he has lately revived some outdated Leninist arguments about the merging of state and finance, identifying monopoly capitalism as the cause of the malaise. The way out then, for Ferguson, is an economy freed from the fetters of the state (see Ferguson, 2009b).
36 Gramsci (1996, p. 79).
37 See Gowan (2007).
38 See his *Decline of the Dollar: A Marxist view of the monetary crisis* (1972) and his important essay 'Where is America going?' in *New Left Review* (1969). Robert Gilpin began raising the same type of issues in the early 1970s.
39 See Poulantzas (1978a, p. 55, *passim*).
40 Busch (1978), especially Table 57, in which Busch presents the share in industrial production of the United States, Japan, France, Italy, Great Britain and West Germany, as well as their share in exports. His analyses that follow this table argue for a relative hegemonic decline of the United States after 1971.
41 Albo, Gindin and Panitch (2010, p. 22).
42 Albo, Gindin and Panitch (2010, pp. 34–5).
43 All these three points become even clearer in a book Panitch co-edited with Martijn Konings, *American Empire and the Political Economy of Global Finance* (2008). Ray Kiely adopts a similar position, especially with regard to the robustness of US capitalism and its central position in international political economy – see Kiely (2010, esp. ch. 9). An alert group of Greek Marxist scholars working around the quarterly *Thesseis* and under the influence of Poulantzas' and Louis Althusser's works, adopts a similar position; see Lapatsioras et al. (2009).
44 See Nahusch and Wackermann (2009). Many analysts, especially in Germany and Austria, follow this approach, at times blended with a Minskyan analysis (Minsky was Schumpeter's student).
45 Kautski's thesis of 'ultra-imperialism' suggests that all great powers, due to the inherent tendency of capital to concentration, would agree to form a global cartel to rule the world together, rather fighting each other in dividing it. Lenin and Bukharin vehemently rejected this idea.

46 Among others, see Foster and Magdoff (2009, pp. 16–18 ff.)
47 Foster and Magdoff (2009, p. 54, *passim*).
48 We are referring to the key works by Michel Aglietta, *A Theory of Capitalist Regulation: The US experience* (2000; first published in France in 1976), especially Chapter 5, and Alain Lipietz, 'Behind the crisis: the exhaustion of a regime of accumulation' (1986).
49 Poulantzas (1976, pp. 19–55) (1976 is the date it first appeared in French).
50 Moseley (1991). Moseley argued that the fall in the rate of profit in the United States is linked to a pronounced shift from productive to unproductive labour (in the retailing sector, various services and so on), hence he saw deindustrialization as the key variable in explaining the policy shift to financialization.
51 We believe that Brenner is extremely influenced by the work of Philip Armstrong, Andrew Glyn and John Harrison, *Capitalism since World War II* (1984), in which a perceptive and coherent argument about profitability and the over-accumulation crisis is made throughout, covering all the post-war years up to the late 1970s. Brenner's key essay in relation to the current crisis is the Preface to the Spanish translation of his *The Economics of Global Turbulence*, published by Akal in May 2009 with the title 'What is good for Goldman Sachs is good for America: The origins of the current crisis'. This essay builds on his two major works, *The Boom and the Bubble: The US in the world economy* (2003a) and *The Economics of Global Turbulence* (2006). We will treat all these texts as an integrated whole.
52 Brenner (2009, p. 2).
53 Brenner (2003a, pp.14–15).
54 Brenner (2003a, pp. 54–61, *passim*, and 2006, pp. 162–3, 190–2, 206–7). Brenner has been criticized by orthodox Marxists on grounds of not paying particular attention to the antagonism between capital and labour, thereby misusing the Marxist theory of value. Apparently Arrighi developed such an argument too, although he did not insist so much on it as he recognized that in reality capital can outflank competition from labour, yet cannot outflank competition coming from other capitals. For an orthodox critique of Brenner, see especially the contribution by Murray E. G. Smith (2010, esp. ch. 3).
55 Among others, Garrett (2010).
56 Brenner (2006, p. 325).
57 See also his 'Towards the precipice' (Brenner, 2003b) and the Preface to Brenner (2006).
58 Brenner (2006, p. xxvi).
59 For an account of how Wallerstein uses Kondratieff waves to explain the current crisis, see his 'Dynamics of (unresolved) crisis' (2009) as well as his contributions to *New Left Review* and elsewhere. Wallerstein, however, used Kondratieff waves all along to periodize capitalist development and crises – see, for example, 'The global

possibilities, 1990–2025' (Wallerstein, 1996). With regard to Arrighi, we are referring to his *The Long Twentieth Century* (Arrighi, 1994), *Chaos and Governance in the Modern World System* (Arrighi and Silver, 1999) and *Adam Smith in Beijing* (Arrighi, 2007). Interestingly, the last volume of the trilogy is dedicated to Andre Gunder Frank (1929–2005), whose latest insights in his late work, *ReOrient* (1998a), have rather been overlooked by contemporary scholarship. On Arrighi's scepticism about using Kondratieff waves in his analyses, see his Introduction to Arrighi (1994).

60 Arrighi (2007, pp. 120 ff.).

61 Arrighi (2007, p. 132).

62 See especially Arrighi (1994, pp. 231–300).

63 Arrighi (2007, p. 134).

64 Arrighi (2007, p. 139).

65 See http://data.worldbank.org/indicator/NV.IND.MANF.ZS

66 Value added is the net output of a sector after adding up all outputs and subtracting intermediate inputs. It is calculated without making deductions for depreciation of fabricated assets or depletion and degradation of natural resources. See the section with the technical notes of UN statistics division: www.unido.org/fileadmin/user_media/Services/Research_and_Statistics/Technical_notes.pdf

67 Brenner (2003a, p. 68).

68 Arrighi (2007,p. 142).

69 Brenner (2003a, p. 67).

70 See, for instance, the contribution by Gobal Balakrishnan and his notion of the 'stationary state' in 'Speculation on the stationary state' (2009) and 'The convolution of capitalism' (2011).

71 Balakrishnan (2011, p. 216).

72 See Kliman (2007, 2009). Kliman observes that the rate of profit continued to fall in the 1981–2004 period to an average 14.2 per cent. This is mainly because debt cannot be used to 'grow the economy' faster than is warranted by the underlying flow of new value generated in production.

73 Aglietta (2008).

74 Arrighi and Beverly Silver (1999) and Arrighi (1994).

75 We are referring to his 'Postscript to the second edition of *The Long Twentieth Century*' (2009) and Arrighi and Silver (2011).

76 We do not wish to relaunch here the old, but always relevant, discussion about the definition of capitalism in history. For the unaware, we would like to recall an old debate between Wallerstein and Frank, on the one hand, and Ernesto Laclau on the other, which dwells precisely on this issue – see, Brewer (1980, chs 8, 9, 10).

77 Exceptionally relevant here is the pioneering work by Ronan Palan on offshore business (2002).

78 Important in this respect is the work by Robert Wade; see, among others, Wade and Veneroso (1998).

79 See Gowan (1999). Robert Wade added the IMF into the equation, yet the IMF *is* effectively the US Treasury.

80 Hobsbawm (1995, p. 87).

81 One of the most erudite and rather unknown attempts at theorizing Kondratieff waves through a theory of conjuncture is the work of the young Soviet economist Pavel Maksakovsky, *The Capitalist Cycle: An essay on the Marxist theory of the cycle* (2009). Maksakovsky's premature death in 1928 at the age of 28 prevented him from seeing his work published by the Communist Academy and the Institute of Red Professors in 1929.

82 Benno Teschke, in *The Myth of 1648* (2003), criticizes Arrighi precisely on this point. Quite rightly, Teschke blames Arrighi, for example, for the fact that he considers Holland an hegemonic global power in the eighteenth century, whereas in fact she was just a global player (see especially pp.133–6). But if this is the case, then how we can generalize a 'theory' of cyclical hegemonic transitions comparing, *mutatis mutandis*, Genoa or Holland with the United States today?

83 See Fouskas and Gökay (2005).

84 In *The Long Twentieth Century* (1994) and elsewhere, Arrighi outlines three possible future scenarios. The first is that the United States and its European allies use their military power to extract a 'protection payment' from the new emerging centres of Asia, a scenario that would lead to the formation of a truly global empire, the first ever in history. The second possibility is that East Asian centres and China – the centrality of China becomes clear in *Adam Smith in Beijing* (Arrighi, 2007) – assume global leadership, albeit not in a manner that mirrors the US imperium and indeed the entire Western system of dominance over the last 500 years. And the third scenario is endless worldwide chaos.

85 In 'Postscript to the second edition of *The Long Twentieth Century*' (2009).

86 This is explained superbly in the work of Robert Wade and Peter Gowan. See, for instance, Gowan (1999, esp. pp. 92–3).

2 FROM BRETTON WOODS TO THE ABYSS OF GLOBALIZATION

1 Quoted in Williams (1959, p. 29).

2 Williams (1959, p. 30).

3 Quoted in Arrighi (1994, p. 241).

4 Hudson (2003, p. 2).

5 Hudson analyses well the link between German reparations and inter-ally war debts (2003, pp. 47 ff). In *The Economic Consequences of the Peace* (1995), Keynes explains why the 'war guild' clause of the Treaty of Versailles makes no sense and that the terms of the Treaty are very harsh on Germany which, after all, won the war in the East – a point

made in A. J. P. Taylor's work too. More to the point, he explains why with such harsh terms the recovery of Germany would be impossible, pushing her to adopt a revisionist position in European politics to undo the Treaty of Versailles. Overall, Keynes argued that Europe's recovery is impossible if the industrial power of Germany is curtailed, as the French mostly wanted.

6   Quoted in Arrighi (1994, p. 271).

7   Among others, Eichengreen (2008, pp. 43 ff.). See also his *Exorbitant Privilege: The Rise and Fall of the Dollar and the Future of the International Monetary System* (2011). Eichengreen sees the Suez crisis of 1956 as the landmark event undermining once and for all the importance of British sterling.

8   US pressure on European powers to allow it to participate in Middle Eastern oil ventures, especially over Baku and Mosul, were immense during the San Remo conference in Italy in April 1920; see Kent (1993).

9   For this periodization see, among others, Cesarano (2006, pp. 43 ff.).

10   Eichengreen (2008, p. 45).

11   Polanyi (2001, p. 26) (first published in 1944).

12   Kindleberger's argument is in *The World in Depression, 1919–1939* (1986, first published in 1973). The quote is from Hobsbawm (1995, p.100). Kindleberger argues that the Great Slump was mainly caused because of the absence of a central system-wide stabilizer to act, among others but above all else, as a lender of last resort. This point of view resulted in the so-called 'hegemonic stability theory', which became very dear to mainstream IR theorists from the 1970s onwards. This 'theory' suggests that the system achieves equilibrium only if there is a central hegemon in it.

13   Hudson (2003, p. 65).

14   Irwin (2011).

15   Hobsbawm (1995, p. 100).

16   Among others, Beasley (1987). Beasley's work, written from a non Marxisant perspective, is especially relevant as it highlights the differences between Western and Japanese imperialism, a theme that we meet again in Arrighi's *Adam Smith in Beijing* (2007).

17   Among others, Eichengreen (2008, esp. ch. 4) and Cesarano (2006, esp. ch. 5). In a similar vein are works by Gilpin, Krasner, Keohane, Nye and others, most of whom have links with the Council on Foreign Relations and the mainstream publication *Foreign Affairs*.

18   Gardner (1956).

19   This point is fully grasped, among others, by Arrighi (1994, pp.278 ff.), Kiely (2010, pp. 101 ff.), as well as Leo Panitch, Peter Gowan and other Marxisants.

20   Hudson (2003, pp.123–4).

21   The objections of the Soviet Union were quite understandable. In the beginning, they objected to the veto power of the United States and the right of the IMF to fix the exchange rate of the ruble. Finally, they did

not sign the Treaty as they refused to disclose economic data by joining a US-dominated international institution; see van Dormael (1978).

22 Eichengreen (2008, p. 94).

23 Schild (1993, esp. pp. 220 ff.). See also the very useful account by Arman van Dormael (1978).

24 Hudson (2003, pp.138, 143).

25 Mandel (1975, p. 463).

26 Hudson (2003, p. 148).

27 Aldcroft (1993, p. 118), Killick (1997, esp. pp. 14–64), Hogan (1997, pp. 1–87), Milward (1984, pp. 1–167).

28 See, among others, Van Der Vee (1986, esp. the table on p. 30), Armstrong, Glyn and Harrison (1984) and Marglin and Schor (1990).

29 Hobsbawm (1995, p. 258).

30 As we pointed out in Chapter 1 drawing from Marx's own work, the rate of profit is the relationship between surplus value and the sum-total of constant and variable capital involved in the production of this surplus value. In other words, the rate of profit is the percentage return on capital employed. As Armstrong, Glyn and Harrison note, 'a constant profit share maintains a constant profit rate only if the ratio of output to capital remains constant. This ratio in turn depends on the relative rate of growth of capital employed and of output produced' (1984, p. 171). See also Brenner (2006).

31 Glyn et al. (1990, pp. 69–70).

32 Van Der Vee (1986, p. 197).

33 Okumura Shigetsugu, quoted in Ikeda (1996, pp. 47 ff).

34 Ikeda (1996, p. 51).

35 Hobsbawm (1995, p. 263).

36 See, among others, Brenner (2006, pp. 70, 82).

37 Glyn et al. (1990, p. 42); Brenner (2006).

38 This development, it should be noted, led the communist parties of the West at the time, with the exception of the Italian Communist Party (PCI), to put forth the theory of 'state-monopoly capitalism', whereby the private and the state-bourgeois capital merged in an inseparable whole and yet this phase was preparing the road to socialism. This theory was severely criticized by Nicos Poulantzas, especially in his *Classes in Contemporary Capitalism* (1978a).

39 Hobsbawm (1995, p. 262).

40 Armstrong et al. (1984, pp. 174 ff.).

41 Armstrong et al. (1984). Brenner adopts the same thesis: the fall in profitability is not related to wages but lies in the inability of manufacturers to fully realize (reify) their investments as a result of the increased downward pressure on prices that resulted from competition; see, among others, Brenner (2006, p. 108, *passim*).

42 Holloway (1996, p. 15). This edited volume contains useful analyses on the crisis of Keynesianism, but most of the contributors reduce developments since 1971 to the contradiction between capital and labour. In

our view – and although we gained a lot by studying their work – this leads to a relative failure on the part of the contributors to grasp the global and asymmetrical complexity of US-centred international finance and dollarization post-1971.

43 Linhart (1976).

44 See Gramsci (1971, pp. 279–318). The Italian movement of 'operaismo' in the 1960s, including the left-wing faction of the Italian Communist Party under Pietro Ingrao and the group of 'Il Manifesto' (Luigi Pintor, Lucio Magri, Rossana Rosanda, Luciana Castellina and others), produced excellent critical essays on the functions of Taylorism/Fordism, as well as on Marxist theoretical traditions; see among others Tronti (1971). Key texts by Raniero Panzieri, Antonio Negri and many others can also be found in *Quanterni Rossi* and *Quanterni Piacentini*, two important journals almost unknown in the English-speaking world. For an overview in English placing these themes in theoretical and historical context, see Toscano (2009) and Fouskas (1998).

45 Galbraith (1967).

46 Keynes (1936, p. 378).

47 Keynes (1936, p.159).

48 See Fouskas and Gökay (2005, esp. ch. 2).

49 For a courageous attempt to relaunch the concept see the latest contribution to the debate by John Hobson, *The Euro-centric Conception of World Politics; Western International Theory 1760–2010* (2012).

50 Armstrong et al. (1984, p. 219), and Brenner (2006, pp. 39 ff.).

51 Armstrong et al. (1984, p. 220).

52 Hobsbawm (1995, p. 452).

53 Brenner (2006, p. 101).

54 Armstrong et al. (1984, p. 219).

55 Donald Sassoon details the revival of working class militancy in eleven West European countries by counting the working days lost per 100,000 non-agricultural workers; see *One Hundred Years of Socialism* (1996, pp. 357 ff.).

56 Mandel (1972, pp. 39–40). Panitch and Gindin identify Charles P. Kindleberger (1981) as the first economist pointing this out (2005, note 21).

57 On this, see in particular Robert Gilpin's disapproving comments in his *The Political Economy of International Relations* (1987, pp. 348 ff., *passim*). For Gilpin this very fact constituted the main reason for the collapse of the Bretton Woods system.

58 Quoted in Paul Volcker and Toyoo Gyohten (1992, p. 81 ff.).

59 Eichengreen (2008, pp.113–14).

60 This Gaullist strategy, it should be noted, did not come out of the blue. It was in the footsteps of previous French governments at least since the First World War, which favoured a strategy of gold accumulation; see Cesarano (2006, p. 51, *passim*).

61 Eichengreen and Kenen (1994, p. 34).

62 In metric units, the numbers are as follows: at the end of 1953 the United States still had 20,000 metric tonnes (mt) of gold and continental Europe 4.840 mt of gold, but in 1967, the last full year of dollar–gold parity, Europe's stock jumped to 18.640 mt, whereas the US stock was down to 10.722 mt.
63 The best comparative work on this, tackling the issue before 1973, is by James O'Connor, *The Fiscal Crisis of the State* (1973).
64 Gilpin (1987, p. 344).
65 We follow Armstrong et al. (1984, pp. 225 ff.).
66 Armstrong et al. (1984).
67 Unemployment rates in Western Europe and Japan between 1950 and 1969 averaged less than 2 per cent; see Van Der Vee (1986, p. 76) and Sassoon (1996, p.450, Table 16.2) (Sassoon's data are drawn from Maddison, 1982).

3 THE FAILURE OF FINANCIAL STATECRAFT (1), 1971–91

1 Steil and Litan (2006).
2 Conveniently and typically, Benn Steil and Robert E. Litan distinguish between 'microeconomic' and 'macroeconomic' financial statecraft. The former looks at specific financial institutions, the latter at cross-border capital flows. However, neither of the two analytical dimensions examined in their work tackles the role of the state in deregulation, as well as the long-term negative impact of this role on economic growth and employment.
3 Mandel (1969). For an opposite contemporary view, see Poulantzas (1974, pp. 53, *passim*). As we saw earlier, Leo Panitch, Sam Gindin and others around the journal *Socialist Register* build their arguments on Poulantzas's analyses, arguing against the decline of the US empire-state today.
4 This is a thesis Mandel repeats in all his subsequent work, such as *Late Capitalism* (1972/1975), as well as *The Long Waves of Capitalist Development* (1980).
5 See in particular Brenner (2006, pp. 208 ff.).
6 'Valorization' is the way in which capital, via the process of its reification in the commodity market, sustains and increases the surplus value created during the process of production. It is thus distinguished from the process of extraction of surplus value, which takes place in the sphere of production alone.
7 Mandel (1975, pp. 464–5).
8 Mandel (1975, p. 466).
9 Between 1950 and 1970, total employment rose in line with population growth. Industrial workers grew faster than total employment. As Glyn and colleagues argued (Armstrong et al., 1984, pp. 236 ff.), 'while civilian employment in the ACCs rose by 46 million, the number of self-employed

and "family workers" fell by 20 million. In 1954, 31% of those officially classified as in work were in this category. By 1973 the proportion had fallen to 17%.'

10 It should be noted that this business strategy was not new at all. In fact, it was precisely this unfettered function of the Anglo-American markets the led to the collapse of the credit system in the late 1920s, an event rehearsed in 2007–08; see, among others, Andrew Glyn's *Capitalism Unleashed: Finance, Globalisation, and Welfare* (2007), a work also indispensable for understanding the evolution of 'rentier capitalism' since the 1970s; and Robert Kuttner, 'Testimony before the Committee on Financial Services' (2007). Kuttner looks at the 'alarming parallels', as he calls them, between 1929 and 2007.

11 Poulantzas (1974, p.114, *passim*). We discuss their contribution to the debate below. We should point out that it is no accident that Peter Gowan, in his attempt to propose a 'public-utility model' for banks in Anglo-American capitalism, brings up examples from German, Japanese and Chinese banking systems, all of which are operating and steered by the state; see his 'Crisis in the heartland' (2009). Herein also lies our disagreement with an important Marxist contribution to the discussion on the financial crisis of 2007–9, written for *Radical Notes* – see Lapatsioras et al. (2009).

12 Other national capitalist formations can be brought into context too. See, for example Salvati (1981).

13 It is interesting to note that some authors, working on various types of measurements of the profit rate, show that the falling tendency of the rate of profit was not confined to the United States alone, but it extended to other G-7 countries too; see in particular Dumenil and Levy (2001).

14 From Mandel and Poulantzas (particularly in his last theoretical statement, *State, Power, Socialism*, 1978b) to Arrighi, Panitch, Van Der Pijl, Brenner, Harvey, Rosenberg, Callinicos and Gowan, there seems to be a solid agreement on this very point in neo-Marxist and Marxisant discourses. Constructivists, such as Alexander Wendt, have a very flippant definition of the state, whereas realists, such as Gilpin, typically defined the state as a political unit separate from economic and social relations.

15 Gowa (1983).

16 The Johnson administration had started Strategic Arms Limitation Talks (SALT) but had given them very low priority. Nixon and Kissinger were, in effect, starting them anew. The SALT I agreement was finally signed in 1972, freezing the deployment of intercontinental ballistic missiles (ICBM). As is well known, the SALT agreements, in practice, came to naught because the United States disagreed on a number of issues. The advent of Reagan in office in 1981 destroyed the entire SALT structure.

17 See their *The Global Political Economy of Israel* (Nitzan and Bichler, 2002, pp.24–7, 202, 268–73, *passim*).

18 Under Volcker, all three series of interest rates rose: the Federal funds rate, the one-year Treasury bill rate and the ten-year Treasury bond rate. See, among others, Goodfriend and King (2004) and Panitch and Gindin (2005).

19 Some of the issues we tackle here are well presented in Salvatore et al. (2003). The same thesis is also proposed by Joseph Stiglitz (2002, p. 239).

20 As well as Panitch's and Kiely's works quoted and discussed above, see also Seabrook (2001).

21 See Fouskas and Gökay (2005, ch. 1); also 'An agenda for the next American President' (Fouskas and Gökay, 2008) , pp. 100–1.

22 See Spiro (1999).

23 Gowan (1999, pp. 20–21 ff.).

24 Eichengreen (2008, p. 151). The Werner Report, in vain, tried to articulate a response to the declining dollar and the Smithsonian agreements, which tripled the width of fluctuation bands against the dollar, 'allowing intra-European exchange rates to vary by as much as 9%' (ibid.). The Europeans sought to restrict this by half, creating the so-called 'snake'.

25 See, among others, Gilpin (1987, pp. 140–1).

26 Eichengreen and Kenen (1994, p. 46).

27 In their effort to undermine US open door imperialism certain state elites of the global South (led for example by Peron in Argentina and Vargas in Brazil) attempted to implement a populist type of socialism by way of boosting domestic industries and markets. The Greek socialists in the 1980s under Andreas Papandreou had also attempted, unsuccessfully though, to resort to such a strategy.

28 See in particular, Moran (1990) and Tolchin and Tolchin (1992).

29 Nitzan and Bichler (2002, p. 25).

30 Nitzan and Bichler (2002, p. 261, fn 26).

31 See Lasswell (1997). We have deployed this concept to explain the state of affairs in Cyprus since 1959–60 – see Fouskas and Tackie (2009).

32 Apart from our work on this point, see also the perceptive comments by Chalmers Johnson (2004, pp. 142–4). Bondsteel was named after Army Staff Sergeant James L. Bondsteel, a Medal of Honour winner in Vietnam. In fact, Bondsteel is the largest and most expensive base the United States built since the Vietnam war. Kellogg Brown & Root continues to be involved in the maintenance costs of the base.

33 We do not wish here to give the impression that the war between NATO and Yugoslavia in 1999 was because of US energy and military economic interests in the Balkans. This is certainly one factor but, as we have explained elsewhere, US objectives in the region included, significantly, matters regarding European security and the assertion of US primacy in Europe via NATO's eastward enlargement. The United States simply could not allow Serbia, a client state of Russia, to be in its underbelly as a hostile force, at a moment when NATO and the United

States were incorporating Hungary, Poland and the Czech Republic into their security policy.

34 Gökay (2005).

35 Frank (1999).

36 In 1982, OPEC adopted the 'quota system' to limit its oil supplies and thereby keep oil prices from falling below certain levels. Under this system, each OPEC country is allocated a specific quota for oil production. This did not prevent the 1986 oil price collapse, however, because most OPEC countries did not respect their quotas. See Gökay (2006b).

37 The dominance of the dollar is not simply the result of the size of the US economy; it is also the result of two other things, politics and finance. See Gökay and Whitman (2004, p. 65).

38 Spiro (1999, p. 121).

39 See William Greider's detailed account of the 1979–83 crisis, which he identifies as the beginning of a rapid accumulation of petrodollars in US banks: *Secrets of the Temple: How the Federal Reserve Runs the Country* (1989).

40 Kaiser and Ottaway (2002).

41 For a detailed discussion of this see Black (2005).

42 We draw from OECD (1991), Maddison (1982; 1991, pp.140–2, *passim*), and IBRD (1992, Table 2, p. 220 (for Middle East, Latin America and Caribbean)).

4 THE FAILURE OF FINANCIAL STATECRAFT (2), 1991–2011

1 Hay (2002).

2 Wendt (1987). Wendt's comprehensive constructivist account is *Social Theory of International Politics* (1999).

3 See the English translation of this classic and extremely important work by Rodney Livingstone for Merlin Press (Lukács 1971).

4 See Fouskas and Gökay (2005), especially Chapter 2.

5 Alex Callinicos and Ray Kiley embrace such a problematic perspective – see Callinicos (2009) and Kiely (2010), and our review of these works in the *Political Quarterly* (Fouskas, 2011, 2012). Callinicos adopts a periodization of imperialism into 'classical' (1870–1945), 'superpower' (1945–1991) and 'imperialism after the Cold War' (pp.137 ff.). Kiely's periodization of imperialism goes as follows: the 'pre-1830s' period experienced a mercantile type of imperialism; then there is the period of 'free trade imperialism' (1840s–1870s), followed by a period of 'classical imperialism' (1880s–1945), which is associated with new geopolitical rivalries among core states; then there is 'Cold War imperialism' between the two superpowers (1945–91); and then there is another ten-year period of imperialism which Kiely identifies as 'intensification of neo-liberal international order' (1991–2001); finally, from 9/11 onwards in which 'liberal

humanitarian interventions intensify'. We think that this periodization is highly problematic and even misleading, although this should not detract from the overall scholarly value of both works from which we benefited enormously.

6   Kennedy (1988, p. 534).
7   Gökay and Whitman (2010).
8   Todd (2003).
9   See e.g. Samuel Huntington, *The Clash of Civilizations and the Remaking of World Order* (1996), which offers a US-centred view of international relations; Zbigniew Brzezinski, *The Grand Chessboard: American Primacy and its Geo-strategic Imperatives* (1997), which is organized around residual views of a bipolar world, and Joseph Stiglitz, *Making Globalization Work* (2007), which argues that US and European public policy can successfully manage the global political economy.
10 Among others Helleiner (1994).
11 Eurocentric thinking attributes to the West an almost providential sense of historical destiny, manifested in its continuous advances in science, technology, industrialism, rationality and economic institutions from time immemorial. It takes European experience as universal and envisions the world from a single privileged point that is Europe. The world is thus bifurcated into 'the West' and 'the Rest', and a system of knowledge is constructed around a series of binary hierarchies with Europe invariably occupying the higher position: Western nation, non-Western tribe; Western religion, non-Western superstition; Western capitalism, non-Western petty commodity production; Western technology, non-Western craftsmanship; Western progress, non-Western stagnation, so on and so forth; see Guang (2002). This view has been expressed by both Marxist and non-Marxist scholars; see, for instance, Brenner (1977) and Landes (1998). The larger global context is simply not discussed on the assumption that it was unimportant as compared to European developments. Andre Gunder Frank and other critical thinkers call this 'tunnel history' derived from a tunnel vision, which sees only 'exceptional' intra-European causes and consequences and is blind to all extra-European contributions to modern European and world history (Frank, 1998b).
12 Harvey (2005, p. 154); Li (2004).
13 See www.worldbank.org/depweb/beyond/beyondco/beg_04.pdf; Bello (2009b).
14 See Brenner (2006, p.7, fig. 0.3 and pp. 198 ff.).
15 Brenner (2006, pp. 206–7).
16 Kotz (2007).
17 Brenner (2006, p. 213).
18 Brenner (2006, p. 215).
19 Bloomberg and Schumer (2007).
20 On this, see the perceptive comments by Arrighi (2007, pp. 171 ff.) and Brenner (2009).

21 See Fouskas and Gökay (2005, pp.59–60), with the findings of Arrighi, (2007) and Hudson (2003).

22 We are referring to disposable income after taxes being paid; see Board of Governors of the Federal Reserve System, Fourth Quarter 2005 (March 2006), www.federalreserve.gov/releases/Z1/Current/

23 Foster and Magdoff (2009, p. 46).

24 Hayek (1960), and Friedman (1962), and also his very significant policy article, 'The role of monetary policy' (1968). For a perceptive critique see Chomsky and McChesney (2007).

25 See e.g. Pauly (1994).

26 For the Gramm–Leach–Bliley Act, see http://banking.senate.gov/conf/. 'Casino capitalism' was a term coined by Susan Strange in the mid-1980s to describe the unbridled speculation that was developing in the wake of neoliberal economics and financialization (Strange, 1986).

27 Jim Jubak's Journal, January 18, 2008, 'The next banking crisis on the way', MSN Money, http://articles.moneycentral.msn.com/Investing/JubaksJournal/TheNextBankingCrisisOnTheWay.aspx. A seasoned investment advisor, Jubak observed that 'the more investors who bought in [to speculative investments such as credit default swaps], the more of these new products Wall Street could sell and the more money it was willing to lend to home builders, home mortgage lenders and credit card companies; to the savings and loans and banks that created the raw materials (mortgages, credit card debt, auto loans) that Wall Street needed to manufacture its products; and to the hedge funds and structured investment vehicles that bought what Wall Street produced …. It worked out just fine until reality stuck a pin in the bubble.'

28 China, for instance, is especially vulnerable to local government debt, as local governments have borrowed heavily to invest in property and infrastructure. Some estimates put this debt as high as 40–50 per cent of the country's GDP: see, Editorial, 'China's mountain debt', World Socialist Web Site (WSWS), July 12, 2011.

29 Chernow (2001).

30 Barth, Brumbaugh and Wilcox (2000).

31 The yin and yang of these crisis displacement strategies can be clearly seen in William Greider's (1989) account of the struggle between neoliberal monetarism and liberal regulation during the extended inflation-deflation crisis of 1979–83.

32 On this issue, see the perceptive article by Iraj Hashi, 'The disintegration of Yugoslavia: regional disparities and the nationalities question' (1992).

33 Woodward (1995, pp. 15, 380).

34 See Gowan (1999).

35 From our work with the Editorial team of the Journal of Balkan and Near Eastern Studies, we would distinguish the contributions by Jovo Ateljevic and Jelena Budak, 'Corruption and public procurement: example from Croatia' (2010), and other articles by Ateljevic on the issue of

corruption. We should also mention here Schierup (1999), especially the contributions by Vesna Bojičič and Branka Likič-Brborič.

36 See in particular Attali (1997). From 1981 to 1991 Attali was special adviser to François Mitterrand.
37 There are further comments on this issue in Fouskas (2003, ch. 3).
38 Sachs quoted in Gowan (1995a, p. 5) (the same text is also in Gowan, 1999b, ch. 9).
39 See e.g. Gowan (1995a).
40 Glenny (2008). Glenny argued that global transnational crime, and not just East European, may account as much as 20 per cent of world GDP.
41 Gowan (1995a, p. 83).
42 Bello (2009b).
43 Bello (2009a).
44 Foster (2006).
45 Gowan (2009, p. 15).
46 Pressley (2008).
47 From 2000 to 2005, the rise in after-tax income was barely one third of the rise in home prices.
48 The complexity of shadow banking is well analysed by Pozsar et al. (2010).
49 Hoogvelt (2010, p. 57) (in a special issue edited by Barry Gills).
50 Dicken (2007, pp. 379–409).
51 The Editors, 'Working class households and the burden of debt', *Monthly Review*, 50(1), May 2000, http://monthlyreview.org/500editr. htm; Foster (2006)
52 'The true extent of Britain's debt', *Spectator,* December 10, 2008, http:// www.spectator.co.uk/coffeehouse/3078296/the-true-extent-of-britains-debt.thtml (accessed in January 2009).
53 Dowling (2007), Tabb (2008).
54 Tabb (2008).
55 See, e.g. Crotty and Epstein (2008). The authors in this case argue that the elimination in 1999 of the 1930s Glass–Steagall legislation, which segregated commercial and investment banking, was the culmination of two decades of radical deregulation that created what is often called the 'New Financial Architecture' (NFA).
56 See especially Strange's *Casino Capitalism* (1986) and also her *Mad Money: When Markets Outgrow Governments* (1998).
57 See Greider (1989). In his account of home loan practices in the high interest era of the early 1980s, Greider notes that adjustable rate mortgages (ARMs) were developed to accommodate low-income borrowers and increase home sales, with these ARMs shifting risk from the lenders to the borrowers, much as did the subprime loans of the 2000s (1989, p. 589).
58 In the case of petro-dollar lending, developing countries were treated in much the same way, with loans offered at very high interest rates that were made not to support development, but to profitably recycle

petro-dollars (see e.g. Greider, 1989, p. 435). In the second case, as the term 'subprime' suggests, loans were offered at below market rates of interest to home buyers who could not otherwise qualify for a loan, with the loans to reset to market rates after an initial loan period, usually three to five years depending on the loan terms. Also, many if not most of these loans were made with little or no down payment, instead of the 5 per cent or 10 per cent usually required in standard home mortgages, with down payments effectively folded back into the original loan together with closing costs and fees, leading to loans that exceeded the stated price of the house.

59 Gittelsohn (2009).

60 Cooper (1981).

61 The shift of power away from the United States is clearly visible in many spheres, from the growing call to replace the US dollar with a 'more stable currency' (see e.g. Stiglitz, 2009), to a renewed political independence among its one-time allies, such as Japan (see e.g. Dickie, 2009).

62 As William Greider observed, 'In this pivotal instance [when the Federal Reserve raised interest rates in 1984 to choke off a nascent economic recovery], as it had done so often in its history, the central bank was deciding to defend wealth and let workers take the loss. The financial side of capitalism would be protected from risk, even excessively enhanced. Enterprise in the productive economy would be restrained, even injured' (1989, p. 620).

63 US Federal Deposit Insurance Corporation, October 8, 2009, http://www2.fdic.gov/idasp/KeyStatistics.asp?tdate=10/8/2009&pDate=10/7/2009

64 The US Federal Reserve is only marginally a public institution in that appointments to its Board are made by the President and confirmed by Congress. However, in practice the Board works closely with the 12 regional Federal Reserve Banks, all of which are managed by private bankers for the purpose of serving banking interests. See, US Federal Reserve, http://www.federalreserve.gov/aboutthefed/default.htm, and Greider (1989).

65 The Federal Reserve influences economic activity not only by adjusting interest rates, but also by making money available to member banks through its Discount Window. However, to maintain membership in the Federal Reserve system, banks have to maintain ready access to a specified amount of capital, which is intended to act as a cushion against withdrawals. The Federal Reserve varies the amount required, known as 'reserves', according to what the Fed believes prudent, which it often increases in times of financial crisis to allay fears about bank solvency.

66 All data from Eurostat as given by BBC's useful graph: www.bbc.co.uk/news/business-13361934

67 www.bankofengland.co.uk/publications/quarterlybulletin/public99.pdf

68 Adungo (2011).
69 www.telegraph.co.uk/news/newstopics/spending-review/8079232/
    Spending-Review-2010-750000-public-sector-workers-could-lose-their-
    jobs.html, 22 Oct 2010.
70 www.direct.gov.uk/prod_consum_dg/groups/dg_digitalassets/@dg/@en/
    documents/digitalasset/dg_186415.pdf
71 www.statcan.gc.ca/pub/11-010-x/2011003/part-partie3-eng.htm,
    March 2011
72 www.instituteforgovernment.org.uk/pdfs/Canada's_deficit.pdf(accessed
    August 2011).
73 BBC News, March 21, 2002, http://news.bbc.co.uk/1/hi/business/187
    1493.stm
74 BBC News, June 30, 2010, www.bbc.co.uk/news/10457352. (accessed
    August 2011).
75 CBI press release, May 9, 2011, www.cbi.org.uk/ndbs/press.nsf/0363c1
    f07c6ca12a8025671c00381cc7/0a60682f7ed3e0c580257887004b930
    d?OpenDocument (accessed August 2011).

5   THE POWER SHIFT TO THE GLOBAL EAST

1   In an article published in *New Left Review*, Hung Ho-fung (2009)
    argues that the Chinese export-led classes concentrated in the coastal
    areas are basically working in the service of US imperialism, provid-
    ing cheap exports, while using hard-earned savings to finance the
    US purchases of those exports via acquisition of US debt. This, we
    argue, is mapping out the degree of interdependence between Chinese/
    Southeast Asian and US political economies, not the aggregate dyna-
    mism of both economic constellations – China/Southeast Asia on the
    one hand, and the United States on the other. This interdependence,
    we argue, works to the advantage of China as it can fall back to a
    domestic pro-growth policy of high wages and alternative currency
    adoption, abandoning the fetter of the US debt at any time and at
    any pace. The methodological perspective of Hung – a rigorous class
    analysis – which is reflecting, in many respects, Mao's worries in the
    beginning of China's industrialization after the Second World War,
    misrepresents the overall dynamics of Asian (rising) and Western
    (declining) economies.
2   The actual quote attributed to Napoleon was in 1803 (before he became
    emperor). He is said to have pointed to a map of China and said: 'Ici
    repose un géant endormi, laissez le dormir, car quand il s'éveillera, il
    étonnera le monde' – 'here lies a sleeping giant (lion in other versions), let
    him sleep, for when he wakes up, he will shock the world': *Asia Times*,
    November 7, 2009, www.atimes.com/atimes/China/KK07Ad01.html
3   Frank (1998a).
4   Kastner (2008, p. 786).

5   China is the world's most populous country, with about 1.32 billion people, according to 2007 figures.

6   Quoted in Klare (2008, p. 67).

7   *China Daily*, September 30, 2007, www.chinadaily.com.cn/china/2007-09/30/content_6148252.htm

8   'Report: US power will fade By 2025. National Intelligence Council predicts scarce resources, loose nukes, a rising China', CBS News, November 20, 2008, www.cbsnews.com/stories/2008/11/20/world/main4622166.shtml

9   National Intelligence Council (2008).

10 China Country Analysis Brief, August 2005, Energy Information Administration, US Government, www.eia.doe.gov/emeu/cabs/china.html.

11 Quite useful here are the essays in Shambaugh (2005).

12 'Oil price not to restrain China, India growth', www.chinadaily.com.cn/english/doc/2005-09/01/content_474283.htm; 'China, India are highest-growth economies', www.chinadaily.com.cn/english/doc/2006-01/25/content_515525.htm

13 'A New World Economy. The balance of power will shift to the East as China and India evolve', *Business Week Online*, August 22, 2005, www.businessweek.com/magazine/content/05_34/b3948401.htm.

14 Dicken (2007, p. 320).

15 'India, China to hold joint military exercises', *China Daily*, May 29, 2007, www.chinadaily.com.cn/china/2007-05/29/content_882845.htm

16 In 'Facing unemployment, China's biggest challenge during the global crisis', *ChinaNewswires*, February 17, 2009, www.chinaknowledge.com/Newswires/CA.aspx?id=208

17 Bagley (2006).

18 Bhattacharya (2008).

19 Kaplinsky (nd).

20 Lewis (2009). REEs or rare earth metals are a collection of 17 chemical elements in the periodic table. REEs are incorporated into many modern technological devices, including superconductors, miniaturized magnets, electronic polishers, refining catalysts and hybrid car components. The use of REEs in modern technology has increased dramatically over the past years.

21 Lague (2006).

22 *China Daily*, September 1, 2004, www.chinadaily.com.cn/en/doc/2004-01/09/content_296976.htm; Oster (2006).

23 Developing Telecoms, October 13, 2008, www.developingtelecoms.com/content/view/1481/100/

24 'It's getting hotter in the East', *Business Week Online*, August 22, 2005, www.businessweek.com/magazine/content/05_34/b3948456.htm

25 National Intelligence Council (2008, p. 27).

26 Dicken (2007, p. 43).

27 Prestowitz (2005).

28 Frank (1994).
29 Cody (2007); World Bank, 'World Development Indicators 2006 (2004 data)', at devdata.worldbank.org/wdi2006/contents/Table1_1.htm; CIA (2006).
30 Dicken (2007, p. 32).
31 *Financial Times*, May 23, 2011, www.ft.com/cms/s/0/b0366ce4-829a-11e0-8c49-00144feabdc0.html#axzz1Ucw4oGxb
32 Council on Foreign Relations, 'Making room for Brazil's growing clout', July 12, 2011, www.cfr.org/brazil/making-room-brazils-growing-clout/p25461
33 BBC World Service, www.bbc.co.uk/worldservice/sci_tech/features/essentialguide/theme_pol.shtml
34 PricewaterhouseCoopers UK (2011 p. 8).
35 www.carnegieendowment.org/files/World_Order_in_2050.pdf (accessed August 2011).
36 *Financial Times*, 'The new Seven Sisters: oil and gas giants dwarf western rivals', FT.com, March 11, 2007, www.ft.com/cms/s/2/471ae1b8-d001-11db-94cb-000b5df10621.html
37 'There are likely to be notable shifts in relative growth rates within the E7, driven by demographic trends. In particular, both China and Russia are expected to experience significant declines in their working age populations over the next 40 years. In contrast, countries like India, Indonesia, Brazil, Turkey and Mexico (being relatively younger) should on average show higher positive growth over the next 40 years', the PwC report says (PricewaterhouseCoopers UK, 2011, p. 24).
38 Gökay (2006a), Dicken (2007, pp. 225–8, 282–5, 313–15).
39 Kennedy (2009).
40 China's banking sector is controlled by the so-called 'Big Four' (China Construction Bank Corp., Industrial and Commercial Bank of China, Bank of China Ltd, Agricultural Bank of China).
41 Chinese banks have recently cemented their position as the most highly valued financial institutions, taking four of the top five slots in a ranking of banks' share prices as a multiple of their book values. China Merchants Bank, China Citic, ICBC and China Construction Bank lead the table, followed by Itaú Unibanco of Brazil, all with a price-to-book multiple of more than three. (*Financial Times*, January 10, 2010, www.ft.com/cms/s/0/1c13f7f2-fe16-11de-9340-00144feab49a.html?nclick_check=1).
42 http://video.ft.com/v/664780463001/Gold-standard
43 Keidel (2008).
44 Altman (2009).
45 BBC News, September 13, 2011.
46 Simpkins (2009).
47 Hoffman (2009).
48 Ford (2009), Navarro (2009).
49 Kennedy (1988, pp. 17, 29). Despite the fact that the rise and relative

decline of the United States is not the same as that of other European empires, Kennedy's account is important as it highlights the importance of economic structures in understanding the decline of empires in history.

50   Mearsheimer (2001), Zakaria (2008). See also his 'The rise of China won't be peaceful at all' (2005) and 'Imperial by design' (2010). Other mainstream intellectuals and practitioners, such as Richard Haas, Zbigniew Brzezinski, Joseph Nye, Robert Keohane, John Ikenberry and Barry Buzan, have periodically expressed concerns about the viability of the US empire-state and proposed solutions that could arrest its long-term decline. We reviewed their works in *Political Quarterly* from 2003 to 2010, and the reader can find out views about their approach there. Briefly, we would like to point out that eventually these approaches, coming from liberal, constructivist and institutionalist schools of thought in IR, are intellectual symptoms of the structural crisis of the United States, whose disintegrative tendencies are impossible to arrest. See in particular our review of Barry Buzan's *The United States and the Great Powers: World politics in the twenty-first century* (Fouskas, 2005).

51   For a critical review of this historically problematic work, see Gowan (2002) now also in Gowan (2010).

6   RESOURCE DEPLETION AND ENVIRONMENTAL DEGRADATION

1   The ideas contained in this chapter are drawn from Bülent Gökay, 'How oil fuels world politics', in Gökay (2006, pp. 3–10); and Gökay and Whitman (2009, pp.31–7).

2   'How does oil influence world politics?', *BBC News*, September 6, 2002, http://news.bbc.co.uk/1/hi/talking_point/2221917.stm

3   See M. King Hubbert's original 1956 prediction of world petroleum production rates: http://en.wikipedia.org/wiki/Hubbert_peak_theory

4   'IEA report & peak oil', *Energy Bulletin*, November 16, 2008, www.energybulletin.net/node/47229

5   Klare (2008, p.13).

6   Klare (2008, pp. 33–6, 39–40). For details of oil reserves by region, see BP (2003).

7   Roberts (2004).

8   Simmons (2003).

9   The report forecasted that the price of oil will soon exceed $100 again, which it did.

10   Kemp (2008).

11   National Intelligence Council (2008, p. 27).

12   Dicken (2007, pp. 27–8).

13   Kennedy (1993, p. 96).

14   McGourty (2009).

15 See e.g. Nandy (1987), Agarwal and Narain (1990) and Escobar (1997).
16 Among others, Foster (2002).
17 See e.g. Dolsak, Ostrom and MaCay (2003).
18 See e.g. Daly and Farley (2003).

CONCLUSION

1   The tendency of the rate of profit to fall is one of the most contentious elements in Karl Marx's intellectual legacy. He regarded it as one of his most important contributions to the analysis of the capitalist system, calling it 'in every respect the most important law of modern political economy' (see Marx, 1973, p. 748). We can divide the post-Second World War period into three distinct phases: a) 1941–56, where the rate of profits was 28 per cent, b) 1957–80, where the rate of profits was 20 per cent and c) 1981–2004, where the rate of profits was 14 per cent. As if history today repeats itself, with the new E-7 playing the same outcompeting role as Western Europe and Japan played in the 1960s. The difference between the present and the 1960s is that the competition is now much more broad-based and substantial, and is being accompanied by emerging alternative trading, finance and currency patterns that are associated with a shift of the centre of activities to Southeast Asia, not only in terms of production, but also of trade and finance.
2   See Chan (2011).
3   Marx wrote in *Capital* that 'the public debt becomes one of the most powerful levers of primitive accumulation'. And he continued: 'As with the stroke of an enchanter's wand, it endows unproductive money with the power of creation and thus turns it into capital, without forcing it to expose itself to the troubles and risks separable from its employment in industry or even usury. The state's creditors actually give nothing away, for the sum lent is transformed into public bonds, easily negotiable, which go on functioning in their hands just as so much hard cash would' (Marx, 1976, p. 919).
4   See Sassoon (1996).
5   For Vice President Joe Biden's entire speech at Sichuan University, see http://thecritical-post.com/blog/2011/08/vice-president-bidens-speech-at-sichuan-university-chengdu-china-21-august-2011-transcript-text-tcpchicago/
6   Fouskas and Gökay (2005, pp. 30–1).
7   Frank (2004, p. 125).
8   Bonner and Wiggin (2005).

REFERENCES

We include here only the sources that are cited in the text, as it is impossible to list all the material that we have consulted while researching and writing the book.

Adungo, Robert (2011) 'Redundancies set to rise in 2011 as public sector cuts hit', *UK Net Guide*, February 14. www.uknetguide.co.uk/ Latest-News/Redundancies-set-to-rise-in-2011-as-public-sector-cuts-hit-800403747.html

Agarwal, Arun and Narain, Sunita (1990) *Global Warming in an Unequal World – A Case of Environmental Colonialism*, New Delhi.

Aglietta, Michel (2000) *A Theory of Capitalist Regulation: The US Experience*, London.

Aglietta, Michel (2008) 'Understanding the structured credit crisis', *La Lettre du CEPII*, 275, Centre d'Etudes Prospectives et d'Informations Internationales, Paris, February.

Aglietta, Michel (2008) 'Into a new growth regime' (Symposium on 'the economics of global turbulence'), *New Left Review*, Nov.–Dec.

Albo, Greg, Gindin, Sam and Panitch, Leo (2010) *In and Out of Crisis*, Oakland.

Aldcroft, Derek H. (1993) *The European Economy, 1914–1990*, London and New York.

Allen, Franklin and Gale, Douglas (2001) *Comparing Financial Systems*, Cambridge, Mass.

Altman, Roger (2009) 'The great crash, 2008: a geo-political setback for the West', *Foreign Affairs*, Jan./Feb. www.foreignaffairs. org/20090101faessay88101/

Anderson, Perry and Gowan, Peter (eds) (1997) *The Question of Europe*, London.

Armstrong, Philip, Glyn, Andrew and Harrison, John (1984) *Capitalism since World War II: The Making and Break-up of the Great Boom*, London.

Arrighi, Giovanni (1994, 2nd edn 2009) *The Long Twentieth Century: Money, Power, and the Origins of Our tTimes*, London.

Arrighi, Giovanni (2007) *Adam Smith in Beijing: Lineages of the Twenty-first Century*, London.

Arrighi, Giovanni and Silver, Beverley (1999) *Chaos and Governance in the Modern World System*, Minneapolis.

Arrighi, Giovanni and Silver, Beverley (2011) 'The end of the long twentieth century', in Craig Calhoun et al. (eds), *Business as Usual: The Roots of the Global Financial Meltdown*, New York and London.

Ateljevic, Jovo and Budak, Jelena (2010)'Corruption and public procurement: example from Croatia', *Journal of Balkan and Near Eastern Studies* 12(4).

Attali, Jacques (1997) 'A continental architecture', in Perry Anderson and Peter Gowan (eds), *The Question of Europe*, London, pp. 345–56

Bacevich, Andrew J. (2002) *American Empire: The Realities and Consequences of U.S. Diplomacy*, Cambridge, Mass.

Bacik, Gokhan and Aras, Bülent (eds) (2004) *September 11 and World Politics*, Istanbul.

Bagley, James W. (2006) '90% of the world's engineers Asian residents by 2010?', *Control Engineering*, January 4. www.manufacturing.net/ctl/index.asp?layout=articlePrint&articleID=ca6296224

Balakrishnan, Gobal (2009) 'Speculation on the stationary state', *New Left Review*, 59, Sept.–Oct.

Balakrishnan, Gobal (2011) 'The convolution of capitalism', in Craig Calhoun et al. (eds), *Business as Usual: The Roots of the Global Financial Meltdown*, New York and London.

Barth, James, Brumbaugh, R. D. Jr., and Wilcox, James (2000) 'The repeal of Glass-Steagall and the advent of broad banking', *Journal of Economic Perspectives* 14(2) (Spring), pp.191–204.

Beasley, William G. (1987) *Japanese Imperialism, 1894–1945*, Oxford.

Bello, Walden (2009a) 'Afterthoughts: the global collapse: a non-orthodox view', *Philippine Daily Inquirer*, February 11.

Bello, Walden (2009b) 'Capitalism's crisis and our response', Transnational Institute, April. www.tni.org/archives/act/19430

Bhattacharya, Arindam. (2008) 'China and India: new innovation and talent forces', *Business Week*, Nov. 17. www.businessweek.com/global-biz/content/nov2008/gb20081117_964178.htm?chan=top+news_top+news+index+-+temp_global+business

Black, William K. (2005) *How to Rob a Bank: How Corporate Executives and Politicians Looted the S&L Industry*, Austin.

Bloomberg, Michael R. and Schumer, Charles E. (2007) *Sustaining New York's and the US' Global Financial Services Leadership*, report to the US Senate, http://schumer.senate.govhttp://schumer.senate.gov/SchumerWebsite/pressroom/special_reports/2007/NY_REPORT%20_FINAL.pdf (

Bonner, William and Wiggin, Addison (2005) *Empire of Debt: The Rise of an Epic Financial Crisis*, Hoboken, N.J.

BP (2003) *Statistical Review of World Energy 2003*, www.bp.com/subsection.do?categoryId=95&contentId=2006480

Brenner, Robert (1977) 'The origins of capitalist development: A critique of neo-Smithian Marxism', *New Left Review* 104 (Jul.–Aug.), www.newleftreview.org/A185 (accessed February 6, 2012).

Brenner, Robert. (2003a) *The Boom and the Bubble: The US in the World Economy*, London.

Brenner, Robert (2003b) 'Towards the precipice', *London Review of Books*, February 6.

Brenner, Robert (2006) *The Economics of Global Turbulence*, London.

Brenner, Robert (2009) 'What is good for Goldman Sachs is good for America', Center for Social Theory and Comparative History UCLA, April 18.

Brewer, Anthony (1980) *Marxist Theories of Imperialism*, London.

Brzezinski, Zbigniew (1997) *The Grand Chessboard: American Primacy and its Geo-strategic Imperatives*, New York.

Busch, Klaus (1978) *Die Krise der Europäischen Gemeinschaft*, Hamburg.

Calhoun, Craig and Derluguian, Georgi (eds) (2011) *Business as Usual: The Roots of the Global Financial Meltdown*, New York.

Callinicos, Alex (2009) *Imperialism and Global Political Economy*, London.

Campbell, Colin J. and Laherrère, Jean H. (1998) 'The end of cheap oil', *Scientific American*, March. http://dieoff.org/page140.htm

Central Intelligence Agency (CIA) (2006) *World Factbook 2006*, Washington, D.C. www.cia.gov/cia/publications/factbook/geos/ch.html

CIA (2012) *World Factbook*. www.cia.gov/library/publications/the-world-factbook/maps/ch_largelocator_template.html

Cesarano, Filippo (2006) *Monetary Theory and Bretton Woods: The Construction of an International Monetary Order*, Cambridge.

Champonnois, Sylvain (2006) *Comparing Financial Systems: A Structural Analysis*, European Central Bank Working Paper Series 702, Dec.

Chan, John (2011) 'Biden's visit to China underscores America's decline', *WSWS*, August 24.

Chernow, Ron (2001) *The House of Morgan: An American Banking Dynasty and the Rise of Modern Finance*, New York.

Chomsky, Noam and McChesney, Robert W. (2003) *Profit Over People: Neo-liberalism and global order*, New York.

Cody, Edward (2007) 'China boosts military spending; senior U.S. official presses Beijing to clarify "plans and intentions"', *Washington Post*, March 5. www.washingtonpost.com/wp-dyn/content/article/2007/03/04/AR2007030400401.html

Cooper, Wendy (1981) 'Bankers claim the danger of global collapse is receding', *Multinational Monitor* 2(11).

Crotty, James and Epstein, Gerald (2008) 'The costs and contradictions of the lender-of-last resort function in contemporary capitalism: the sub-prime crisis of 2007–2008', University of Mass., unpublished paper, October. http://dec84.univ-paris13.fr/ccepn/Texte_Epstein_101008.pdf

Daly, Herman and Farley, J. (2003) *Ecological Economics: Principles and Applications*. Washington DC.

Dicken, Peter (2007) *Global Shift: Mapping the Changing Contours of the World Economy*, London.

Dickie, Mure (2009) 'Shift in dealing with the US on cards', *Financial Times*, Aug. 30.

Dolsak, Nives, Ostrom, Elinor and MaCay, Bonnie J. (eds) (2003) *The Commons in the New Millennium: Challenges and Adaptation*, Cambridge.

Dormael, Arman van (1978) *The Bretton Woods Conference: Birth of a Monetary System*, New York.

Dowling, William A. (2007) 'Retirement imperiled: the case of HELOCs', *Journal of Business Case Studies* 3(4).

DuRand, Cliff (nd) 'The exhaustion of neo-liberalism in Mexico', www.globaljusticecenter.org

Dumenil, Gerard and Levy, Dominique (2001) 'Costs and benefits of neo-liberalism. A class analysis', *Review of International Political Economy* 8, pp. 578–607.

Eichengreen, Barry (2008) *Globalizing Capital: A History of the International Monetary System*, Princeton, N.J..

Eichengreen, Barry (2011) *Exorbitant Privilege: The Rise and Fall of the Dollar and the Future of the International Monetary System*, New York.

Eichengreen, Barry and Kenen, Peter B. (1994) 'Managing the world economy under the Bretton Woods system: an overview', in Peter B. Kenen (ed.), *Managing the World Economy: Fifty Years after Bretton Woods*, Institute for International Economics, p. 34.

Engels, Friedrich (1876) 'The part played by labour in the transition from ape to man', available at www.marxists.org/archive/marx/works/1876/part-played-labour/index.htm (accessed February 2, 2012).

Escobar, Arturo (1997) 'The making and unmaking of the Third World through development', in M. Rahnema et al. (eds), *The Post-Development Reader*, London.

Ferguson, Niall (2005) 'The unconscious colossus: limits of (and alternatives to) American empire', *Daedalus*, Spring, pp. 18–33.

Ferguson, Niall (2009a) *The Ascent of Money: A Financial History of the World*, London.

Ferguson, Niall (2009b) 'Too big to live; why we must stamp out state monopoly capitalism', Centre for Policy Studies, Surrey.

Ford, Peter (2009) 'China's buying spree in global fire sale', *Christian Science Monitor*, February 23.

Foster, John Bellamy (2002) *Ecology Against Capitalism*, New York.

Foster, John Bellamy (2006) 'The household debt bubble', *Monthly Review*, 58(1), May. http://monthlyreview.org/0506jbf.htm

Foster, John Bellamy and Magdoff, Fred (2009) *The Great Financial Crisis: Causes and Consequences*, New York.

Fouskas, Vassilis K. (1998) *Italy, Europe, the Left: The Transformation of Italian Communism and the European Imperative*, Aldershot.

Fouskas, Vassilis K. (2003) *Zones of Conflict: US Foreign Policy in the Balkans and the Greater Middle East*, London.

Fouskas, Vassilis K. (2005) 'Review of Barry Buzan's *The United States and the Great Powers: World Politics in the Twenty-First Century,*' *Political Quarterly* 76(2) (Apr.–Jun.), pp. 307–309.

Fouskas, Vassilis K. (2011) 'Timely meditations: explaining France's lead in the Libyan crisis.' www.globalfaultlines.com

Fouskas, Vassilis K. (2012) 'Review of Ray Kiely's *Rethinking Imperialism*', *Political Quarterly* 83(1).

Fouskas, Vassilis K. and Gökay, Bülent (2005) *The New American Imperialism: Bush's War on Terror and Blood for Oil*, Connecticut.

Fouskas, Vassilis K. and Gökay, Bülent (2008) 'An agenda for the next American President', *Mediterranean Quarterly* 19(3) (Summer), pp. 99–114.

Fouskas, Vassilis K. and Tackie, Alex (2009) *Cyprus: The Post-imperial Constitution*, London.

Frank, Andre Gunder (1994) 'World system history', preliminary draft prepared for presentation to the annual meeting of the New England Historical Association, Bentley College, Waltham, Mass., April 23. www.hartford-hwp.com/archives/10/034.html

Frank, Andre Gunder (1998a) *ReOrient: Global Economy in the Asian Age*, Berkeley, Calif.

Frank, Andre Gunder (1998b) 'A Review of David Landes', November 28. www.reorient.net/html/frank_on_landes.html

Frank, Andre Gunder (1999) 'NATO, Caucasus/Central Asia oil', *WSWS*, June 16.

Frank, Andre Gunder (2004) 'US economic overstretch and military/political imperial blowback', in Gokham Bacik et al. (eds), *September 11 and World Politics*, Istanbul.

Friedman, Milton (1962) *Capitalism and Freedom*, Chicago.

Friedman, Milton (1968) 'The role of monetary policy', *American Economic Review*, 58.

Frye, Timothy (2002) 'The perils of polarization: economic performance in the post-Communist world,' April, http://siteresources.worldbank.org/INTDECINEQ/Resources/frye.pdf

Galbraith Kenneth, John (1967) *The New Industrial State*, Harmondsworth.

Gardner, Richard N. (1956) *Sterling-Dollar Diplomacy: Anglo-American Collaboration in the Reconstruction of Multilateral Trade*, Oxford.

Garrett, Geoffrey (2010) 'G2 in G20: China, the United States and the world after the global financial crisis', *Global Policy* 1(1), (Jan.).

Gilpin, Robert (1987) *The Political Economy of International Relations*, Princeton, N.J.

Gittelsohn, John (2009) 'Ex-sub-prime exec works flip side of the market', *Orange County Register*, March 16. www.ocregister.com/articles/span-style-font-2334783-weight-bold

Glenny, Misha (2008) *McMafia: Crime without frontiers*, London/New York.

Glyn, Andrew (2007) *Capitalism Unleashed: Finance, Globalisation, and Welfare*, Oxford.

Glyn, Andrew, Hughes, Alan, Lipietz, Alain and Singh, Ajit (1990) 'The rise and fall of the Golden Age', in Stephen A. Marglin et al. (eds), *The Golden Age of Capitalism*, Oxford, pp. 69–70.

Gökay, Bülent (2005) 'The beginning of the end of the petrodollar: what connects Iraq to Iran', *Alternatives: Turkish Journal of International Relations*, 4(4) (Winter).

Gökay, Bülent (2006a) 'The power-shift to the East: the "American Century" is ending', *Pravda*, May 18. http://english.pravda.ru/opinion/feedback/80536-east-0

Gökay, Bülent (ed.) (2006b) *The Politics of Oil: A Survey*, London.

Gökay, Bülent and Whitman, Darrell (2004) 'Ghost dance: the US and illusions of power in the 21st century', *Alternatives: Turkish Journal of International Relations* 4.

Gökay, Bülent and Whitman, Darrell (2009) 'Mapping the fault-lines: a historical perspective on the 2008–2009 world economic crisis', *Cultural Logic*, pp. 31–7.

Gökay, Bülent and Whitman, Darrell (2010) 'Lineages of the 2008–10 global economic crisis: exposing shifts in the world economic order ', *Journal of Balkan and Near Eastern Studies* 12(2).

Goodfriend, Marvin and King, Robert Graham (2005) 'The incredible Volcker disinflation', National Bureau of Economic Research.

Gowa, Joanne (1983) *Closing the Gold Window: Domestic Politics and the End of Bretton Woods*, Ithaca, N.Y.

Gowan, Peter (1995a) 'East-Central Europe's headless hegemon', *Labour Focus on Eastern Europe* 50.

Gowan, Peter (1995b) 'Neo-liberal theory and practice for Eastern Europe', *New Left Review* 213.

Gowan, Peter (1999a) 'The NATO powers and the Balkan tragedy, *New Left Review* 234 (Mar.–Apr.).

Gowan, Peter (1999b) *The Global Gamble*, London.

Gowan, Peter (2002) 'A calculus of power', *New Left Review* 16 (Jul.–Aug.), pp. 47–67.

Gowan, Peter (2007) 'Economics and politics within the capitalist core and the debate on the new imperialism', mimeo.

Gowan, Peter (2008) 'Global economy', in Michael Cox et al. (eds), *US Foreign Policy*, Oxford.

Gowan, Peter (2009) 'Crisis in the heartland: consequences of the new Wall Street system', *New Left Review* 55 (Jan.–Feb.).

Gowan, Peter (2010) *The Calculus of Power*, London.

Gramsci, Antonio (1971) 'Americanism and Fordism', in *Selections from the Prison Notebooks*, London.

Gramsci, Antonio (1996) *Selections from the Prison Notebooks*, London.

Greider, William (1989) *Secrets of the Temple: How the Federal Reserve Runs the Country*, New York.

Guang, Lei (2002) '*ReOrient*: Andre Gunder Frank and a globalist perspective on the world economy', *Perspectives* 3(4) (Mar.). www.oycf.org/oycfold/httpdocs/Perspectives2/16_033102/re_orient.htm

Hanusch, Horst and Wackermann, Florian (2009) 'Global financial crisis: causes and lessons: a neo-Schumpeterian perspective', Discussion Paper Series 303, Augsburg University, Institute for Economics.

Harvey, David (2005) *A Brief History of Neo-liberalism*, Oxford.

Harvey, David (2010) *The Enigma of Capital and the Crisis of Capitalism*, London.

Hashi, Iraj (1992) 'The disintegration of Yugoslavia: regional disparities and the nationalities question', *Capital and Class* 48, pp. 41–88.

Hay, Colin (2002) 'Crisis and the structural transformation of the state: interrogating the process of change', *British Journal of Politics and International Relations* 1(3).

Hayek, Friedrich A. (1960) *The Condition of Liberty*, London.

Helleiner, Eric (1994) *States and the Re-emergence of Global Finance: From Bretton Woods to the 1990s*, Ithaca, N.Y.

Hilferding, Rudolf (1910/1981). *Finance Capital: A Study of the Latest Phase of Capitalist Development*, London.

Hirst, Paul and Thompson, Grahame (1996) *Globalisation in Question*, Cambridge.

Ho-fung, Hung (2009) 'America's head servant', *New Left Review* 60.

Hobsbawm, Eric (1995) *Age of Extremes: The short twentieth century 1914–1991*, London.

Hobson, John (2012) *The Euro-centric Conception of World Politics: Western International Theory 1760–2010*, Cambridge.

Hoffman, Andy (2009) 'Cash-rich China on buying spree', *Report on Business*, February 20. www.theglobeandmail.com/servlet/story/LAC.20090220.RCHINA19/TPStory/Business

Hogan, Michael J. (1997) *The Marshall Plan: America, Britain, and the Reconstruction of Western Europe 1947–1952*, Cambridge.

Holloway, John (1996) 'The abyss opens: the rise and fall of Keynesianism', in Werner Bonefeld et al. (eds), *Global Capital, National State and the Politics of Money*, London.

Hoogvelt, Ankie (2010) 'Globalisation, crisis and the political economy of the international monetary (dis)order', *Globalisations* 7(1–2).

Hopkins, Terence K., Wallerstein, Immanuel et al. (eds) (1996) *The Age of Transition: Trajectory of the World System 1945–2025*, London and New Jersey.

Hudson, Michael (2003) *Super Imperialism: The origin and fundamentals of US world dominance*, London.

Huntington, Samuel (1996) *The Clash of Civilizations and the Remaking of World Order*, New York.

Ikeda, Satoshi (1996) 'World production', in Terence K. Hopkins et al. (eds), *The Age of Transition*, London and New Jersey, pp. 47 ff.

International Bank for Reconstruction and Development (IBRD) (1992) *World Development Report 1992*, Washington DC.

Irwin, Douglas (2011) *Peddling Protectionism: Smoot-Hawley and the Great Depression*, Princeton, N.J.

Johnson, Chalmers (2004) *The Sorrows of Empire: Militarism, Secrecy and the End of the Republic*, London.

Jubak, Jim (2008) 'The next banking crisis on the way', *MSN Money*, January 18.

Kaiser, Robert G. and Ottaway, David (2002) 'Oil for security fueled close ties. But major differences led to tensions', *Washington Post*, February 11.

Kaplinsky, Raphael (nd) 'Is globalization all it is cracked up to be?' *Review of International Political Economy* 8.

Kastner, Scott L. (2008) 'The global implications of China's rise', *International Studies Review*, Dec.

Keidel, Albert (2008) 'The global financial crisis: lessons for the United States and China', Carnegie Endowment for International Peace, October 16. www.carnegieendowment.org/files/China_and_the_Global_Financial_Crisis3.pdf

Kemp, John (2008) 'Oil industry running faster just to keep up?', Reuters, November 19. www.reuters.com/article/reutersComService4/idUSTRE 4AI3TP20081119

Kenen, Peter B. (ed.) (1994) *Managing the World Economy: Fifty years after Bretton Woods*, Institute for International Economics.

Kennedy, Paul M. (1988) *The Rise and Fall of the Great Powers: Economic Change and Military conflict from 1500 to 2000*, London.

Kennedy, Paul (1993) *Preparing for the Twenty-First Century*, London.

Kennedy, Paul (2009) 'American power is on the wane', *Wall Street Journal*, January 14. http://online.wsj.com/article/SB123189377673479433. html

Kent, Marian (1993) *Moguls and Mandarins: Oil, Imperialism and the Middle East in British Foreign Policy. 1900–1940*, London.

Keynes, John M. (1919/1995) *The Economic Consequences of the Peace*, Harmondsworth.

Keynes, John M. (1936/1973) *The General Theory of Employment, Interest and Money*, Cambridge.

Kiely, Ray (2010) *Rethinking Imperialism*, London.

Killick, John (1997) *The United States and European Reconstruction 1945–1960*, Keele.

Kindleberger, Charles P. (1981) *International Money: A Collection of Essays*, London.

Kindleberger, Charles (1986) *The World in Depression, 1919–1939*, Berkeley, Calif.

Klare, Michael (2008) *Rising Powers, Shrinking Planet*, Oxford.

Kliman, Andrew (2007) *Reclaiming Marx's 'Capital'; A Refutation of the Myth of Inconsistency*. Lanham, Md.

Kliman, Andrew (2009) 'The destruction of capital and the current economic crisis', *Radical Perspectives on the Crisis*, Department of Economics, Pace University, New York, January 15.

Kotz, David M. (2007) 'Contradictions of economic growth in the neo-liberal era', May http:///people.umass.edu/dmkotz/Contradictions_07_05.pdf

Krugman, Paul (2008) *The Return of Depression Economics*, London.

Kuttner, Robert (2007) 'Testimony before the Committee on Financial Services', US House of Representatives, Washington DC, October 2.

Lague, David (2006) 'China corners market in a high-tech necessity', *International Herald Tribune*, Jan. 22. www.iht.com/articles/2006/01/22/business/rare.php (accessed September 2008).

Landes, David S. (1998) *The Wealth and Poverty of Nations: Why are Some so Rich and Others so Poor?* New York.

Lapatsioras, Spyros, Maroudas, Leonidas, Michaelides, Panayiotis G.,

Milios, John and Sotiropoulos, Dimitri (2009) 'On the character of the current economic crisis', *Radical Notes*, April 10.

Lapavitsas, Costas (2010) 'Financialisation and capitalist accumulation: structural accounts of the crisis of 2007–9', RMF discussion paper 16, SOAS, University of London, February.

Lasswell, Harold D. (1997) *Essays on the Garrison State*, New Brunswick.

Layne, Christopher (2006) *The Peace of Illusions: American Grand Strategy from 1940 to the Present*, Ithaca, N.J.

Lewis, Leo. (2009) 'China builds rare-earth metal monopoly', *The Australian*, March 9. www.theaustralian.news.com.au/business/story/0,28124,25158871-5005200,00.html

Li, Minqi (2004) 'After neo-liberalism: empire, social democracy, or socialism?', *Monthly Review*, January. www.monthlyreview.org/0104li.htm

Linhart, Robert (1976) *Lénine, les paysans, Taylor. Essai d' analyse matérialiste historique de la naissance du système productif soviétique*, Paris.

Lipietz, Alain (1986) 'Behind the crisis: the exhaustion of a regime of accumulation', *Review of Radical Political Economics*,18.

Lukács, Georg (1923/1971) *History and Class Consciousness*, trans. R. Livingstone, London.

Maddison, Angus (1982) *Phases of Capitalist Development*, Oxford.

Maddison, Angus (1991) *Dynamic Forces in Capitalist Development*, Oxford.

Madoff, Bernard Lawrence (2011) 'From behind bars, Madoff spins his story', *Financial Times Weekend Magazine*, April 9–10.

Maksakovsky, Pavel (2009) *The Capitalist Cycle: An Essay on the Marxist Theory of the Cycle*, Chicago, Ill.

Mandel, Ernest (1969) 'Where is America going?', *New Left Review* 54 (Mar.-Apr.).

Mandel, Ernest (1972) *Decline of the Dollar; A Marxist View of the Monetary Crisis*, New York.

Mandel, Ernest (1975) *Late Capitalism*, London.

Mandel, Ernest (1980) *The Long Waves of Capitalist Development*, Cambridge.

Marazzi, Christian (nd) *The Violence of Financial Capitalism* (semiotext), London.

Marglin, Stephen A. and Schor, Juliet B. (eds) (1990) *The Golden Age of Capitalism: Reinterpreting the Post-war Experience*, Oxford.

Marx, Karl (1857–8/1973) *Grundrisse*, Harmondsworth.

Marx, Karl (1867/1976) *Capital*, vol. 1, Harmondsworth.

McGourty, Christine (2009) 'Global crisis "to strike by 2030"', *BBC News*, March 19. http://news.bbc.co.uk/1/hi/uk/7951838.stm

Mearsheimer, John (2001) *The Tragedy of Great Power Politics*, New York.

Milward, Alan S. (1984) *The Reconstruction of Western Europe*, London.

Moran, Theodore (1990) 'The globalisation of America's defence industries', *International Security* 15.

Moseley, Fred (1991) *The Falling Rate of Profit in the Post-War United States Economy*, London.

Nahusch, Horst and Wackermann, Florian (2009) 'Global financial crisis: causes and lessons. A neo-Schumpeterian perspective', mimeo, University of Augsburg, February.

Nandy, Ashish (1987) *The Intimate Enemy: Loss and Recovery of Self under Colonialism*, Bombay.

National Intelligence Council (2008) *Global Trends 2025: The National Intelligence Council's 2025 Project*. www.dni.gov/nic/NIC_2025_project.html

Navarro, Peter (2009) 'Power in Beijing balance sheet', *Asia Times Online*, March 6.

Nitzan, Jonathan and Bichler, Shimshon (2002) *The Global Political Economy of Israel*, London.

O'Connor, James (1973) *The Fiscal Crisis of the State*, New York.

Organisation of Economic Cooperation and Development (OECD) (1991) *Economic Outlook: Historical Statistics 1960–1989*, Paris.

Oster, Shai (2006) 'As China auto market booms, leaders clash over heavy toll', *Wall Street Journal*, June 13.

Palan, Ronan (2002) 'Tax heavens and the commercialization of state sovereignty', *International Organisation* 1(56) (Winter).

Panitch, Leo and Gindin, S. (2005) 'Finance and the American empire', *Socialist Register*.

Panitch, Leo and Konings, Martijn (2008) *American Empire and the Political Economy of Global Finance*, New York.

Parthasarathy, Gopalaswami (2011) 'BRICs summit towards a new world order', *Asian Affairs*, May.

Pauly, Louis W. (1994) 'Promoting a global economy: the normative role of the International Monetary Fund', in Richard Stubbs et al. (eds), *Political Economy and the Changing Global Order*, London.

Pettifor, Ann (2008) *OpenDemocracy*, September 2.

Polanyi, Karl (1944/2001) *The Great Transformation: The Political and Economic Origins of our Time*, Boston, Mass.

Poulantzas, Nicos (1974) *Les classes sociales dans le capitalisme aujourd'hui*, Paris.

Poulantzas, Nicos (1976) 'The transformation of the state today, the political crisis and the crisis of the state', in Nicos Poulantzas (ed.), *The Crisis of the State* [in Greek], Athens.

Poulantzas, Nicos (1978a) *Classes in Contemporary Capitalism*, London.

Poulantzas, Nicos (1978b, UK edn 2000) *State, Power, Socialism*, New York.

Pozsar, Zoltan, Adrian, Tobias, Ashcraft, Adam and Boesky, Hayley (2010) 'Shadow banking', Federal Reserve Bank of New York, staff report 458, July.

Pressley, James (2008) 'Brace for $1 trillion write-down of "yertle the turtle" debt', Bloomberg Press, March 31. www.bloomberg.com/apps/news?pid=newsarchive&sid=aHCnscodO1s0

Prestowitz, Clyde. (2005) 'China–India entente shifts global balance', Yale Global, April 15. http://yaleglobal.yale.edu/display.article?id=5578

PricewaterhouseCoopers UK (2011) 'The world in 2050', January, http://www.pwc.com/en_GX/gx/world-2050/pdf/world-in-2050-jan-2011.pdf (accessed February 2, 2012).

Reich, Robert (2011) 'Dithering as America risks a double dip', *Financial Times*, June 2.

Roberts, Paul (2004) 'Last stop gas: cheap oil, the only oil that matters, is just about gone', *Harper's Magazine*, August. www.harpers.org/archive/2004/08/0080164

Rosenberg, Justin and Callinicos, Alex (2008) Exchange of letters, *Cambridge Review of International Affairs* 1(21) (Mar.).

Rukavishnikov, Vladimir (1999) 'Is Russia becoming a third world country? Unemployment risks in the time of post-Soviet restructuring', in Nikolai Genov (ed.), *Unemployment Risks and Reaction*, UNESCO, Bonn-Sofia.

Salvati, Michelle (1981) 'May 1968 and the hot autumn of 1969: the responses of two ruling classes', in Suzanne D. Berger (ed.), *Organising Interests in Western Europe*, Cambridge.

Salvatore, Dominick, Dean, James W. and Willett, Thomas (eds) (2003) *The Dollarisation Debate*, Oxford.

Sassen, Saskia (2008) 'Mortgage capital and its particularities: a new frontier for global finance', *Journal of International Affairs* 1(62) (Fall/Winter).

Sassoon, Donald (1996) *One Hundred Years of Socialism*, London.

Saunders, Michael (2008) 'The true extent of Britain's debt', *Spectator*, Dec. 10.

Schierup, Carl-Ulrik (ed.) (1999) *Scramble for the Balkans: Nationalism, globalism and the political economy of reconstruction*, London.

Schild, Georg M. (1993) *Bretton Woods and Dumbarton Oaks: American Post-war Planning in the Summer of 1944*, PhD dissertation, University of Maryland.

Seabrook, Leonard (2001) *US Power in International Finance*, New York.

Shambaugh, David L. (ed.) (2005) *Power Shift: China and Asia's New Dynamics*, Berkeley, Calif.

Simmons, Matthew (2003) 'Revealing statements from a Bush insider about peak oil and natural gas depletion', *Wilderness Publications*, June 12. www.fromthewilderness.com/free/ww3/061203_simmons.html

Simpkins, Jason. (2009) 'China continues its commodities binge with Brazilian oil deal', *Money Morning*, Feb. 24. www.moneymorning.com/2009/02/21/china-brazil-oil/

Smith, Murray E. G. (2010) *Global Capitalism in Crisis*, Toronto.

Smith, Adam (1776/1965) *The Wealth of Nations*, New York.

Spiegel, Peter and Blitz, James (2011) 'Gates warns allies over NATO burden', *Financial Times*, June 11–12.

Spiro, David E. (1999) *The Hidden Hand of American Hegemony: Petrodollar Recycling and International Markets*, Ithaca, N.Y.

Steil, Benn and Litan, Robert E. (2006) *Financial Statecraft: The Role of Financial Markets in American Foreign Policy*, New Haven, Conn.

Stiglitz, Joseph (2002) *Globalisation and its Discontents*, London.

Stiglitz, Joseph (2007) *Making Globalization Work*, New York.

Stiglitz, Joseph (2009) 'We're in a whole new territory', *Newsweek*, April 6.

Strange, Susan (1986) *Casino Capitalism*, Oxford.

Strange, Susan (1998) *Mad Money: When markets Outgrow Governments*, Ann Arbor, Mich.

Stubbs, Richard and Underhill, Geoffrey (eds) (1994) *Political Economy and the Changing Global Order*, London.

Tabb, William K. (2008) 'The financial crisis of US capitalism', *Monthly Review*, Oct. 10. www.monthlyreview.org/mrzine/tabb101008.html

Teschke, Benno (2003) *The Myth of 1648: Class, Geopolitics, and the Making of Modern International Relations*, London.

Thaler, Richard H. (2011) 'A simple fix for budget: just grow up', *International Herald Tribune*, Aug. 27–8.

Todd, Emmanuel (2003) *After the Empire: The Breakdown of the American order*, London.

Tolchin, Susan and Tolchin, Martin (1992) *Selling our Security: The Erosion of America's Assets*, New York.

Toscano, Alberto (2009) 'Chronicles of insurrection: Tronti, Negri and the subject of antagonism', *Cosmos and History* 1(5).

Tronti, Mario (1971) *Operai e capitale*, Turin.

US Geological Survey (2002) Fact Sheet 087-02, http://pubs.usgs.gov/fs/2002/fs087-02/

Van Der Linden, Marcel (2007) 'The "law" of uneven and combined development: some underdeveloped thoughts', *Historical Materialism* 15.

Van Der Vee, Herman (1986) *Prosperity and Upheaval: The World Economy 1945–1980*, Harmondsworth.

Volcker, Paul and Gyohten, Toyoo (1992) *Changing Fortunes*, New York.

Wade, Robert and Veneroso, Frank (1998) 'The Asian crisis: the high debt model versus the Wall Street-Treasury-IMF complex', *New Left Review* 228 (Mar.–Apr.).

Wallerstein, Immanuel (1996) 'The global possibilities, 1990–2025', in Terence K. Hopkins, Immanuel Wallerstein et al., *The Age of Transition: Trajectory of the World System 1945–2025*, London and New Jersey, pp. 226–43.

Wallerstein, Immanuel (2009) 'Dynamics of (unresolved) crisis: where do we go from here?' the Harold Wolpe Lecture, University of KwaZulu-Natal, November 5.

Wallerstein, Immanuel (2011) 'Dynamics of (unresolved) crisis', in Craig Calhoun and Georgi Derluguian (eds), *Business as Usual: The Roots of the Global Financial Meltdown*, New York and London, pp. 69–88.

Waltz, Kenneth (1954/2001). *Man, the State and War*, New York.

Wendt, Alexander (1987) 'The agent-structure problem in international relations theory', *International Organisation* 3(41).

Wendt, Alexander (1999) *Social Theory of International Politics*, Cambridge.

Williams, William Appleman (1959/1972). *The Tragedy of American Diplomacy*, New York.

Woodward, Susan (1995) *The Balkan Tragedy,* Washington DC.

Zakaria, Fareed (2005) 'The rise of China won't be peaceful at all', *The Australian*, Nov. 18.

Zakaria, Fareed (2008) *The Post-American World*, New York.

Zakaria, Fareed (2010) 'Imperial by design', *The National Interest*, 111 (Jan.–Feb.), pp. 16–34.

WEBSITES

Not all websites used in the book are included in this list; others can be found in the notes and sources in the graphs and tables.

http://data.worldbank.com
http://english.pravda.ru
http://yaleglobal.yale.edu
www.atimes.com (Asia Time Online)
www.bankofengland.co.uk
www.bbc.co.uk
www.bloomberg.com
www.businessweek.com
www.carnegieendowment.org
www.cbi.org.uk
www.cfr.org (US Council on Foreign Relations)
www.chinadaily.com.cn
www.dni.gov (Department of National Intelligence)
www.eia.doe.gov (US Department of Energy)
www.fdic.gov (US Federal Deposit Insurance Corporation)
www.federalreserve.gov
www.globalfaultlines.com
www.globalresearch.ca
www.globaljusticecenter.org
www.manufacturing.net
www.monthlyreview.com
www.opendemocracy.net
www.radicalnotes.com
www.tni.com (Transnational Institute)

INDEX

A

Acheson, Dean, xv, 78
Afghanistan war, 27
Africa, 6–7, 31, 39, 70, 76, 120, 129, 148
Aglietta, Michel, 20, 25, 27, 155, 157, 158, 176
agriculture, 36, 58, 94, 115, 121, 134
American civil war, 33, 38
Arab–Israel war (1967), 66
Arab–Israeli conflict, 66, 68, 72, 73
Arab nationalism 44, 50, 69
Aramco (national oil company of Saudi Arabia), 123
Argentina, 67, 165
Arrighi, Giovanni, xviii, 3, 6, 8, 21–6, 28–30, 59, 117, 132, 144, 148, 155, 157–60, 164, 168
ASEAN (Association of South East Asian Nations), xii, 129, 130
Asian financial crisis, 88, 129
Atlantic Charter, 40
Australia, 23, 124, 129
Austria, 4, 35, 156
authoritarianism, 8, 37–9, 95, 146, 151

B

bailout, 13, 85, 105–7, 128, 149
balance of payments and debt, 50, 129, 147
Balkans, 70, 71, 91, 93–4, 165
Bank of America, 103
Bank of England, 84, 110
Bear Stearns, 103

Bolshevik Revolution, xx, 38
bond market, 1, 3, 10, 12, 52, 62, 67, 73, 85, 99–100, 105, 165, 175
Braudelian historiography, 21–2, 25–8, 31
Brazil, 6–7, 9, 31, 34, 67, 79, 111, 114–15, 120–8, 148, 165, 173
  GDP, 115, 121–2, 126
Brenner, Robert, xviii, 5–6, 11, 19–25, 59, 65, 75, 83, 85–6, 90, 143, 157–8, 161–2, 164
Bretton Woods institutions, *see* General Agreement on Tariffs and Trade (GATT), IMF, World Bank
Bretton Woods system, 2, 10, 15, 22, 33, 38–9, 40–3, 45–6, 53, 55, 60–1, 63, 65, 67–8, 71–4, 81, 87–8, 91–2, 94–5, 99, 103, 153, 162, 179
Britain, 4, 10, 15, 18, 26–7, 29, 30, 34–5, 37–40, 42, 44, 45, 51, 54, 63–4, 81–3, 85–6, 93, 96–7, 99–100, 106, 108–9, 126, 130, 143, 145, 149, 156
  GDP, 100, 107–8, 110, 126, 130
British Empire, 26, 29, 30, 35, 37, 40, 150
budget deficit, 54, 106–10
Bush, George W., 70

C

capitalist accumulation/capital accumulation, 3, 7, 11, 15, 18,

26–7, 29–30, 33, 36, 47, 52, 69,
  77, 83, 175
capitalist modernity, 3, 6, 18, 36,
  78
Carter administration, 67, 85
casino capitalism 49, 55, 88, 168–9,
  187
Castro, Fidel, 50
Central Asia, 70–1, 96, 148
Chartered Institute of Personnel and
  Development (CIPD), 106
Chase Manhattan Bank, 166
cheap labour power, 21, 46, 117
Chile, 67
China, xvii–xviii, xv–xvi, 3, 6–7, 9,
  18, 20–2, 24, 26, 31, 33, 78–9,
  81–2, 86, 89, 97, 100, 111–32,
  137–8, 142, 144–5, 147–8, 159,
  164, 168, 171–4
    GDP, 120–3, 126, 168
    manufacturing, 7, 21, 100,
      114–15, 117–19, 126
China Development Bank, 128
China Minmetals, 129
China National Petroleum
  Corporation (CNPC), 123
China Petrochemical Corporation,
  129
Chrysler, 85
Churchill, Winston, 40
Cisco Systems (American multi-
  national corporation), 119
City of London, 62, 98
class interest, 2, 8, 10, 12, 18–19,
  27–31, 34, 36, 38, 43, 61, 63–6,
  90, 110, 112, 131–2, 142
Clinton, Bill, xviii, 2, 19, 20, 58,
  79, 82–3, 94
Cold War, 49–50, 56, 67, 72, 74,
  78, 81, 87, 94, 103, 112–13,
  153, 166
colonialism, 27, 44, 50, 73, 87,
  112, 176, 185
COMAC (Commercial Aircraft
  Corporation of China), 7
COMECON/Council for Mutual

Economic Assistance, xii, 41, 86,
  87, 94, 151
commercial banking, 37, 86,
  99–100, 169, 173
commercialization/globalization of
  the arms trade, 38, 66, 69–70,
  72, 95, 164
commodity money, 37, 39, 65, 155
Communism, 19, 49, 56, 78, 86,
  94, 95, 161
Confederation of British Industry,
  xii, 110
Conservative–Liberal Democrat
  coalition government, UK,
  106–10
Council on Foreign Relations, 57–8,
  160, 173
Crash of 1929–32, 26, 29, 99
credit crunch, 10, 14, 104, 106,
  128, 154
credit default swaps (CDS), xiii, 57,
  62, 98, 168
credit rating agencies, 13, 98
crisis of 2007–08, xv, 9–10, 30, 37,
  89, 100–1, 104, 106–7, 122,
  127, 146, 155, 164
Cuba, 50, 86, 133

D
de Gaulle, Charles, 36, 52–3, 162
debt mechanism, 95
debt payments, 34
deindustrialization, 11, 54–5, 86,
  157
depreciation of currencies, 35–6,
  158
derivatives, 3, 57, 62
détente, 44, 49, 66
Dexter White, Harry, 40–2
Dicken, Peter, xx, 121, 169, 172–4
dollar–glut problem, 47, 52–3, 72
dollar–gold parity, 3, 37, 41, 43,
  163
dollar primacy, 4, 7, 26, 29, 40,
  55–6, 111
dollar standard, 3, 57, 65, 69, 72

dollarization, 3, 46–7, 58, 63, 67–8, 73, 162
Dollar–Wall Street Regime (DWSR), xii, 28, 154
'dot.com' bubble, 11–12, 14, 20–1, 88, 96

E
Eastern Europe, 43, 79, 82, 94–5
ecological crisis, 8, 11, 31, 45, 133, 140–1, 145–6, 151
economic instability, 12, 17, 35, 37, 71, 90
Eisenhower, Dwight, 61
Energy Information Administration (EIA), 114, 172
Eurasia, x, 2, 50, 55, 125–6
eurocentrism, xix, xx, 2, 50, 81, 112, 141, 145, 167
European Central Bank (ECB), xii, 105
European Economic Community (EEC), 46
European markets, 5, 36, 52, 93–4
European producers, 36, 52, 66
European Union, 2, 8, 16, 46, 93–4, 105, 112, 129
Eurozone, 4, 8, 10, 29, 105, 107, 109, 128, 146
ExxonMobil (American multi-national oil and gas corporation), 123

F
Fannie Mae (Federal National Mortgage Association), 10, 98
feminism, 45
fiat money, 65–6
finance capital, 4, 12, 24, 46
Financial Services Modernization Act (USA, 1999) (Gramm–Leach–Bliley Act), 88, 99, 168
financial speculation, 37, 99, 136
financialization, xviii, xv, xviii, 1–6, 10–12, 15–20, 24, 26, 28–9, 32, 35, 38, 57, 62–3, 66, 79, 82–3,

86, 88–90, 96, 98–101, 120, 127, 132, 142–5, 157, 168
FIRE (finance, insurance and real estate), 85
fiscal crisis, 44, 83, 144
Fitch, 99
fixed exchange rates, xviii, 3, 22, 41, 43, 63–4
floating exchange rates, 35, 41, 66, 68, 165
Fordism, 36, 48–9, 55, 62, 162
Fordney Tariff (1922), 36
foreign debt, 36, 58, 65, 93
foreign direct investment, 19, 21, 34, 45, 49, 52
France, xii, 3, 6, 15, 18, 34–5, 37, 39–40, 44, 51–3, 63, 65, 68, 100, 124, 126, 154, 156–7
Frank, Andre Gunder, xvii, 72, 80, 112, 144, 158, 167, 180
Freddie Mac, 10, 98
free trade agreement (FTA), xii, 129
Friedman, Milton, 87, 99, 168, 180

G
Galbraith, John Kenneth, 49, 59, 62
gas, 24, 31, 71, 125, 134–6, 138–9, 148
Gazprom (Russian natural gas company), 123
General Agreement on Tariffs and Trade (GATT), xii, 4, 39, 42, 45, 88
General Motors, 85, 115
geopolitics, xviii, xvi, 9, 38, 120, 126, 145, 148, 166
Germany, xii, xvi, 3–4, 8, 12, 15–16, 22, 34–7, 39, 42, 44, 46, 49–51, 63, 75, 84, 92–3, 119, 124, 126, 130, 142–3, 156, 159–60, 164
    GDP, 46, 75, 126, 130
Glass–Steagall Act (USA, 1933), 37, 88, 90, 99, 102, 169

Glenny, Misha, 95, 169, 180
global banking system, 73–4, 88, 91, 104, 106, 127–8, 164
Global East/Emerging Seven (E-7), 6–7, 9, 25, 27–9, 31, 79, 81, 86, 89, 111–12, 114–15, 117, 120, 122–3, 125–8, 142, 144–6, 148–9, 159, 175
global fault-lines, 7–8, 27, 30–1, 44, 50, 56, 79–81, 88–9, 91, 103, 111, 125, 132, 143–6, 149, 151
global governance, 26–7, 29, 38, 139
global 'triad', 52
global warming, 45, 134, 139, 140
globalization, xv–xvi, xviii, 1–3, 5–7, 10, 15, 25, 27, 31, 33, 57–8, 62, 64, 66, 69, 82, 99, 106, 113, 120, 142, 145, 153
   and financialization, xv, 2–3, 62, 99, 120, 142
gold convertibility, 35, 37, 43, 67
gold standard, 4, 20, 35, 41, 72
Golden Age of Capitalism, xii, xviii, 19, 21, 43–56, 92
Goldman Sachs, 85, 157
Gowan, Peter, v, ix, xi, 28, 59, 68, 94–5, 153–4, 156, 159–60, 164–5, 168–9, 174
Gramsci, Antonio, 15, 22, 48, 156, 162, 181
Great Depression, 29, 35, 38, 44, 75, 89–90, 99, 102, 104
Greece, xvi, 21, 31, 37, 46, 75, 105, 107, 128, 143–4, 146, 156, 165, 185

H
haute finance, 37, 49, 142
Hayek, Friedrich, 87, 168
hedge funds, 3, 62, 84, 98, 168
hegemonic transitions, xvii–xx, 8, 28–30, 77, 144, 159
housing bubble, 10–11, 14, 20–1, 37, 58, 97, 99, 105, 144
hub and spoke system, 2, 29, 39

Hungary, 35, 95–6, 166
hyperinflation, 35, 71, 73

I
immigration, 46
imperial expansion, 9, 17, 21, 25–6, 34, 37, 40, 42–3, 79, 90, 108, 125, 127, 153
India, xii, xvi–xvii, 6, 7, 9, 24, 31, 70, 79, 81–2, 89, 112–27, 137–8, 145, 148, 172–3
Indonesia, 6, 7, 9, 122, 124, 126, 130, 173
industrial capital, 4, 6, 10–12, 18, 23, 25–6, 28, 33–4, 36, 44, 46, 49, 58, 61, 63, 103
industrial cycle, 60, 133
industrial production, 37, 43, 44, 72, 111, 156
Industrial Revolution, 58, 81, 112, 132
inflation, 22, 33, 35, 37, 47, 53–4, 58–63, 65, 67, 71, 73–4, 83, 92, 94, 137, 144, 168
Inland Revenue System (IRS), 27
Intel (American multinational semi-conductor corporation), 119
inter-capitalist competition, 7, 20, 22, 33, 36, 52, 59–60, 64–5, 79, 112, 117, 125–6, 148, 175
interest rates, 10–11, 13, 16, 41, 47, 55, 58, 60, 67, 74, 84, 97, 100, 110, 155, 165, 170
International Energy Agency (IEA), xii, 138, 174
international/imperial order, xv, xvi, 6, 9, 25, 27, 31, 39–41, 43, 77, 81, 112, 120, 134, 149, 155, 167
International Monetary Fund (IMF), xii, 39, 41–3, 58, 68–9, 83, 86, 88, 92, 94–5, 159, 161, 187
international political economy (IPE) 5, 14, 30, 39, 55–7, 65–6, 69, 78, 81–2, 86, 142

International Standard Industrial
Classification (ISIC), 23, 24
investment banks, 3, 10, 62, 84,
90, 99, 102–4, 128, 169
Iran, 70, 125
Iraq, 27, 70, 134
Iraq–Iran war, 70
Israel, 66, 68, 70, 72–3, 126, 138,
165
see also Arab–Israel conflict
Italy, xii, 21, 26, 35, 37, 46, 51,
105, 124, 126, 128, 143, 156,
160, 179
Italian Communist Party, 48,
161, 162, 179

J
Japan, xii, xvi, 2–3, 11–12, 15–16,
19–20, 22–3, 29, 38–9, 44–8,
50–2, 54, 60, 63–8, 72–3, 75,
79, 81–2, 84, 86, 100, 111–12,
114–15, 119, 124, 126, 129,
142–4, 154, 156, 160, 163–4,
170, 175
GDP, 46, 75, 79, 126

K
Kennan, George, 78
Kennedy, Paul, xx, 79–80, 127,
129–30, 169, 173–5, 183
Keynesianism, xviii, 6, 11–13, 15,
17, 33–4, 37–8, 40–2, 47–9,
55, 62–4, 71, 74–5, 87, 90, 94,
106, 108, 110, 141, 143, 155,
159–60, 162
Kiely, Ray, 58, 67, 143, 153, 156,
160, 165–7
Kindleberger, Charles P., 36, 160, 162
Kissinger, Henry, 68, 164, 183
Kondratieff waves, 21, 28, 157–9,
164
KPMG, 106

L
laissez faire capitalism, 7, 49, 57
Latin America, 2, 35, 38–9, 43–4,
50, 67, 69, 74, 76, 95, 121,
123, 129, 166
Lehman Brothers, 10, 104
Lenin, Vladimir, 33, 35, 48, 63,
156–7, 184
Libyan war, 6, 27, 148, 154

M
M–C–M', 18, 155
M–M', 13, 18, 25, 155
Mandel, Ernest, vii, xix, 42, 44, 53,
57–62, 102, 155, 161–4, 184
manufacturing sector, 5–6, 18–21,
23–4, 42, 45–6, 50–1, 54, 57,
75, 83–6, 98, 100, 109, 112,
114, 115, 117–19, 122, 126,
133, 134, 142, 161, 168
Mao Zedong, 111, 113, 132, 171
Marshall Plan, 42, 44, 91, 94, 182
Marx, Karl, xix, 3, 4, 16, 19, 25, 77,
83, 140, 143, 147, 155, 161, 175
Mearsheimer, John, 130–1, 174, 185
Mexico, xii, 9, 67, 122, 124, 126,
173, 179
Microsoft (American multinational
corporation), 119
Middle East, 2, 7, 31, 35, 38, 66,
70, 71, 76, 132, 138, 148, 160,
166
military–industrial complex, 61
military power, 27, 38, 64, 113,
129, 159
monetary system, 36, 39, 61, 128
Moody's (credit rating agency), 99
mortgage market, 10–11, 14, 62,
97–102, 104, 127, 168–70
Motorola (American multinational
telecomms company), 119
multilateral trade, 40, 66
multinational corporations, 19, 27,
45, 55, 62, 69, 116
multipolar phase, 9, 29, 31

N
NAFTA (North American Free
Trade Association), xii, 129

NATO (North Atlantic Treaty Organization), xii, 6, 27, 45, 64, 78, 94, 125, 148, 165, 166
Negri, Antonio, 11, 17, 162
neo-conservatism, 2, 12
neoliberalism, xv, xviii, 2–4, 7, 10, 12, 16–18, 20, 32, 43, 49, 58, 64, 69, 71, 74–6, 79, 82–3, 86–93, 98, 102–3, 106, 108, 125, 139–40, 142–3, 150, 154, 168
   neoliberal reforms, 4, 37, 69, 85, 90–4, 107, 113
Netherlands, 37, 75, 123
new industrial state, 49
Nitze, Paul, xv, 61, 78
Nixon, Richard, 3, 53, 57–8, 62, 65–8, 164
Nokia (Finnish multinational comms corporation), 119
Northern Rock, 10, 107
NSC-68, 61

O
Obama, Barack, 104, 154
Occupy Wall Street movement, 31
OECD, xiii, 27, 64, 72–75, 88, 166, 185
offshore business, 27, 45, 54 158
oil, 3, 8, 31, 34–5, 47, 54, 61, 66–73, 114, 121, 123, 128–9, 133–40, 145, 148, 160, 166, 174
   oil embargo, 72
OPEC, xiii, 54, 68, 72, 166
open door imperialism, 4, 7, 27–30, 32–3, 35–6, 39–40, 43, 46, 50, 58, 61, 63–4, 93–5, 113, 153–4, 165
Ostpolitik, 44, 49, 93
over-accumulation crisis, 7, 10–12, 16–18, 26, 33, 50, 61, 74, 79, 86–7, 100, 127, 143, 157
over-production, 20, 36
OZ Minerals (Australian zinc producer), 129

P
Pakistan, 70
Panitch, Leo, xviii, 16, 17, 58, 67, 143, 155–6, 160, 162–5
PDVSA (Venezuelan petroleum company), 123
peak oil, 135–7, 174
Petrobras (Brazilian multinational energy corporation), 123, 128
petrodollar system, 65, 67–8, 71–4, 81, 91, 102, 166, 170
Petronas (Malaysian oil and gas company), 123
pipelines, 70–1, 128–9
Poland, 35, 95, 96
Polanyi, Karl, 22, 35, 57, 160
politicization of oil sector, 66, 69
Portugal, 31, 37, 105, 143
PPP (purchasing power parity), 122–4, 126
profitability, xvii–xviii, 11, 19–20, 25, 47, 50–1, 53–4, 63, 65, 70, 112, 143, 157, 161
protectionism, 37, 39, 42, 146

R
rare earth elements (REE), xiii, 117
Reagan, Ronald, 2, 12, 20, 67, 71, 74–5, 83, 85–6, 165
real estate speculation, 37, 71, 74–5, 102
realism in IR, 1, 5, 14, 74, 81, 131, 143, 164
recession, 13, 61, 71, 73, 75, 83–4, 92, 96–98, 101, 105, 107–9, 115, 122–3, 137–8, 146
relative decline of USA, xxi, 19, 22, 27, 30, 50, 55, 59–60, 71, 79, 96, 109, 112, 119, 125, 129–30, 156, 174
rentier activities, 1, 5, 10, 62, 85, 100, 135, 164
revolts of 2011–12, 132
Ricardo, David, 83
Rockefeller, William, 34
   see also Standard Oil

Roosevelt, Franklin D., 37, 40, 53
Rosneft (Russian oil company), 128
Royal Bank of Scotland (RBS), 107
Royal Dutch Shell, 123
Russia, xii, xv–xvi, 6–7, 9, 31, 35,
   71, 78–9, 82, 95–6, 111, 120,
   122–6, 128–9, 138, 145, 148,
   166, 173

S
Sachs, Jeffrey, 82, 87, 93–4, 169
Saudi Arabia, 3, 47, 61, 67–8, 70,
   72, 86, 123
Saudi Oil, 3, 47, 61, 68, 72, 86, 123
Seabrook, Leonard, 49, 59, 62
seigniorage, 66, 71
shadow banking sector, 4, 12, 62,
   98, 146, 169
shock therapy policy, 43, 82, 87,
   90–1, 93–4, 143, 169
Smith, Adam, 3, 64, 83, 154
Smoot–Hawley Act (1930), 36
social movements, 31, 45, 140
South Korea, 38, 115, 124
Southeast Asia, xv, 7, 11, 18,
   20–21, 24, 27, 33, 45, 50, 52,
   55–6, 64, 70, 112, 125, 130,
   171, 175
Soviet bloc, 79, 82, 86, 113, 151
Soviet Union (USSR), xii, 7, 20,
   41, 44, 48–50, 56, 66, 71–2,
   74, 78–9, 81–2, 86–7, 91–2, 95,
   102, 113, 143, 145, 151, 160
Spain, 31, 37, 46, 105, 124, 143
speculation, xvii, 3–5, 11–12, 16,
   20, 25, 36–7, 49, 52, 58–9, 62,
   66, 71, 74–5, 82, 88–90, 97–9,
   101–2, 104, 127, 135–6, 138
speculative bubble, 10–12, 16,
   20–1, 49, 62, 71, 75, 85, 98,
   143, 150, 154, 157, 168
stagflation, 22, 61–5, 67, 74, 92,
   143
stagnation, 18–20, 22, 55, 60–1,
   73, 75, 112–13, 144, 146, 167
Standard & Poor's, 98, 147

'Star Wars' project, 71, 74
state–finance nexus, 28, 94
state–industry nexus, 28
sterling–dollar diplomacy, 3, 34,
   72, 132, 147
stock market, 3, 10–11, 20–1, 24,
   37, 62, 71, 75, 88, 97, 165
   bubble, 3, 10–11, 20–1, 37,
      71, 88, 97
Strange, Susan, 59, 102, 168–9
structural contradictions, 7, 10, 12,
   15, 27, 36–7, 44, 50, 59–61,
   64–5, 72–3, 79, 81, 88–91,
   100–1, 104, 141, 148, 162
structured investment vehicles
   (SIVs), xiii, 98, 168
Suez Canal crisis, 61, 160

T
tariffs, 4, 36, 39–40, 46, 57
Taylorism, 48–9, 162
terminal crisis, 16, 26–9, 144
Thatcher, Margaret, 2, 12, 75, 83,
   106, 107
'Tiger States' of Southeast Asia, 27
Tito, Josip, 91
Toxic Asset Relief Program, 104
toxic assets, 10, 104–5, 127–8
Transneft (Russian pipeline
   operator), 128
Trotsky, Leon, xvi, xix–xx, 50, 155
Turkey, 7, 9, 21, 46, 120, 122,
   124, 126, 173

U
unemployment, 37, 42, 51, 55, 75,
   83, 94–5, 105–7, 109–10, 121,
   125, 144, 163
uneven and combined development,
   xvi–xvii, xix–xx, 7–8, 19, 27,
   30, 39, 44–50, 53, 60, 78, 89,
   132, 145, 155
unipolar phase, 9, 20, 30, 131
United States
   accumulation regime, 30, 33,
      60, 64, 69

consumer debt, 84, 86, 100, 143
debt, 3, 9, 36, 41, 50, 52–5, 58–60, 65, 84–6, 89, 91, 95, 98, 100–1, 104, 143, 147, 171
elites, 7, 27–8, 34, 46, 61–2, 64, 78, 85, 113, 165
Federal Reserve System, 35, 57, 62, 67, 84, 103, 170
global supremacy, 2, 15–17, 30, 32, 34, 38, 50, 64, 71, 114, 126, 150
GDP, 54, 79, 85–6, 99–101, 123–4, 126, 130, 147
GNP, 34, 44
hegemonic system, xvii–xx, 2, 16–17, 25–8, 30, 68, 85, 87, 89, 109, 113, 126, 144, 147–50, 156
manufacturing, 18–20, 23–4, 42–3, 45–6, 50–1, 54, 57, 75, 83, 85–6, 98, 112, 126, 168
military bases, 45, 150
neo-imperialism, 9, 15, 28–9, 32–3, 143, 155
political power, 37, 41
producers, 36, 54, 84
Savings & Loan fiasco (1987), 88
Treasury, 3, 20–1, 40, 43, 53, 65, 67–8, 70, 73, 83, 86–8, 91–2, 95, 143, 159, 165
US–UK special relationship, 42

V
valorization of capital, 59, 61, 163

Vietnam war, 22, 49, 50, 53, 65, 91, 96, 130, 165
Volcker, Paul, 16, 55, 58, 63, 66–7, 71, 74–5, 155, 162, 165
vulnerabilities of the Empire, xvi, xvii, 89, 99, 132, 142, 145, 149,168

W
Wallerstein, Immanuel, 5, 21, 157–8
Walmart, 28, 85
war reparations, 35–36, 42, 159
weapon–dollar system, 65–6, 71, 73, 91, 114
Western Europe, 15, 20, 22–3, 39, 44–7, 50, 52, 60, 65, 68, 78, 125, 144, 163, 175
Woodward, Susan, 91–2
World Bank, 23–4, 39, 42–3, 68–9, 83, 88, 92, 127
WEO (World Energy Outlook), 138
WTO (World Trade Organization), 88
World War, First, 21, 34, 36, 39, 48
World War, Second, 9, 15, 21–2, 26, 35, 38–40, 44, 58, 110, 111, 123

Y
Yom Kippur War (1973), 68, 72–3
Yugoslavia (former), 43, 91, 92, 93, 95, 165, 168

Z
Zakaria, Fareed, 131, 174, 188

Lightning Source UK Ltd.
Milton Keynes UK
UKOW01f1852200917

309577UK00002B/17/P